The Plan

Epstein, Maddon, and the Audacious Blueprint for a Cubs Dynasty

David Kaplan

First Triumph Books paperback edition 2021

Library of Congress Cataloging-in-Publication Data available upon request.

This book is available in quantity at special discounts for your group or organization. For further information, contact:

Triumph Books LLC
814 North Franklin Street
Chicago, Illinois 60610
(312) 337-0747
www.triumphbooks.com

Printed in U.S.A.
ISBN: 978-1-62937-882-4

Design by Patricia Frey
All photos are courtesy of AP Images.

I want to dedicate this book to my late father, Marshall, and my late mother, Lila. Because without his love of baseball and the love of sports that he instilled in me and my brother at a young age I would not be doing what I'm doing today. My mom was my biggest fan and No. 1 cheerleader. But, above all she was always honest with me and she demanded I develop a passion for reading and writing.

Thank you both for your unwavering belief in me. Hey Dad, can you believe it? The Cubs won the World Series! I miss you both more than you can imagine, and I love you.

Contents

Foreword

Being a part of the Chicago Cubs' first World Series championship team since 1908 will be an experience that I will cherish for the rest of my life. To get to this point, however, our team had to go through a lengthy overhaul that involved the entire franchise. I made my debut with the Cubs in 2012, and those early days were incredibly tough. That year we lost 101 games, yet as soon as I joined the team I could feel a positive vibe throughout the organization. I just knew that the Cubs were in the process of building one of the best teams in Major League Baseball.

I truly believe that the Chicago Cubs are one of the most incredible organizations in the entire world of sports. With the Cubs, it all starts right at the top with Tom Ricketts and the Ricketts family. They give us everything that a club needs to be successful and that is all you can ask for from ownership. Our front office, headed up by Theo Epstein, Jed Hoyer, and Jason McLeod, are proven winners and they have built the best team in baseball by adding great young players who play like veterans and outstanding veterans who play like youngsters. I am confident that the mix of talent that we have will lead to many more winning seasons and hopefully several more World Series championships.

David Kaplan, who has been around our team for over 20 years, gives the reader a real perspective of how the Chicago Cubs were able to go from being called the "lovable losers" to the best team in baseball. We ended a drought of 108 years without a World Series title and we did it by playing for each other and playing for our fans and the city of Chicago.

When we arrived in Mesa, Arizona, in February 2016, our team knew what we could accomplish and what was expected of us. Our manager, Joe Maddon, told us that we had to meet those expectations head-on. Thus, our mantra, "Embrace the Target," was born and we did just that all season long. We got off to a 25–6 start and we met every challenge along the way against tremendous competition. Although a 162-game season is a grind, every player who wore our uniform, our coaching staff, and our front office never took our eyes off of the ultimate prize, winning a World Series championship.

This is an accomplishment that many didn't believe could happen. It did happen, and this is David Kaplan's story of how he watched us become champions.

–Anthony Rizzo
World Series champion
and three-time All-Star first baseman,
November 2016

Special Introduction

The author, David Kaplan, has masterfully captured the drama of one of baseball's most compelling stories, the resurgence of the Chicago Cubs over the past few years. Mr. Kaplan, a distinguished and popular Chicago sports broadcaster, artfully describes how a franchise, known as the "lovable losers" for its unparalleled record of futility that had existed for more than a century, is transformed into the World Series champion.

After 108 years of despair, dating back to the Cubs' previous World Series victory in 1908, hope, which had been the allure that had driven fans to root for the Cubs in the first place, no longer is fleeting, if not rare. It is now so abundant and thick that you can reach out and touch it. The unbending loyalty of Cubs fans is remarkable. And they are not just from Chicago. There are Cubs fans everywhere, in every corner of our great country. Finally, they have been rewarded.

As it should be in baseball, the players receive and certainly deserve the bulk of the credit when a team is successful. But in the case of the Cubs, a great deal of credit is also due to the foresight and vision of the Ricketts family and especially the Cubs' chairman, Tom Ricketts.

This is Mr. Kaplan's story, one that began more than a decade ago, when Tom Ricketts, a die-hard Cubs fan, first had his eye on the purchase of the Cubs. During the summer of 2006, before the Cubs were even for sale, Tom, knowing he would need the approval of his family to make his dream come true—particularly his father, the patriarch of the family—threw a giant family party across four rooftops facing Wrigley. Before the day was out, he had convinced his father and the rest of the clan that owning the Cubs would be good for the Ricketts.

The author describes how Tom spent the next few years working behind the scenes to buy the club. Finally, in 2009, the family's purchase of the Cubs from the Tribune Company came to fruition. As Commissioner, I recognized the value of the Ricketts family and knew it would be a positive influence on the game, and was instrumental in gaining baseball's approval of the sale. The Cubs had just completed a season in which they had finished out of the playoffs. That, unfortunately, began a streak of five consecutive losing seasons and Cubs fans surely felt like it was—in the immortal words of Yogi Berra—"déjà vu all over again."

But through the next few years, Mr. Kaplan reports, Tom had begun working on a long-term plan for rebuilding the club as well as rejuvenating Wrigley Field. As a former owner of the Milwaukee Brewers, I know how difficult it is to build a ballclub from the bottom up. It takes a great deal of intelligence, creativity, hard work, and patience—not to mention a bit of luck. After enduring several difficult seasons, Mr. Kaplan details how the Cubs began to turn it around following the 2011 season. That's when Tom made the first of his brilliant front office hires, bringing Theo Epstein to Chicago from the Boston Red Sox as the Cubs President of Baseball Operations.

Even before his purchase of the Cubs, Tom had begun to reach out to me, usually for advice and historical perspective about the game. After the 2011 season, it was clear he was looking for a general manager. According to the author, Tom had already conducted a study of every franchise's minor league system and their draft records to determine who was signing and developing the best young talent. In his view, that franchise was the Boston Red Sox–and Theo Epstein was the reason.

It turned out that Theo was ready to move on after a decade in Boston. Once Tom got permission from the Red Sox to talk to Theo and made his pitch, I got involved as an intermediary in the discussions between the two clubs and helped make it happen. The hiring of Theo caught a lot of people in baseball by surprise. Theo had been a fixture in Boston. Hired as its general manager in 2002 at the age of 28, he became, at the time, the youngest GM in the history of the game. Theo was an immediate success and became a legend overnight when the Red Sox won the World Series in 2004, his first season with the club. It was Boston's first World Series victory in 86 years and finally brought to an end the curse of Babe Ruth that had plagued the club and the city for all those years. In 10 years with the Red Sox, Theo's club won two World Series championships and reached the playoffs six times.

As Mr. Kaplan describes, it wasn't going to be easy for Theo to duplicate that kind of success in Chicago. He and his brain trust began putting together the pieces, player by player, over the next few seasons. But he needed the right person to run the club on the field, and that person was Joe Maddon, who joined the Cubs as manager prior to the start of the 2015 season. And they haven't looked back since. Joe had significant success as manager of the Tampa Bay Rays even though he had to deal with the financial constraints that all small market clubs must deal with.

And now the Cubs have pulled off a miracle just as historic as the one Theo was instrumental in pulling off in Boston. There, Theo helped erase the "Curse of the Bambino," and, in Chicago, he helped dismantle the "Curse of the Billy Goat." This one is equally as momentous, if not more so, and will bring the same kind of joy and happiness to loyal and patient Cubs fans that those fans in Boston experienced a dozen years ago.

David Kaplan has done great work in putting this story together, focusing first with the arrival of Tom Ricketts and his family and then with the arrivals and contributions of Theo Epstein and Joe Maddon. But, more importantly, as a longtime Cubs fan, David has lived through and certainly understands the pain and torment that Cubs fans have endured over many, many decades. He appreciates the import of the moment now that the Cubs have erased 108 years of futility and recognizes that it is joyously welcomed by all Cubs fans, those who are present and, in spirit, those who are gone.

—Allan H. "Bud" Selig
Former Milwaukee Brewers owner (1970–1992)
and MLB Commissioner (1992–2015),
November 2016

Author's Note

What would possess a man to take nearly a billion dollars of his family's fortune to buy a baseball team that is the worst in the league, has a stadium that is going to need nearly $700 million worth of renovations, and has spring training and Latin American facilities that are also substandard compared to most of Major League Baseball?

Add in that the man and his siblings, wife, and children would also go from an extremely comfortable life of privilege, a life that they have enjoyed without a hint of public scrutiny, to a life where their every professional move would be second guessed by a fan base as large as any in all of professional sports and an intense media throng who cover the team on a 24/7 basis.

In addition, the political dealings to renovate the most iconic stadium in American sports will be as difficult a process to navigate as any transaction the family has ever had to endure throughout their professional lives. There will be opportunities to move the team out of its famous stadium, battles with politicians and neighbors alike, all hoping to capitalize on your team's success to line their pockets.

To top it off, the deal to buy that baseball team will be so complex that it will hamstring the franchise for several years as they attempt to completely overhaul the organization from top to bottom all the while knowing that their failures will be splashed across the sports pages on a daily basis.

Once they would assume control of the franchise they would find an organization that was out of touch with the way most of Major League Baseball conducted its business. The Cubs were behind in so many areas Tom Ricketts and his family would have no idea where they should begin. The infrastructure was far below major league standards. The computer age had arrived and left the Chicago Cubs in the dark ages. Plus, most importantly, the talent level from the minors to the major league roster was so deficient that the future was exceptionally bleak to even the most die-hard fan.

That's how strong the lure of owning the Chicago Cubs is, the lure of being the one to end the longest championship drought in sports history. A franchise known as the "lovable losers," with all of its warts, had many billionaires lusting to own it. One bidder emerged on top, paying $845 million for the challenge of winning a World Series.

However, it would take time, there would be hundreds of losses and last-place finishes along the way and there would be many days the fan base and the media would question if the owners were committed to winning. Many would wonder if ownership was willing to spend what it would take to rebuild the franchise and to field a championship caliber team.

This is the inside story of how the Chicago Cubs went from laughingstock and a team called the "lovable losers" to World Series champions and the envy of all of Major League Baseball.

1

Tom Ricketts and the New Cubs

> *"Buying the Cubs in 2009 was like buying a house after a great party. There's empty pizza boxes, empty beer cans everywhere, and some guy you don't know sleeping on your couch. Then you realize,* I didn't buy the party, I just bought the hangover.*"*
>
> —Tom Ricketts, 2016

Owning a professional baseball team is a dream that many young men have as they go through their childhood and formative years playing Little League and participating in fantasy baseball. What baseball fan hasn't romanticized what they would do if they owned their favorite MLB team?

We all think we would make better decisions than the current management and we all think it's easier than it really is. For Tom Ricketts, the dream to own a team started at a young age. "The dream really has two levels," he told me in his Wrigley Field office in June of 2016.

"There are really two levels–the fantasy level, which I always fantasized about and in fact, my business school essay was about me wanting to own a Major League Baseball team. As a kid I was a baseball fan and then when I became an investment banker and trader I got into some fantasy baseball leagues and I started reading Bill James and all of his abstracts and I really got into it. I lived across the street from Wrigley Field and my dream job became owning a major league team."

Then there is the second level that Ricketts spoke about, and that is when you have the assets to legitimately entertain the notion of owning a baseball team. With his father having started T.D. Ameritrade and the entire family experiencing tremendous financial success, the dream of owning a team suddenly didn't seem so far-fetched. Being the astute observer of the financial world that he is, he had his eyes on the Cubs more than a year before the team hit the market.

"From a family standpoint it was a once-in-a-lifetime opportunity. If it happened and if we didn't act upon it then we would be kicking ourselves for having missed a golden opportunity. My company, Incapital, was going very well but I was traveling on business all over the world and I was looking for a way to step back and be around home more. Owning the Cubs would keep me just as busy, but instead of being in Hong Kong, London, or somewhere else, I would just be down the street, so to speak. In fact, before I ever talked to my siblings and our dad I sat down and talked about it with my wife," Ricketts said.

At this point in time it seemed a mere pipe dream that the Ricketts family could win the bidding for the Cubs if the franchise even hit the open market. However, taking a run at the Cubs was exactly what Tom Ricketts was planning to do.

"I told my wife I might think about running this out and seeing how it goes. She gave me her blessing but I'm sure running the calculus in her head she probably thought this has no chance of ever happening. Then I talked with my dad, who is not a big sports fan. He was not excited about it at first but we have this family trust that is fairly inert. It just sits there. I said to him that we should have the family trust be one of the bidders," Ricketts said.

However, at this point the Chicago Cubs were not yet up for sale. There were rumors about that possibility and there were reports of financial problems throughout the Tribune Company. In fact, the Tribune was eventually headed towards bankruptcy and needed to liquidate assets, with the Cubs as one of their most valuable properties. But, that part of the equation was still a ways away.

"It was late 2005 and I remember hearing through my contacts in the financial world that the Tribune was looking for a private equity investor. They needed somebody to put a slug of money into their company and this was all pre Sam Zell. However, the typical financial return profile that a private equity investor is looking for is either you sell it in a few years for a large multiple or you get some type of excellent cash flow that makes it very valuable. A baseball team has neither of those. You don't take any cash out and they don't appreciate at a rate that a private equity investor would have interest in. It is an investment that only appreciates years down the road," Ricketts explained to me.

As that process began to unfold it was still a long way away from seeing the Chicago Cubs with a "for sale" sign on the franchise. And, it was still more than a year away from an eventual sale of the Tribune Company to maverick Chicago billionaire Sam Zell.

"Then, in August of 2006, we threw a giant party on four rooftops because that's what we do, the Ricketts throw giant parties," he joked. However, that day swayed Joe Ricketts, the patriarch of the family.

"My dad had never done anything like having a party on a rooftop and he loved it. He told us it was much cooler than he had ever imagined. The Cubs weren't very good that season but the park was packed, as were all of the rooftops. The vantage point that we had, you could see the whole neighborhood, and my dad's buy-in was this was pretty amazing and it looked to be a good investment. My siblings were a lot easier to convince, but that day on the rooftops it was all just an idea because the Cubs weren't for sale. I just knew what was going on in the financial world and what I was hearing about the Tribune Company and from that point the process took three more years to buy the team."

Where does one start when they want to buy a baseball team and where does one start when that team isn't even on the market yet? "Before the team was ever up for sale we flew out to New York to see our bankers in the fall of 2006 and we hired Sal Galatioto, who is the president of GSP [Galatioto Sports Partners], who became our sports banker. Then we met with the sports partners at Lehman Brothers and we told them we wanted to retain them as well to help us buy the Cubs. All of them told us the Cubs weren't for sale and I told them, okay, they are not for sale but if they go up for sale–and I believe they will be–we want to hire you to help us buy them," Ricketts told me.

With Ricketts looking ahead to what he believed would happen as the Tribune faced mounting pressure to liquidate some of the company's assets, he and his siblings put a plan in motion so that when the Cubs did hit the market they would have a jump on what was sure to be a large field of interested and well-funded groups who all wanted a chance to pursue the Holy Grail of winning a championship with the Chicago Cubs.

"So we actually signed up our bankers in November or December of 2006 and the team didn't hit the market until April of 2007. I just knew what was going on with the sale of the company to Sam Zell and with the financial structure of his deal that unless there was a miraculous recovery in the print media world, I knew the team would have to be put up for sale," Ricketts said.

When I spoke with Sal Galatioto in August of 2016 he provided tremendous insight into why he decided to work with the Ricketts family as opposed to the countless other groups who tried to retain his services as they tried to buy the Cubs. "The Ricketts are so well organized and they really think things through. They plan everything before they make a decision and they take the long-term view as opposed to so many others who take a short-term approach."

GSP is perhaps the best company in the United States in the sports acquisitions industry and while the competition to purchase the Cubs was going to be tough, Ricketts also faced competition to convince Galatioto that he and his family were the right people to own the Cubs. "Tom made it clear to me from day one that the family was all Cubs fans and that they didn't want to buy just any professional baseball team. They wanted to own the Chicago Cubs and that was very important to me. I wanted to represent someone who really had a passion for the team they were buying. They were obviously wealthy and that combined with the reputation of the family and their love for the Cubs were huge factors in working together to help them acquire the franchise," Galatioto said.

"I didn't think that Tom was crazy when he approached me about buying the Cubs, but at that point the Tribune Co. was telling everyone who inquired that the team wasn't for sale. Throughout all of my years in this business I've come to realize that things that look nuts today aren't nuts tomorrow. The Cubs are one of the most iconic franchises in all of sports and they are more of a national brand rather than a local brand as so many other teams are. Teams like the Cubs don't usually come on the market," Galatioto said.

But as the Ricketts and GSP continued to meet and to strategize as they pursued the Cubs, rumors started to run rampant that the iconic franchise was indeed going up for sale. Tom Ricketts' intuition had been right on the money years earlier.

"Tom was very astute and his knowledge of the financial picture of the Tribune Company gave him and his family a head start on the process of pursuing the Cubs if they were to hit the market. The team was owned by a large corporation and large corporations, more than individuals, sometimes they decide for whatever reason they are going to sell assets.

"I knew if a team like the Cubs came on the market there was going to be a lot of competition. It's not like you're trying to sell a team in Podunk. It's Chicago, which is a great market, and it's the Cubs, which is a great brand, and so you have a lot of investors who want to buy the team," Galatioto said.

However, having money and loving a team as a fan is far from enough to get into the club of billionaire owners of professional baseball teams. It is quite possibly the most exclusive club in the world and no matter how wealthy a prospective owner is, Major League Baseball and the other 29 owners have to be comfortable with who they are admitting to their club or the deal will never get the required approval.

"Tom knew nobody in Major League Baseball so we had to introduce him to the important guys in baseball so that they would get comfortable with him. I called Jerry Reinsdorf and he was so gracious to the Ricketts family. He had Tom and his siblings and dad up to his skybox for a White Sox game and he cleared the box so we could all have a very honest and frank discussion.

"We spent three hours talking philosophy and the baseball business. Jerry wanted to know why they wanted to buy a team and why they wanted to buy the Cubs. And the family showed really, really well. Jerry really liked them and he felt that they would be great owners. They understood that owning a baseball team was a marathon not a sprint. Having Jerry in their corner was really important because owning a team is like trying to get into a really exclusive country club. You have to have someone of great stature in the game who feels comfortable with you and is willing to stand up in a meeting and say, 'These are good people and they will be good for our sport,'" Galatioto said.

Having Reinsdorf in their corner was important, but the Ricketts family needed more than just Reinsdorf if they were going to win the bidding for the Cubs and gain approval from the hierarchy of Major League Baseball. They had to meet several of the most influential people in the sport so they could be a group that the baseball insiders who run the sport would be comfortable approving, if and when the Ricketts could come to terms with the Tribune Company to buy the franchise.

"We went around the game meeting different key owners so they would get comfortable with Tom," Galatioto said. "We met with Bob DuPuy, who was the deputy commissioner of Major League Baseball, so he and his family really became a known entity throughout the upper levels of Major League Baseball.

"Also, you have to remember that when the Cubs came on the market it was at a very dark time in American economic history. The world was falling apart. The banks weren't lending and the Tribune Company had issues and people thought it would be difficult to raise money. You name it, it was going on. It was a mess.

It took a long time to get this deal done–plus, the Tribune was difficult to deal with," Galatioto said.

"Then, if you remember the Tribune filed for bankruptcy in the middle of the sale process and so we had to navigate that. The Cubs were part of that bankruptcy and while it was a prepackaged bankruptcy we still had to navigate that. Major League Baseball didn't want that stigma but we all understood that it had to be done. We had to distance ourselves from all the other junk that was falling around in the Tribune system," Galatioto added.

The Ricketts family was one of a handful of groups that expressed serious interest in the Cubs when the Tribune Company, faced with mounting financial problems, finally decided to put the team up for sale on Opening Day of 2007. The Tribune had gone from corporate ownership with one of the most conservative leadership teams to a company on the brink of financial ruin, until maverick real estate mogul Sam Zell rode in and bought the company in a highly leveraged deal that eventually caused the century old publishing and media giant to collapse and file bankruptcy in 2008.

You might say that the "rebirth" of the Cubs wouldn't have been possible if it weren't for the intervention of a man known as the "Grave Dancer."

Born in 1941 in Chicago, Sam Zell built a reputation for reviving struggling companies, earning his nickname for, as he puts it, "dancing on the skeletons of other people's mistakes." In April of 2007, Zell made an $8.2 billion deal to take control of Tribune Co., which included the *Chicago Tribune*, the *Los Angeles Times*, and several other newspapers; several television stations (including the WGN Super Station); websites such as CareerBuilder.com; and of course the Chicago Cubs.

Zell's intentions of selling the Cubs were made clear almost immediately and he planned on unloading the team and Wrigley

Field by Opening Day 2008. That, however, wasn't to be. In order to maximize the return, Zell initially wanted to sell the team and the ballpark separately, with Wrigley Field going to the Illinois Sports Facilities Authority (ISFA).

However, with the fate of Wrigley Field in limbo, he would be hard-pressed to find a buyer. Negotiations between the Tribune Co. and ISFA stalled mostly over details regarding renovation of the nearly 100-year-old ballpark. Eventually in May, Zell made the decision to scrap the idea and package the Cubs and Wrigley together. That decision helped to jumpstart the sale process.

When it finally came time for serious bidders to get involved, the list included several potential ownership groups. Real estate investor Hersch Klaff jumped into the fray, as did a New York partnership of Marc Utay (Clarion Capital) and Leo Hindery Jr. (InterMedia Partners, former head of YES Network, who even dabbled in race car driving). Michael Tokarz (MVC Capital investment firm), multimillionaire Don Levin (owner of the Chicago Wolves minor league hockey team), a group including attorney Thomas Mandler and businessman Jim Anixter (the "Pink Hat Guy" who is often spotted sitting behind home plate wearing his trademark pink hat at Wrigley Field), even a group led by Sports Acquisition Holding Corp., with Hank Aaron and Jack Kemp aboard, all expressed interest.

However, once the team was officially put up for sale on Opening Day of the 2007 season, most observers thought that the group of Andy McKenna and John Canning were a slam dunk to win the bidding. Both McKenna and Canning had longtime ties to MLB, dating back to McKenna's time as the president of the Cubs from 1981 to 1984 and his time as a part of the ownership group of the Chicago White Sox.

Canning was also very well-connected because he was, and remains to this day, part of the ownership group of the Milwaukee

Brewers, a franchise that was at one time owned by baseball commissioner Bud Selig. The path to owning the Cubs appeared to lead right to the McKenna/Canning group, but early in the process they withdrew their interest in purchasing the franchise.

The news was stunning to baseball insiders but Canning is convinced they made the right decision despite the value of the franchise nearly tripling in just seven years. In an interview in 2010 with *Chicago* magazine, Canning had this to say about not ending up as one of the owners of the Chicago Cubs:

"Our bid was $800 million. We were the low bidder. [Tribune Company, which owned the Cubs] wanted way too much. The financial markets collapsed. By waiting as long as they did, they might have left $200 to $300 million on the table. The Ricketts [paying $845 million] ended up right where we were. But, you know–they're the right owner. They have a lot of patience. Major League Baseball likes family owners. They'll be good for the team."

Canning cherishes his privacy, and the media glare that comes with owning the Cubs was also something that dissuaded him from continuing to pursue ownership of the Cubs. "I didn't enjoy and I wouldn't have enjoyed the prominence. While we were identified as a bidder, all of a sudden, at this country club I belong to, people wanted to play golf with me. Valet guys put my car in front. I didn't enjoy that," he told *Chicago* magazine.

Canning also told *Crain's Chicago Business* in 2013 that he is glad he avoided the scrutiny that an owner of the Cubs would undoubtedly have had to endure. "I couldn't stand the spotlight. I started to really dislike that part of it. Besides, I'm a Sox fan."

Andrew McKenna is one of the most powerful men in the history of Chicago sports and he is also one of the classiest, with a stint running the Cubs early in Tribune's tenure as owner in the early '80s on his resume. He is also a part owner of the Chicago

Cubs Ownership History
(via Cubs Media Guide)

1876	William A. Hulbert
1882	Albert Spalding & John Walsh
1905	Charles Murphy
1914	Charles Taft
1916	Charles Weeghman
1919	Wrigley Family
1919	William Wrigley Jr.
1932	Philip K. Wrigley
1977	William Wrigley
1981	The Tribune Company
2009	Ricketts Family

Bears and his connections around the sports world and the Chicago business community made him a natural fit as a potential owner of the Cubs.

However, looking back on his group's decision to pull out of the bidding for the franchise, McKenna says he has no regrets. "We made the best decision for our group. The Ricketts have been excellent owners and I am really happy for them that they bought the team. I think they have done a great job rebuilding the franchise. What they have accomplished during their time as owners of the team has truly been outstanding," McKenna told me.

With the front-runner making a surprising decision to pull out, the race was suddenly wide open. The Canning/McKenna group appeared to have everything that baseball wanted in an owner. They were well-capitalized, they had no member of their group that was considered questionable by baseball's hierarchy, and they were local.

The other partners in the group were all major names in the Chicago business world and all were exceptionally wealthy: Larry Levy, Rich Melman, Pat Ryan, and John Rogers all would have been acceptable to Major League Baseball.

Mark Cuban, a very successful businessman who also owns the NBA's Dallas Mavericks, was popular with the Cubs' massive fan base and had been spotted in the bleachers at Wrigley Field after the team was put on the block, but his rebellious personality and showmanship meant he had no chance of being approved by the other 29 MLB owners who must give their blessing on any sale of a franchise.

The Ricketts group, consisting of Tom and siblings Laura, Pete, and Todd, were all Cubs fans but none more so than Tom, who holds a bachelor's degree and MBA from the University of Chicago and first met his wife in the Wrigley Field bleachers.

"My family and I are Cubs fans. We share the goal of Cubs fans everywhere to win a World Series and build the consistent championship tradition that the fans deserve," said Ricketts in a statement issued upon winning the bid (reported at the time as "nearly $900 million") in January 2009.

But the deal still wasn't done.

"This deal took a long time to complete but Tom hung in there no matter what happened. He was really focused. They wanted to buy the team and he never got down despite all of the issues and problems that kept popping up. He had a plan and a vision and most importantly he had the staying power, even though there were people who had serious doubts about their ownership at the start when the team struggled," Galatioto said.

In February 2009, the Ricketts family sold $403 million dollars of TD Ameritrade stock to help finance the purchase of the Cubs and Tom resigned from the TD Ameritrade board. The arranging of finances and disagreements over the value of Cubs' broadcast contracts among other things delayed the deal into June, at which point the Tribune Co. reopened talks with Utay and Hindery in a move which most observers figured was a method of pressuring Ricketts into accepting a deal more to Tribune's liking.

On August 21, Tribune Co. announced that they had signed an agreement to sell the Cubs to the Ricketts family. The sale was reported to be $800 million (later updated to $845 million) to acquire a 95 percent interest in the team, full ownership of Wrigley Field, and 25 percent of Comcast SportsNet Chicago. The Tribune retained a 5 percent interest in the joint venture but a clause in the deal allows the Ricketts family to buy out the 5 percent stake in 2018 if they so choose.

A few final steps to complete the sale followed. Delaware federal bankruptcy judge Kevin Carey approved Tribune Co.'s request for quick court action on August 31, 2009. Carey gave court approval to the sale on September 24, 2009. MLB clubs unanimously granted their approval of the transfer from the Tribune Company to the Ricketts Family Trust on October 6.

Next, the Cubs officially filed for Chapter 11 bankruptcy on October 12, to ensure the sale was free of any debt from Tribune Co. (to protect the Ricketts family from creditor claims against Tribune Co.); the team remained in bankruptcy for only one day, due to the August 31 request for an expedited process. The process usually takes 30 to 45 days.

At last, on October 27, 2009, the Ricketts family officially assumed control of the Chicago Cubs, Wrigley Field, and 25 percent of Comcast SportsNet. In a statement, Tom Ricketts said: "My family and I are thrilled that this day has finally come and we thank [Major League Baseball] Commissioner Bud Selig and Major League Baseball owners for approving our ownership. Now we will go to work building the championship tradition that all Cubs fans so richly deserve."

Tom Ricketts' Opening News Conference October 30, 2009:

We're very excited to get started. There's a lot of work to do. But everyone needs to know that we are here for the long-term. And we are here to win.

> *I think you're gonna see all of us...around the stadium a lot. I don't think we're gonna change too much. We're gonna walk around, we're gonna see folks, we're gonna be in the stands. I can't imagine that anyone who comes to a lot of games won't see myself, or my siblings.*
>
> *Most of all, we'd like to thank the fans. Through this long process, the best part was how much support we received from fans like us, who would send a note or reach out to say hang in there, you're the guys we want to see win.*
>
> *Number one is, we're gonna win the World Series. We're gonna win the World Series by striving every day in every way to be the best franchise in baseball. We're going to invest in the best facilities in baseball. We're going invest in the best personnel and we're gonna hold them to the highest standards of excellence and accountability.*
>
> *The second thing we want to say to the fans is that we love Wrigley Field, and we're going to do everything we can to improve the Wrigley Field experience for the fans that are coming today and to preserve the Wrigley Field experience for the future generations of fans to come, so that they can share in that special unique magic that is Wrigley Field.*
>
> *Thirdly, we want to tell everyone how much we love the city of Chicago....*
>
> *We intend to reinvest in the stadium, in the team, in the organization to keep building toward that goal of a consistent winner. We don't have any quarterly results to worry about or year-end balance sheets. Our shareholders are our fans.*

A former Tribune employee who was privy to the details of the sale chuckled when I asked him about the lengthy sale process that eventually culminated in the Ricketts family landing the team.

"After Tom closed on the deal to buy the team he would open up a cabinet and more crap would fall out. He really had no idea how many problems he would encounter as he began to navigate owning the team. From the stadium to the struggle to get a deal done for a new spring training facility to the radio deal, things just kept popping up. Their perseverance to get to this point is very impressive."

Another Tribune Company source told me shortly after the sale closed and the Ricketts family held their first press conference that all of the complexities of the deal made it extremely likely that Tom Ricketts would regret buying the Chicago Cubs shortly after beginning to run the franchise on a day-to-day basis. "I am convinced that once Tom rolls up his sleeves and gets his hands on the team and sees how screwed up everything is he will regret ever getting involved in the process," he said.

However, when I referenced that opinion to Tom Ricketts when we sat down in April of 2013 and again in June of 2016 and went over all of the problems and roadblocks that he and his family had encountered since purchasing the team, he was more convinced than ever that he would make the same decision to purchase the Cubs again. In fact, it is remarkable to see how his perspective didn't change despite one of baseball's worst teams in 2012 and 2013 and one of baseball's best teams in 2016.

"I knew this process was going to be long and difficult but there truly has never been a moment where I regretted buying the franchise. Yes, there were times that the road seemed much longer than I ever imagined but there was never a moment that I wished I was doing something else with my life," he said in June 2016.

Compare that to this quote in April 2013, when he sat down for an interview with me on Comcast SportsNet. "I know that we have a long way to go but I am convinced that we have the best front office in Major League Baseball and I know that in time Theo and Jed will have us competing to win the World Series. Yes, it is going to take some time for us to get our organization where we want it but we bought the Chicago Cubs to keep it in our family for a long time," he told me.

So with the team now officially owned by the Ricketts family it was time to learn the world of Major League Baseball from the ground up. It was also time to learn the ins and outs of the Chicago Cubs and to find out why they had failed to win a World Series for over 100 years. Tom Ricketts knew the franchise had a long way to go but he was about to learn it was a lot further than he had ever imagined.

2

Worse Than They Thought

> *"We will win the World Series. That is our goal and we will achieve it."*
>
> —Tom Ricketts, October 30, 2009

On a gorgeous Saturday afternoon in the summer of 2009, a man stood next to the statue of Cubs legend Ernie Banks and waited to meet some family and friends who would sit with him as his favorite team as a youngster, the Cubs, played their archrivals, the St. Louis Cardinals.

No one recognized the man, as he looked like any other fan entering venerable Wrigley Field that day. However, as he stood there he knew something only a very few people were privy to. That he and his family were about to purchase his favorite team, the ballpark in which they played, and other assorted assets for the staggering sum of $845 million. A fee that at the time was one of the most expensive prices paid for an American professional sports franchise.

Tom Ricketts was about to go from invisible multimillionaire to a man who would quickly feel the searing heat of a fan base and media horde that believed the Cubs needed to be fixed and fixed quickly. No one wanted to hear about long-term rebuilding plans or the need to build new facilities for spring training and in Latin America. They just wanted to win and win quickly.

Tom Ricketts, though, had to learn the baseball business to find out why the franchise had failed so spectacularly. That would take time–along with a staggering number of losses on the field–and he would be subjected to intense criticism that said he had no idea what he was doing. That he was a rich man operating with family money who bought his favorite team and wasn't really in it to win the World Series. That he was cheap and unwilling to spend money to build his team.

"The fans that I spoke to on an almost daily basis, whether it was as I walked around the stands at Wrigley Field or on the streets of Chicago as I went to work every day, were almost always supportive. They were willing to be patient as we rebuilt the franchise as long as we actually had a plan and stayed loyal to that plan," said Ricketts in 2015 as his Cubs finally showed the fruits of their labor with a 97-win season and a trip to the National League Championship Series.

However, back in 2009, Tom Ricketts and his siblings, sister Laura and brothers Pete and Todd, had no idea what it would take to rebuild the crumbling foundation of the Chicago Cubs. The franchise needed work in multiple areas. The baseball operations department was struggling at all levels, whether that was the performance of the major league team or–the lifeblood of any good franchise–the minor league system, where low cost labor is harvested and seasoned into the components of a championship-level team.

The business side was also lagging behind, with a staff that was smaller than any other team in Major League Baseball and revenues that were a fraction of what they could be if the team played at an elite level. Add in that Wrigley Field, while a popular tourist attraction and the one thing that the franchise could successfully sell on a year-to-year basis, was crumbling and was in need of a major renovation. A renovation that would need to be tremendously extensive and a renovation that would be wildly controversial.

"We had this asset that was in a time capsule for 30 or 40 years. Not only did the baseball operations side need a lot of work but the overall infrastructure needed a lot of work as well. We needed to upgrade almost every area of the franchise to compete with what the other teams in baseball were doing," Cubs President of Business Operations Crane Kenney told me.

The Cubs spent as much as $10 million a year just to maintain Wrigley Field. Netting had to be installed to prevent chunks of concrete from falling on fans. Office space was so sparse that media relations was housed in an old donut shop that once operated on the Wrigley Field grounds before it was relocated into a trailer that provided more space. The Cubs' substandard IT department, including the team's computer servers, were protected from water leaks by what Kenney told me was called a "rain hat" that was actually a tin foil bonnet devised by a co-worker, according to a Bloomberg report in April 2015.

Group ticket sales were recorded in triplicate using carbon paper while season ticket renewals were done by fax machine. In fact, multiple employees confirmed to me that sales and ticket renewal progress were tracked by how often the fax machine was refilled. "When we would ask how renewals were going, one of our former staffers literally said, "Pretty well. We've gone through three packages of fax machine paper," a Cubs executive told me.

The franchise literally had no computer programs to track sales, renewals, or to help them market to their customer base. In short, the Cubs were working in the dark ages while the rest of baseball was operating in the 21st century.

Add in all of the structural issues at Wrigley Field, along with the antiquated way that the franchise operated their business on a day-to-day basis and the Ricketts family had no idea at that time how tough a job lay ahead of them as they looked to completely overhaul the franchise in every area. And none of that involved the on-field performance of a team that was a long way from contending for a World Series and was about to head into one of the least successful periods in franchise history.

All the average fan knew was that the major league team was coming off three straight winning seasons when the Ricketts family purchased the team, as well as division titles in 2007 and 2008. Tom Ricketts himself even felt the team was a contender, saying at the press conference to announce the purchase of the franchise, "I'll be honest, I think we have a team that can do it next year."

There was no shortage of advice for Tom Ricketts as the sale of the Cubs to his family became more of a fait accompli and even more so after the sale closed in October of 2009. Almost all of that advice included firing incumbent general manager Jim Hendry and his staff immediately after assuming control of the franchise.

Hendry was an old-school baseball guy who relied on his scouting instincts and legion of contacts throughout the game to put together a team that he told me many times would be filled with tough SOBs who play hard. Hendry did have some great moments as Cubs GM, including during his first full season in charge in 2003 when the Cubs came within five outs of Chicago's first World Series appearance since 1945. Then the Steve Bartman fiasco happened and the Cubs melted down and the fan base had their hearts ripped from their chests once again.

The near miss in 2003 stung Hendry deeply and by his own admission took him months to recover from. "I've lost some tough games during my career, both in college and in the major leagues, but that really knocked me for a loop. It took me a long time to recover from that disappointment and there are still times now that it pops back into my mind," Hendry told me.

The crushing manner in which the Cubs lost in the 2003 National League Championship Series put incredible pressure on the 2004 Cubs to finish the job that had been started one season earlier. Off-season additions meant to strengthen the everyday lineup and the bench came in the way of first baseman Derrek Lee and outfielder Todd Hollandsworth, who'd both been part of the 2003 Florida Marlins world championship team.

"I talked to D-Lee before I made my decision and we both looked at the Cubs and said we want to win it all there. That team is young and that team is loaded. And to win it all in Chicago with the Cubs would be the greatest place you could possibly be," Hollandsworth told me.

"Then D-Lee got traded to the Cubs and I signed there and I really thought that was the most talented team I had ever been a part of. I still can't figure out how we didn't even make the playoffs. We had everything a team needed to win a title. However, we choked. There's nothing else I can really call it. It was there for the taking and we got sidetracked and we didn't get the job done," Hollandsworth said.

The pressure reached a crescendo when *Sports Illustrated* put the 2004 Cubs on the cover of their magazine with the headline: "Hell Freezes Over / The Cubs Will Win the World Series." However, the 2004 Cubs didn't even make it to the playoffs. They failed not for lack of talent but for a lack of team character and an inability to block out the distractions that come with playing in the city of Chicago and for the Chicago Cubs.

That team let what the media wrote—and what their own broadcasters said about them—distract them and ultimately derail them. From players calling the press box to complain about what an announcer said to in-fighting among teammates, it all combined to derail one of baseball's most talented teams in 2004.

The 2005 and 2006 seasons were failures on the field and also saw the end of the Dusty Baker regime as the Cubs manager. Baker had arrived amid tremendous fanfare in the fall of 2002 and despite him getting the Cubs so close in 2003, his four-year tenure is looked at as a tremendous failure by much of the Cubs fan base.

In fact, when he has returned to Chicago as the manager of both the Cincinnati Reds and the Washington Nationals he is routinely booed by Cubs fans at every opportunity. That despite the fact that Baker brought the Cubs closer to a World Series appearance than any other manager had before Joe Maddon, and he's one of the nicest guys in baseball.

But the failure in 2003, when the team was so close, and then the total collapse in 2004, soured the fan base, who were no longer willing to settle for a cold beer and a party at Wrigley Field. They wanted to win and they wanted to win immediately.

At the end of 2006, Tribune executives had seen enough and pulled the plug on team president Andy MacPhail, whose ultra-conservative nature had not led the Cubs to much success during his 12-year tenure. In fact, MacPhail had been hired with a directive to overhaul the Cubs farm system while building a foundation for long-term success at the major league level. Instead he presided over a franchise that in 2006 had one of the worst ranked farm systems in Major League Baseball.

A high-level Tribune Co. executive told me shortly after the 2004 season ended that he was stunned by MacPhail's conservative nature. "He gave me a number for that season's budget and I was shocked. I asked Andy if that's all he needed and he said yes. We were prepared to give him significantly more money but he said he didn't need it."

Cubs Opening Day Payrolls

(1995–2016; via *USAToday*)

Year	Payroll	Rank
1995	$32,460,834	12th
1996	$30,954,000	14th
1997	$39,829,333	14th
1998	$49,383,000	10th
1999	$55,368,500	10th
2000	$62,129,333	12th
2001	$64,515,833	15th
2002	$75,690,833	12th
2003	$79,868,333	11th
2004	$90,560,000	7th
2005	$87,032,933	9th
2006	$94,424,499	7th
2007	$99,670,332	8th
2008	$118,345,833	8th
2009	$134,809,000	3rd
2010	$146,609,000	3rd
2011	$125,047,329	6th
2012	$88,677,033	16th
2013	$103,313,676	14th
2014	$83,046,356	23rd
2015	$116,654,522	14th
2016	$154,575,168	7th

Former Cubs broadcaster Steve Stone also experienced the frugal ways of the MacPhail regime. "I went to Andy shortly after he was hired to run the Cubs. My cousin represented Larry Walker, who was a free agent, and he was a guy that I knew would be a great fit in the Cubs outfield. Larry was interested in coming to Chicago and I felt the Cubs were close to being a postseason team.

"I told Andy that I believed Walker would take a little less to play in Chicago but MacPhail wasn't interested. He told me that he didn't believe the Cubs were close to being a contender so he wasn't interested in adding a bigger salary to the roster. That Cubs team was eliminated from the wild-card race on the next-to-last day of the 1995 season. Had they had Larry Walker they probably make the playoffs," Stone told me.

That tight-fisted mentality filtered down from MacPhail to his top lieutenant, then–Cubs GM Ed Lynch, who held fast with the purse strings during his tenure on the North Side of Chicago. "I also went to Ed with a possible deal. A Houston Astros scout sought me out at Wrigley one day before a game. He asked me if the Cubs would be interested in Craig Biggio. I said I'm sure they would be but let me ask Ed Lynch.

"The Astros were considering a drastic reduction in payroll if they fell out of the playoff race and knew that if they traded Biggio, the future Hall of Famer would bring a tremendous haul of young prospects. While the Cubs farm system wasn't great, there were a few highly regarded prospects in it at that time. Houston wanted a handful of those guys and was willing to consider a deal, according to one of their scouts," Stone told me over lunch in May of 2016.

"I walked into Ed's office and I relayed the conversation that I had just had with Houston. Ed wheeled around, typed something into his computer, and turned back and said something I will never forget: 'We have Rey Sanchez locked up for three years real cheap. No, I won't do that,' he told me.

"I said to Ed, 'Maybe you're misunderstanding me. I'm not talking about Myron Biggio. I'm talking about Craig Biggio. You know, one of the best players in baseball?' However, you have to understand that at that time the Tribune Co. wasn't spending the kind of money they would eventually spend later in their ownership. That was the mentality at that time," Stone added.

The Cubs in the Draft Under Andy MacPhail

A look at the Cubs first round draft picks during MacPhail's tenure shows dismal failure during a period of time that saw the Cubs pick in the top 10 of the draft an astounding six times in his 12 years. Of those six picks, only one played in an All-Star Game as a Chicago Cub and of the 12 first round picks he was responsible for, five *never* played a game in the major leagues.

Ed Lynch GM (MacPhail was team president)

1995	4th overall	Kerry Wood	RHP, Grand Prairie HS (TX)
1996	17th overall	Todd Noel	RHP, North Vermillion HS (LA)
1997	10th overall	Jon Garland	RHP, Kennedy HS (CA)
1998	3rd overall	Corey Patterson	OF, Harrison HS (GA)
1999	26th overall	Ben Christensen	RHP, Wichita State University (KS)
2000	3rd overall	Luis Montanez	SS, Coral Park HS (FL)

Andy MacPhail GM (he was also team president)

2001	2nd overall	Mark Prior	RHP, USC (CA)
2002	21st overall	Bobby Brownlie	RHP, Rutgers University (NJ)
2002	32nd overall	Luke Hagerty	LHP, Ball State University (IN)
2002	36th overall	Chadd Blasko	RHP, Purdue University (IN)
2002	38th overall	Matt Clanton	RHP, Orange Coast College (CA)

Jim Hendry GM (MacPhail was team president through the end of the 2006 season)

Year	Pick	Player	Position, School
2003	6th overall	Ryan Harvey	OF, Dunedin HS (FL)
2004	No first-round pick (lost as compensation for signing free agent LaTroy Hawkins)		
2005	20th overall	Mark Pawelek	LHP, Springville HS (UT)
2006	13th overall	Tyler Colvin	OF, Clemson University (SC)
2007	3rd overall	Josh Vitters	3B, Cypress HS (CA)
2007	48th overall	Josh Donaldson	C, Auburn University (AL)
2008	19th overall	Andrew Cashner	RHP, Texas Christian University (TX)
2008	41st overall	Ryan Flaherty	SS, Vanderbilt University (TN)
2009	31st overall	Brett Jackson	CF, UC Berkeley (CA)
2010	16th overall	Hayden Simpson	RHP, Southern Arkansas University (AR)
2011	9th overall	Javier Baez	SS, Arlington Country Day School (FL)

shaded = Made Major Leagues

Perhaps knowing that their ownership days were numbered, the fall of 2006 saw dramatic changes in how the Chicago Cubs went about their business. Gone were the spending restrictions that had hampered the Cubs for so long. Instead, the business plan was replaced by almost reckless spending, knowing that the Tribune Co. would likely not be around long enough to foot the bill for much of the long-term contracts the team was agreeing to.

A new team president was named in October 2006. Out was Andy MacPhail and in was the game's best marketing mind, Cubs Marketing VP John McDonough, who immediately told the starving fan base "It's Time to Win" at his first press conference in October of 2006. McDonough retained Hendry as GM and the two went about rebuilding the major league team on the fly.

The Cubs re-signed third baseman Aramis Ramirez for $75 million and retained closer Kerry Wood, then they signed a record eight-year, $136-million contract with that off-season's top prize, OF Alfonso Soriano. Also added was reliable starting pitcher Ted Lilly, multitalented IF/OF Mark DeRosa, pitcher Jason Marquis, and celebrity manager Lou Piniella, who arrived amid tremendous fanfare.

Suddenly, the Cubs meant business. Gone were their tight-fisted ways; they were ready to take a seat at the big boy table. Piniella, though, had been chosen by Hendry over two other candidates that might have been better hires. Current Yankees manager Joe Girardi, a former Cubs catcher, wanted the job badly and was the favorite choice of team president McDonough.

Current San Francisco Giants manager (and future Hall of Famer) Bruce Bochy also interviewed for the job and wanted the chance to pilot the Cubs. However, Hendry wasn't as enamored with Girardi and felt that Piniella was the "sexier" hire, so he tabbed the colorful and bombastic former Yankees skipper as the Cubs manager in November 2006, giving him a mandate to turn the Cubs into winners.

Piniella and Hendry made a gallant run at changing the Cubs from "lovable losers" to world champions. The 2007 and 2008 Cubs went to the playoffs and in 2008 their 97 wins was the best in the National League. However, the team was built on a crumbling foundation in the minor leagues and as the veterans who agreed to big contracts aged or suffered injuries there was not a stable of low-cost, high-talent replacements waiting in the Cubs minor league system for their chance.

The 2009 season saw the Cubs battle to stay in contention throughout a turbulent year. After being swept by the Arizona Diamondbacks in the 2007 playoffs and the Los Angeles

Dodgers in the 2008 playoffs, Hendry decided that his team needed more offense. He bypassed some of the available options to sign troubled but talented outfielder Milton Bradley to a three-year, $30-million deal when no one else in baseball was willing to guarantee the explosive slugger more than a one-year contract.

The gamble blew up in Hendry's face almost from the start of the '09 season as Bradley feuded with teammates as well as the Chicago media. He was sent home during a game against the White Sox in June after getting into a dugout dispute with teammates and he was suspended for the remainder of the season in late September. Hendry traded him to Seattle for pitcher Carlos Silva after the 2009 season.

With Ricketts taking over after that season, many observers expected Hendry to be fired. Instead, though, Ricketts approved a contract extension for his GM and some of his top lieutenants. Tom Ricketts was a newbie in the baseball world and he wasn't about to embark on his first foray as a team owner by also cleaning house in his front office.

With Hendry still the GM, the Ricketts family hoped that a team that was aging and struggling to contend could turn things around with a few tweaks. Prior to the 2011 season the Cubs signed first baseman Carlos Pena, brought back the wildly popular Kerry Wood to be the team's closer, and traded a cache of prospects to Tampa for starting pitcher Matt Garza.

The signings continued a pattern for the Cubs in the early 2000s of bringing in aging players and hoping to catch lightning in a bottle for the team to be competitive. However, the signings weren't devastating to the team's long-term future. The contracts weren't massive or long-term. The trade for Garza though, was entirely different.

To acquire a solid but unspectacular starter the Cubs gave up two of their top minor league prospects in shortstop Hak Ju Lee and, more importantly, their top pitching prospect in right-hander Chris Archer.

Cubs by Year

Year	W–L	Pct.	Finish
2003	88–74	.543	1st
2004	89–73	.549	3rd
2005	79–83	.488	4th
2006	66–96	.407	6th
2007	85–77	.525	1st
2008	97–64	.602	1st
2009	83–78	.516	2nd
2010	75–87	.463	5th
2011	71–91	.438	5th
2012	61–101	.377	5th
2013	66–96	.407	5th
2014	73–89	.451	5th
2015	97–65	.599	3rd
2016	103–58	.640	1st

"Archer is a future star and I just cannot believe that the Cubs would give him up to acquire a pitcher in Garza who will never be as good as the guy they are giving up on," a former GM now scouting in the American League told me at the time. "They have no chance to contend in 2011 and I don't understand why they would do that. It's the move of a GM [Jim Hendry] who is trying to keep his job. I can't believe that new ownership would sign off on that deal. It's a horrible trade for the Cubs," he went on to tell me.

Ricketts publicly pledged his support for Hendry and his team of scouts but privately he began to assess the landscape in the baseball operations department. He commissioned a study of every team in Major League Baseball and their performance in the amateur draft, knowing that if he wanted to build a solid franchise he would have to start spending big in scouting and player development. Spending in the amateur world is an endeavor fraught with peril, as baseball scouting of 18-year-old prospects is one of the most inexact sciences in the world. It was also an endeavor that the Tribune Co. did not embrace until late in their ownership run.

However, as the franchise continued losing games and falling behind in the standings, the Ricketts quietly went about the business of learning the machinations of Major League Baseball and sizing up what they would need to do to completely overhaul the franchise they had purchased. Tom Ricketts knew he needed new leadership on the baseball side and he knew it had to be someone who understood that the minor league system had to start producing players.

Ricketts was more than willing to spend and spend big in the amateur world. It was a decision that helped convince Epstein to accept the challenge and come to Chicago. During the 2011 draft, which was Hendry's last in charge, Ricketts told his baseball operations team to go for it despite the massive cost to sign all of their top draft picks.

"As the Cubs' draft went on, we were sitting around in [the Red Sox] draft room, and we could tell what they were doing," Epstein said. "We said, 'Hey, they get it. They're finally getting it.'... That got my attention, the attention of a lot of other people in the game.... It was a significant moment."

The Cubs 2011 draft class was loaded with highly rated prospects. From shortstop Javier Baez to first baseman Dan Vogelbach, the Cubs grabbed as many high-ceiling players as they could. No matter the cost, Tom Ricketts approved the signing bonuses it took to add a large collection of talent to the Cubs system. Now there was the matter of getting those players signed to contracts.

Unknown to anyone outside of Ricketts inner circle, Jim Hendry knew in mid-June that he would not be returning to the Cubs as general manager after the 2011 season. However, Ricketts and Hendry had an understanding that he would stay on the job until that prized draft class was signed. The request by Ricketts and subsequent agreement by Hendry to finish the job showed tremendous class on the part of the outgoing GM. He was the linchpin to getting those guys signed and he was a man of his word. I have nothing but the highest regard for Jim Hendry," Tom Ricketts told me.

3

The GM Job

There may be no more affable and accommodating executive in the game of baseball than Jim Hendry, the Chicago Cubs general manager from July 2002 to August 2011. Hendry replaced his boss, Andy MacPhail, as the Cubs GM in July 2002 after the Cubs president fired field manager Don Baylor and stepped away from running the baseball operations of the club on a day-to-day basis with the Cubs just 34–49.

Hendry hit the ground running, taking a team that finished 2002 an abysmal 67–95 and beginning his rebuild almost immediately. He identified the man he wanted above all others to manage his team, and while Dusty Baker still had a World Series appearance to navigate later that season, the rumors around baseball were that he was leaving his job managing the Giants at the end of the season, no matter how his club finished.

Hendry had heard the rumors and had long admired the way Baker managed his teams and how hard his players played for him. He knew that he needed a major hire to instill confidence in his team and he knew he needed a hire that would change the culture around Wrigley Field. "Dusty was a proven winner and I wanted someone who had been around the game and had had success running a team. Dusty checked all of the boxes for us," Hendry told me.

"It started to turn by the end of 2002 and while we weren't ready to be really good yet it wasn't bad anymore. Andy MacPhail had no ego and whenever something went well he'd praise me and when something didn't go well he would take the hit. He was great to work for," Hendry told me when we met at his suburban Chicago home in June 2016.

Hendry finished the 2002 season evaluating the hand that he had been dealt and quickly realized that he needed to add a lot of talent to his roster to turn around a team that had lost 90 games or more three times in the past four seasons. "We came together quickly in '03 and the trade we made with the Dodgers for Mark Grudzielanek and Eric Karros was huge. Both guys played great for us and Eric was a tremendous leader in our clubhouse. The way he conducted himself for our '03 club reminds me a lot of what David Ross is to the 2016 Cubs," Hendry said.

The 2003 season began with very little expectation of the team contending for a World Series championship despite the increased optimism that Baker's hiring had caused among the Cubs' large fan base. The club though, played an up and down first half of the season hanging around the .500 mark into mid-July, which had the team in contention in the National League's Central division.

That sent Hendry into action as he looked to address his club's holes, which included a center fielder who could hit in the leadoff spot and a power hitting third baseman. The savvy GM hit a home run on July 23, 2003, when he acquired veteran outfielder Kenny Lofton and third baseman Aramis Ramirez from the Pittsburgh Pirates.

The Cubs responded almost immediately and began a climb that would see them clinch the division title in late September and then begin a run to the National League Championship Series, before the bizarre events in Game 6 with Cubs fan Steve Bartman that drew worldwide attention. "Once we made the trade with Pittsburgh our team really started to jell. We played great baseball down the stretch and I really felt like we could make a run if we made the playoffs," Hendry told me.

Hendry's Cubs did indeed make a run in the playoffs, beating the favored Atlanta Braves 5–1 in a decisive fifth game in Atlanta in the National League Division Series behind star pitcher Kerry Wood.

Playing at Wrigley Field with a three games to two lead in Game 6 of the National League Championship Series against the then Florida Marlins, the Cubs were just five outs from their first World Series appearance since 1945.

Then, disaster struck the Cubs. Leading 3–0 with their other ace pitcher Mark Prior dominating, a foul ball off the bat of Marlins second baseman Luis Castillo floated towards the seats along the left-field line. Cubs left fielder Moises Alou leaped to make the catch but as fans scrambled to grab the souvenir, one fan made contact with the ball, preventing Alou from making the play.

Alou was furious and his reaction enraged the Wrigley faithful who quickly directed their ire at Cubs fan Steve Bartman, who had touched the ball in flight. The following hitter, Miguel Cabrera, hit a sure-fire double play ground ball to Cubs shortstop Alex Gonzalez, who booted the ball, and before the Cubs would get out of the inning the Marlins had scored eight runs and had the Cubs reeling.

The next night the Cubs lost Game 7 and their dream of going to the World Series was over. The fan base was angry and made

Steve Bartman's life a living hell. He received death threats and he became a convenient scapegoat for a fan base that was livid.

With the Cubs faithful and the Chicago media no longer willing to accept mediocrity as long as the "Wrigley experience" was exceptional, the 2004 season began with tremendous expectations that the franchise's nearly 100-year title drought would finally come to an end. "We could have won in '03 and we should have won in '04. We were the most talented team in the National League and despite some injuries we were really good later in the season," Hendry told me.

As the 2004 season began, a fair number or experts and publications were picking the Cubs to get to or win the World Series. However, injuries hit the Cubs' vaunted pitching staff and some on the club feuded with team broadcasters Steve Stone and Chip Caray. The team found themselves distracted and unlikeable despite a massive amount of talent. "That is the most talented team I have ever been a part of," outfielder Todd Hollandsworth told me despite playing on the Florida Marlins 2003 world champions.

Stone was more direct in his assessment of what happened to that team that kept them out of the postseason. "The Cubs choked their way out of a playoff berth. That's just a fact," the popular TV voice told me. "They directed their anger at Chip and especially me and that was wrong. Dusty, Andy [MacPhail], and Jim did nothing to stop it and the players let that consume them instead of worrying about getting the job done on the field. They lost their focus and in the end they went home instead of being one of the final eight teams standing. That's sad because I really believe that had they made the postseason the Cubs definitely had enough talent to win it all."

"We had some injuries but with a month to go in the season we were playing much better. I really believe we were the best team in the National League once we got healthy but we didn't get in and that season disappoints me as much as any season while I was there because we had a really good team," Hendry said.

There is no doubt that the 2003–04 run of the Chicago Cubs changed the level of expectations for the fan base. Gone was the willingness to sit in the ballpark and cheer as long as the beer was cold, pretty girls were in the bleachers, and Sammy Sosa was belting home runs. The fan base wanted a championship and their tolerance was quickly waning.

Then, in 2005, the crosstown Chicago White Sox won their first World Series since 1917 and now the fan base had even more reason to demand action and high-level spending from the franchise and the Tribune Co. However, in 2006, instead of spending, the Cubs spiraled further out of contention, finishing in last place with an abysmal record of 66–96, which led to the dismissal of Baker as the Cubs manager.

It also led to the dismissal of MacPhail as the team president and it signaled what many believed was a long overdue change in the direction of the Cubs leadership. MacPhail was exceptionally frugal and conservative and many inside the Cubs executive suite believed that he was unwilling to move the Cubs ahead into the modern era. In fact, his frugality bordered on the absurd.

He was known for asking clubhouse staff to disassemble and re-assemble and ship the team's weight room equipment via U-Haul from Wrigley Field to Arizona for spring training every winter. Then the process had to be repeated in late March so that the equipment would be back at Wrigley in time for Opening Day.

"It was ridiculous how the Cubs were being run. Here we were a major market professional sports franchise and we wouldn't buy a second set of weights to keep in Arizona despite the fact that we had minor league players training there and players wanted to work out there in the off-season. Andy thought he was being frugal, but in actuality we were spending more money to disassemble and ship the equipment twice a year than it would have cost to buy new stuff for our Arizona facilities.

"Plus, the set-up we had was lousy. It just continued a pattern of why the franchise was always behind most of our competition. In fact, when Crane Kenney stopped the weights from being shipped to Arizona and instead bought new and better equipment it caused a big fight between Andy and Crane. Crane was 100 percent right but Andy didn't like having his authority usurped," a former front office staffer told me.

While MacPhail had his drawbacks, he's still held in high regard by most who worked for him. Hendry speaks very highly of his old boss and remembers his loyalty and willingness to heap praise on others when things were going well and his willingness to take the blame when things weren't going so well. "Andy was great. He taught me so much about how the job of a general manager should be done. He gave me my opportunity and I will always be grateful to him for that."

Then, in September of 2006, Tribune Co. management decided that major change was finally necessary at the top of the Cubs food chain. MacPhail was out and in his place came one of the brightest minds in professional sports. John McDonough, the club's vice president of marketing and broadcasting, was promoted to president of the team and he immediately reaffirmed his faith in Hendry to begin an immediate infusion of high-level talent at the major league level.

Tribune Co. authorized major spending and Hendry took the company checkbook and set out on a spending spree. From Alfonso Soriano's then–club record eight years, $136 million to four years, $40 million for Ted Lilly to three years, $21 million

Notable Cubs Transactions 2007–08 (Hendry's Last Big Run)

Oct. 25, 2006	Signed Starlin Castro as an amateur free agent
Nov. 14, 2006	Signed Mark DeRosa as free agent
Nov. 16, 2006	Acquired Neal Cotts from White Sox for David Aardsma & Carlos Vasquez
Nov. 20, 2006	Signed Alfonso Soriano as free agent (8 years, $136M)
Dec. 7, 2006	Drafted Josh Hamilton in Rule 5 Draft, sold Hamilton to Reds
Dec. 15, 2006	Signed Ted Lilly as free agent (4 years, $40M)
Dec. 15, 2006	Signed Daryle Ward as free agent
Dec. 19, 2006	Signed Jason Marquis as free agent
Feb. 1, 2007	Signed Cliff Floyd as free agent
July 16, 2007	Acquired Jason Kendall & cash from Athletics for Jerry Blevins & Rob Bowen
Dec. 12, 2007	Signed Kosuke Fukudome as free agent (4 years, $48M)
May 14, 2008	Signed Jim Edmonds as free agent
Jul. 8, 2008	Acquired Rich Harden & Chad Gaudin from Athletics for Josh Donaldson, Sean Gallagher, Matt Murton, & Eric Patterson

for Jason Marquis to re-signing Aramis Ramirez for $75 million, this was unlike anything seen in Chicago sports history. And when the bills were tallied the spending spree totaled $292 million, an obscene amount of money for a franchise that had just months before been exceptionally frugal. What did the spending spree signal? Were the Cubs now actually going for it and was this going to be the new way they did business? Or was there something else afoot that wasn't yet as obvious to observers?

Some in the industry speculated that with the White Sox winning the World Series the Cubs felt tremendous pressure to keep and to maintain their stranglehold on the city's baseball fans. For many years the Cubs had outdrawn their crosstown rivals and in terms of the sheer size of the fan base the difference was massive.

However, with the White Sox winning the title many theorized that a new generation of Chicago baseball fans might switch their allegiance to the team in town with a World Series title. Thus, the Cubs spent and spent big to try to turn around their woeful team in rapid fashion.

Others in and around the game, though, believed something else was at play. A topic that still wasn't gaining as much attention from the mainstream media. The topic involved the Tribune Co. selling the franchise. Tribune had been in a steep decline after the company's $8 billion takeover of the Times Mirror company and the deal which ranked at the time as the largest newspaper acquisition in U.S. history proved to be an almost fatal blow to the company.

"It seems that someone in the Cubs' hierarchy has given Hendry the green light to offer uncharacteristically large sums of money, knowing that the Tribune Company won't be paying the bills for much longer," wrote Murray Chass, the baseball columnist for *The New York Times*.

"The Cubs went out and spent like crazy. It was just like you running up someone else's credit card until it was maxed out but you know that you won't be responsible for paying the bills. They threw money at any player they could get their hands on," a former major league scout told me.

Tribune upper management though, denied that the team was for sale and the preparations for the 2007 season continued with Hendry putting together a vastly improved roster, hiring a new manager in the popular Lou Piniella and a fan base that once again had bought into the hope that "This Is the Year" geared up for what they believed was going to be a championship season.

Then the bombshell news that some had predicted came on Opening Day of 2007, that the Chicago Cubs were indeed for sale. "We did not know what was going on with regards to whether or not the club was for sale," Jim Hendry told me. "We were informed of the news just like everyone else on Opening Day. Lou Piniella and I had to meet with the team to let them know it would not affect them, but it certainly affected how we operated."

While the team struggled to get out of the gate quickly, Piniella was a steady hand at the wheel and Hendry tinkered with his roster enough that the team won 85 games and advanced to the playoffs before they were swept by the Arizona Diamondbacks.

Hendry made more changes in advance of the 2008 season including adding sought-after Japanese outfielder Kosuke Fukudome who signed a four-year $48-million deal with the Cubs, despite having larger offers from several teams including the White Sox and the San Diego Padres. Hendry's recruiting skills were never more evident than in the wooing of Fukudome, who was considered a sure fire major league star by almost every scout who evaluated him and his signing was considered by many the final piece in building a championship team.

The 2008 season was one of the most enjoyable seasons Cubs fans had seen in decades. The team won 97 games and dominated the National League from start to finish and was considered the favorite to win the World Series by oddsmakers and experts alike.

However, like the previous 100 seasons, the postseason ended without a parade in Chicago. The Cubs were swept 3–0 by the Los Angeles Dodgers in a series that was dominated by Dodgers pitching. In fact, in the entire series the Dodgers never used a left-handed pitcher, stymieing the Cubs' vaunted offense with a collection of right handers that shut down Soriano, Ramirez, etc.

Hendry attacked the 2008 off-season like a man possessed, searching for a left-handed bat that he believed would balance the Cubs lineup. He settled on free agent Milton Bradley, a switch hitter who was one of the best pure hitters in the sport.

However, Bradley was mentally unstable and he was a terrible fit in the Cubs clubhouse—not to mention wildly unprepared for the intense Chicago media base that chronicled his every move. The signing was a colossal failure and Bradley finished his lone season in the Windy City on the suspended list before he was traded to Seattle for the equally disappointing Carlos Silva, a starting pitcher who also woefully underachieved.

Hendry also attempted to add a top-flight starter to the Cubs rotation and had a deal basically consummated in December 2008 for San Diego Padres star Jake Peavy. "I received a phone call from my bosses while I was at the winter meetings and they informed me that we were done spending. We had to pull out of the Peavy talks and we had to move money if we wanted to make any deals at all. The back-loaded contracts that we had been giving out because of the company's financial problems along with the way that the sale was structured made it very difficult to make deals after the 2008 season as the company went through the sale process," Hendry told me.

"I will never use any excuses for why we didn't win the World Series while I was the general manager. I would never blame the owner. I was the guy in charge and we had had more than enough resources to put together a quality roster. We came close but we just didn't get over the hump. I had been here long enough. Whatever the financial hurdles were that's what Tom had to deal with to buy the club and whatever issues it caused for me as we put the team together that's part of the gig. I will never make an excuse for why we didn't win," Hendry told me.

"In the last five years I was there we had three different owners. The Tribune people were great to work for. I would have loved to have won it for Jim Dowdle and Dennis FitzSimons and everyone else I worked for. Then we had the Zell years while the club was for sale and then Tom came in and he was great, but no one could have won the last two years I was there because of all of the financial restrictions that were a part of the sale as well as all of the back-loaded deals that we had given out because Tribune wanted to try to win before they sold the club," Hendry said.

"Once you start going down that path by spending a lot of money and back loading deals like we did in '07 and '08 you either have to keep going a little longer than we did if the sale wasn't finalized or you have to do what they eventually did because we weren't going to win in 2010 or 2011," he added.

As Hendry looks at what the Cubs franchise now looks like he is full of praise for the job that Theo Epstein has done overhauling the franchise. "I'm in a good spot," Hendry told me as we talked in his suburban Chicago home one evening during the 2016 season. "I'm not mad at anybody. I don't bitch about anything that didn't go our way.

"Tom Ricketts and I have a tremendous relationship and Theo and I are good friends. You cannot have done a better job than he has done. Tremendous. World class. I do believe that it was time for me to go. It took somebody with the credentials that Theo already had and somebody that had rings. He's done this rebuild brilliantly. God bless him. He is brilliant and on a scale of one to 10 he pulled a 10. There is no way anyone else in the world could have done this better."

When Hendry's dismissal was made public in August 2011 many around the game assumed the Cubs would hire someone on the way up. A respected assistant from a winning franchise appeared to be the pool of candidates that Tom Ricketts would choose from. However, Ricketts had another name in mind, a name that was among the biggest in the game. He wanted to find out if Boston Red Sox GM Theo Epstein would have any interest in moving to Chicago to run the Cubs.

Ricketts had spoken with many people around the game as he tried to learn the world of Major League Baseball both on the baseball operations side and on the business side. His number one confidante was baseball commissioner Bud Selig, who heard from Ricketts on a constant basis. "Tom would call me a lot to ask questions about various issues that he was navigating with the Cubs. Some of those were business related and many of those were baseball related," Selig told me.

Another person that Ricketts spent time with was Oakland A's executive VP and GM Billy Beane. Beane had a stellar reputation around baseball and he knew the inner workings of the game as well as anyone.

After dismissing Hendry, Ricketts began the process of searching for his next baseball operations boss. He did his due diligence, speaking to several people whose opinions he trusted. One of those was Beane. Ricketts flew to San Francisco late in the 2011 season and met with Beane in a downtown hotel.

"I spent quite a bit of time with Tom one day. He had asked my owner if he could talk with me about the Cubs and the process of hiring a general manager. It was not about me taking that job. It was simply about giving him my perspective about the Cubs job, the type of candidates he should be thinking about, and the process of building a new front office," Beane told me.

"I remember our meeting in San Francisco and I remember telling Tom that he had a job that was one of the best in our industry. He needed to know that the position that he was going to be filling was one of the most desirable ones in the game. I told him that warranted some of the best guys in the industry being on his list, not just the next group of up-and-coming guys. Literally, that there was a group of guys at the top of our sport and Theo was one of those guys obviously that anyone would love to have for many reasons," Beane told me.

Beane wanted to make sure that Tom Ricketts knew, despite the losing that had gone on, that the job as GM of the Chicago Cubs was one of the best jobs in Major League Baseball. "The reasons started at the top. The Ricketts family had at that point in 2011 already developed an excellent reputation in the industry and I just told him why the Cubs job would be so attractive to the best guys in our sport. It started at the top with the family but it also included the resources that were going to be available to put the team together. Chicago is a great city to live in and the Cubs have a great fan base. I wanted him to know that he needed to look at those types and not the next group of up-and-coming candidates. Don't settle for the next good up-and-comer. Settle for the best in the business, that's how good the Cubs job is," Beane said.

Beane also counseled Ricketts about the need to have a long-term vision and to have a baseball boss that also embraced that philosophy about handling the bumps in the road as they began the turnaround of the franchise. "Tom had to be patient and he had to have a baseball operations boss who also had patience because the way they rebuilt the franchise takes time," Beane said.

"It was a perfect storm of ownership, a city that had been waiting and had a passionate fan base, and that ultimately you had a guy in Theo that was a young guy and that had the energy that it would take to handle the job. The end result was that it couldn't have played out more perfectly for the Cubs. So much so that before the playoffs started this year I told my oldest daughter, Casey, who lives in Chicago, that I was getting her tickets because it could be historical and you need to be there. When she sent me a picture from one of the games and she had a Cubs hat on, I told her she could have at least snuck an A's hat into the game," he chuckled.

Beane understood what the Cubs' plan was and what they were trying to do as soon as Epstein was hired. "It was clear to me what they were trying to do from the start. Again, it comes down to trying to put something together that was sustainable and could be good or great for a long time. Given how long it had been for that market and where they were as a franchise at that time it needed to be done. But, most importantly, Theo knew going in that he had the backing of the owner and that's the really hard thing to find. To have the guy above you and he buys into what you are doing and you have his support. That's not easy to find because as an owner people around you want that immediate satisfaction of making that one free agent signing that may look good for a year but might not be the best thing for the long-term.

"Again, you literally could not have mapped out more perfectly a vision and have it succeed exactly as was planned. As we go into next year it's hard to imagine that they won't be possibly even better because you're talking about young players. They have guys who are in their early twenties who haven't even reached the prime of their career. It's one of those things that's almost too perfect because in these jobs you always worry for something to happen but this past season couldn't have gone any better with the exception of the injury to Kyle Schwarber," Beane added.

"It goes back to the strength of the plan they had and the discipline to execute that plan. The discipline they showed is very impressive, especially in a very emotional business in a large market like that is very impressive. It's easy to say now that you will stay disciplined but Theo is a competitive guy and it is not easy going through it.

"It's not easy going home every night when you are getting beat. That's not how any of us are built and I know that's not how Theo is built. You don't get into this business–it's not part of your DNA to accept losing. It's still no fun going home every night after getting beat even if it is part of the plan. That being said, that's why it took a lot of discipline. They had it. Credit their entire organization from the top down. It was hard not to admire what they did and it's hard not to enjoy it as someone who has been in the business for over 30 years. Even the guys that they added when they did start spending money they were really perfect additions. It's hard not to enjoy watching what has transpired there. It's been great for the sport and it's obviously been great for the city," Beane told me.

Minor league players are the only cost-effective additions that a team can make because wading into free agency on an annual basis has a certainty to send payroll soaring with very little chance for sustained success. "You pay huge dollars in free agency based on what a player did in the past not on what he does in your uniform. It's a really crazy way to build a team," Ricketts told me in a radio interview I conducted with him in 2011.

So while the 2011 Cubs were floundering on the field, the state of the Cubs minor league system was even worse. The various levels of the Cubs minor league system were devoid of many impact prospects. Players who appeared to be future major league stars were few and far between. Add in an aging stadium, antiquated spring training facilities, and the smallest front office staff in all of baseball and you had a franchise that was one of the worst in the sport. In short, the Chicago Cubs future was as bleak as any in baseball.[1]

Tom Ricketts decided to conduct a study of every team in baseball to see what executives were the best at building through the draft and international free agency. He surmised after talking with dozens of baseball types that unless he had the resources to spend on a par with the New York Yankees and the Boston Red Sox on an annual basis he had to be willing to tear his baseball team down to the foundation and then rebuild it with a series of astute draft picks, trades, and less expensive free agent signings.

He also knew that to execute that plan he had to hire someone with an outstanding record in that department but it also had to be someone with a proven record as winner. That would give his rabid fan base reason to believe the rebuild would work.

It would also buy time for the franchise to rebuild the physical infrastructure of the Cubs facilities in Chicago, Arizona, and the Dominican Republic, where the Cubs were trying to grab their share of that country's incredibly rich teenage talent base.

Who could the Cubs find who had a proven track record of success *and* was willing to leave their current job *and* would want to take on a challenge as great as the Cubs rebuild posed? Several names drew speculation, including New York Yankees GM Brian Cashman, Oakland A's GM Billy Beane, and several up-and-coming executives who had little or no experience running their own baseball operations department. One name though, piqued Tom Ricketts interest more than any other. It was a name that most observers thought would have little or no interest in uprooting his young family and leaving the job that he had as the GM of his favorite team as a child.

---

1. For a full list of Cubs drafts of amateur prospects from 1994 to 2011 see Appendix I.

That name was Theo Epstein and he had already won two World Series as the general manager of the Boston Red Sox and in the process he had helped to end the Curse of the Bambino. A curse which fans of the Red Sox believed in since their team had not won a World Series since then Boston owner Harry Frazee sold Babe Ruth to the New York Yankees in 1920 for $125,000 to finance several Broadway plays he was producing.

After a detailed background investigation into Epstein's availability and after doing informational interviews with a handful of well-respected baseball minds, including current Oakland A's general manager Billy Beane, current Chicago White Sox general manager Rick Hahn, and former Los Angeles Dodgers general manager Dan Evans, Ricketts began his pursuit of the youthful Epstein. The pursuit of Theo was on.

"I only interviewed one person for the Cubs job," Ricketts told me. "I met with a few people as I waited to pursue Theo but those other meetings were informational only or just an opportunity for me to get to know some of the other names who were well-respected in case we couldn't reach a deal with Theo. He was the only candidate that I officially interviewed to work for us."

One thing that most observers of the Cubs don't know is who was quietly advising Tom Ricketts as he went about the process of learning the world of Major League Baseball. With Tom Ricketts and his siblings having absolutely no experience in baseball or having any close confidantes that were well-versed in the inner workings of the game Tom Ricketts needed a sounding board that he could trust. A person who had no hidden agenda. Someone who only wanted the best for Tom, the Cubs, and Major League Baseball.

I said to Tom Ricketts when we met in June 2016, "Someone had to advise you as the process went along. There is no way that you learned the game and the business on your own. So, who was your most trusted and influential advisor?"

Ricketts chuckled as he said to me, "So you don't think I learned all of this by just studying and watching? Of course I had help and almost all of the advice that I got came from Bud Selig. He was tremendous to deal with.

"Bud knows everything about the game and the business of baseball. He helped advise me through the process from the time we became a serious candidate to buy the franchise through the time we decided to pursue Theo. He was always there to answer any question that we had."

In addition, Ricketts had received not only financial advice but, unbeknownst to anyone, excellent baseball advice from an unlikely source as he prepared to buy the franchise. White Sox chairman Jerry Reinsdorf told Ricketts during that US Cellular Field meeting with Sal Galatioto that he didn't need to worry about big decisions on the baseball side of the Cubs.

"Jerry was very nice to me. He invited me down to a game and as we talked he told me to not worry about my GM or my field manager or anything on the baseball side of the business. He told me to concentrate on getting our deal done and finalizing the sale process. He told me there was plenty of time for the rest of the baseball side of the business but not to concern myself with that side at the start. He recommended that I learn the business first. It was great advice," Ricketts said.

"Had I changed GMs right away I would have gone into the search not having any idea what I really wanted in a front office executive. I would have ended up hiring someone who may or may not have been good. But it would have prevented me from making a change after I spent some time learning the business and more importantly the inner workings of our franchise. By waiting, we had a much better idea of what the strengths and weaknesses of our organization were and exactly what type of a person we wanted to lead the baseball operations side of the business," Ricketts said.

4

The Money—Mesa, Wrigley, and the Rooftops

"We used to be a corporate franchise that was run like a family business. Now we are a family-owned franchise that is run like a corporate business. And I mean that in a good way,"

—Crane Kenney, President/Business Operations of the Chicago Cubs, June 2016

While Theo Epstein is the Chicago Cubs President of Baseball Operations and the most well-known executive in Chicago sports, Crane Kenney is the bulldog who is the President of Business Operations for the Cubs. Kenney has endured more than his fair share of barbs from the Chicago media since assuming control of the Cubs in 2003 while he served as General Counsel for the Tribune Company. He has often been on the front line of the Cubs' battles with Chicago's political leaders as the franchise looked to receive approval for an extensive renovation of venerable Wrigley Field. In addition, Kenney has also been the point man on various projects in and around Wrigley Field, including dealing with the rooftop owners whose buildings overlook Wrigley's outfield.

Kenney and his business team have been an integral part of seeing the revenues of the Cubs rise dramatically since the Ricketts family assumed control of the Cubs in 2009. Those revenues have come from several large sponsorship deals that are long-term in their length and are worth nearly half a billion dollars in total. The increase in revenue led Kenney to utter a quote in a *Bloomberg Businessweek* story that has now become a part of Cubs lore. "My job is to fill a wheelbarrow with money, take it to Theo's office, and dump it."

Constructing a winning business plan in baseball involves not only the team on the field but the entire baseball operations side of the business operating in concert with the business side of the franchise. You cannot have a successful team if you can't afford to pay top salaries to attract the best players.

And you cannot sell tickets, negotiate lucrative sponsorship deals, and register large ratings on radio and television if you don't have a very good baseball team. That meant that for the Cubs' new business plan to succeed, Epstein and Kenney had to both have their respective departments synced up to operate at peak efficiency at the same time.

The Legacy Partnerships

The new business philosophy was finally put in place and articulated to the world after Epstein was hired, but the plan had actually been developing since the Ricketts family purchased the team in 2009. It involved many facets of the franchise but the backbone of the improved revenue streams were "legacy partnerships." These were long-term deals in various categories for tens of millions of dollars. An even more lucrative revenue stream, a new Cubs TV deal, was not available to the club because of a pre-existing contract with Comcast SportsNet that predated the sale of the franchise and will not expire until after the 2019 season.

Crane Kenney

- Named Cubs President of Business Operations in 2009
- Born 12/31/1962 in Quincy, MA
- Holds law degree from U of Michigan & Bachelor's degree from Notre Dame
- Began Cubs career in 1994 as an attorney
- Oversees the 1060 Project; the current restoration plan for Wrigley Field

However, when a new TV deal is announced it is expected to bring in revenues that will dwarf the sponsorship side of the Cubs' business plan. Kenney is heading up those negotiations and over the past several years he has investigated every possible opportunity that has expressed interest in the Cubs TV rights knowing that the long-term financial health of the franchise will be greatly affected by the deal the Cubs consummate.

In addition, ticket sales are obviously closely linked to the success of the team on the field and with the Cubs going through a full-scale rebuild after Epstein and his team were hired it was not easy to get fans to pay their hard-earned money to see a team that was not trying their hardest to win as they rebuilt the franchise. The Cubs had struggled in 2010 and 2011 before Epstein was hired and they were a combined 346–464 from 2010 to 2014.

Kenney and the rest of the business team have done yeoman work adding sponsors and increasing revenue streams so that Theo Epstein and Jed Hoyer have as much money as possible to add impact talent to the Cubs organization. Their impact on the Cubs has not been lost on Cubs chairman Tom Ricketts.

"Crane and Colin Faulkner, who succeeded Wally Hayward, have done a tremendous job building the best sales and marketing team in baseball. They've developed deep partnerships with blue chip corporate sponsors who buy into our plan for winning a World Series, becoming a consistent championship contender, and creating a great experience for our fans. They consistently elevate our brand and innovate to bring great corporate partners to the Cubs and our fans," Ricketts told me.

With Kenney and his business team executing the plan that had been put in place, the Cubs were able to close several other deals that brought significant increases in revenue into the Cubs coffers. The deals are all with blue chip companies and all of the deals are very lengthy and in total have generated hundreds of millions of dollars for the franchise.

To attract highly successful companies and to get them to make major financial commitments for multiple years in sponsorship of a baseball team, you would think that team would have to be highly successful on the field. However, the Chicago Cubs proved that on-field success was not crucial to landing a major sponsorship deal.

Instead, the Cubs, through the work of Kenney's business team, sold hope, an elite fan experience, and the vision of what it would be like to be a part of a Cubs team that annually competed for championships. "We sold the chance to be part of something extremely rare and special. The chance to be a legacy partner with the Cubs and to be a part of the Cubs finally winning a World Series," Tom Ricketts said.

The Cubs may not have had a championship-caliber team to sell in 2012, '13, and '14, but they had other attractive things to take to the market that were sure to impress potential advertisers and potential legacy partners. That included iconic Wrigley Field, the Cubs' massive fan base, and the chance to be a part of what *Sports Illustrated* called, "The Last Great American Sports Story," in an article that ran early in the 2016 season.

Potential advertisers were lined up like planes trying to land at O'Hare and the Cubs spared no expense in making their pitch. A $1.1 million dollar "Presentation Center" opened in 2013 and is where Tom Ricketts, Crane Kenney, Colin Faulkner, Wally Hayward before him, and the rest of the Cubs business team made their pitches to various companies for sponsorship opportunities in a renovated Wrigley Field and the future adjacent boutique hotel and plaza. The pitch center offers various perspectives on what an advertiser can expect if they reach a deal with the Cubs.

The front is modeled after a renovated Cubs skybox complete with photos of various Wrigley Field events, including a Bruce Springsteen concert, a Northwestern football game vs. the University of Illinois, and two shots of a packed ballpark, one an aerial shot and one from center field.

To help pay for the several hundred million dollar renovation of the ballpark, called the 1060 Project (Wrigley Field is located at 1060 W. Addison Street), the Cubs were asking for some of the longest commitments–up to 20 years–from corporate sponsors in American professional sports. In return, companies were guaranteed exclusive rights in premier categories such as beer, soft drinks, airline travel, and financial services, as well as banking and investment programs, meaning fewer but far more lucrative deals. In short, they went with a less-is-more approach, making the value of a sponsorship and the use of the Cubs' iconic logo much more valuable to a limited number of sponsors.

However, as the Ricketts began to overhaul the organization they encountered roadblocks at nearly every turn. From the political machinations of the City of Chicago and mayor Rahm Emanuel to the alderman whose ward encompassed Wrigley

Field to the rooftop owners who sought to block some of the renovations and the two video boards that were a key piece of the Cubs' new sponsorship plan, it seemed that every day brought a new challenge that needed to be overcome.

"We would sit up in Tom's suite after games having a beer and we would say, 'Can you believe all of the stuff that we have to overcome?' You couldn't make it up. I mean, I'm in the sports business and you couldn't believe some of the stuff behind the scenes that was taking place," Hayward remembered of his early days with the franchise.

However, the Cubs business team soldiered on and began to make progress with some of the Cubs' existing sponsors. They signed those that wanted to stay involved to one- or two-year bridge deals that were set to expire when other longer term deals that predated the Ricketts family would also be up for renewal.

In essence, it gave the business team a clean slate with which to totally revamp the way the franchise sold its corporate partnership deals. However, the 2009 season saw an aging Cubs team miss the playoffs and had a player in Milton Bradley who was so disliked by people inside and outside of the organization that the Cubs traded him one year into a three-year, $30-million deal.

Popular manager Lou Piniella walked away from his job during the 2010 season and the team began a slide that would see the Cubs finish a combined 118 games under .500 between the 2010 and 2014 seasons, with no division finish higher than fifth place.

So, how do you convince major corporations with balance sheets, shareholders, and corporate checks and balances in place to spend millions of dollars partnering with one of the worst teams on the field in the history of the sport? You present them with the opportunity to embark on a journey of hope and the chance to be part of sports history.

Competition to partner with the Cubs was intense and led to bidding wars in multiple categories, with the total dollars of the legacy partner deals nearing a half billion dollars at the time this book was written. In the beer category, Anheuser Busch beat out a field of deep-pocketed contenders, but with pouring rights in the ballpark and in the under construction adjoining plaza also included in the sponsorship, the deal was especially attractive to the top brands in the industry. Multiple industry sources have pegged the beer deal at $140 million dollars over a 14-year period. The deal gives the company a highly sought-after sign in the right-field bleachers, naming rights of the entire bleacher area, and a right-field bleacher patio.

Under a separate deal with the Ricketts-owned Hickory Street Capital LLC, the Budweiser brand will have signage in the Wrigley Field plaza, and in the hotel that the team is building across the street from the ballpark. In addition, the exclusivity clause in the deal allows only Anheuser Busch (in the beer category) the ability to use the Cubs' highly recognizable logo in their advertising. "It's probably by far the single best presentation that I've seen," Blaise D'Sylva, Anheuser Busch's Vice President of Media, Sports, and Entertainment Marketing told the *Chicago Tribune* shortly after the agreement with the Cubs was announced.

Kenney, Faulkner, and the rest of the Cubs business team, plus Hayward and his offshoot company W Partners, which he started with the backing of the Ricketts family after resigning from the Cubs, worked together to sell sponsors on the opportunity to partner with the Cubs and with Wrigley Field.

Under Kenney's direction the business team completely overhauled the way the Cubs sold sponsorships and they looked to make sponsoring the Cubs something very unique and special.

"We all looked at the Cubs' existing sponsorship model and decided we wanted to make being a sponsor of the Cubs very exclusive at the top levels of our sponsorship program," Kenney told me. "We thought that a less-is-more approach was the way to go and we all spent a lot of time trying to put our business plan together.

"Tom has been great in letting us put the plan together and then going on pitch meetings whenever we asked him to. To be able to have the owner of the team look a prospective advertiser in the eye and explain our plan and his vision is something not every franchise gets to do and we know how fortunate we are to have him," Kenney added.

While the legacy partnerships[1] that Kenney's team negotiated are extremely important to the franchise's bottom line, several other revenue streams are far more lucrative and should have the biggest impact on how much money Theo Epstein and Jed Hoyer have in their baseball operations budget over the next decade.

Those include increased ticket sales, which despite poor teams from 2010 through the end of the 2014 season, saw the Cubs under Faulkner and his ticket office team's direction modernize their approach to selling tickets. They also developed a partnership with ticket re-seller StubHub and they successfully stripped season tickets from several ticket brokers in the Chicago area to prevent them from scalping their seats in the secondary market.

Add in the Major League Baseball Central Fund, which distributes money to all teams from various lucrative league-wide deals and the Cubs media rights deals and the financial picture for the organization has changed significantly since the Ricketts family purchased the team. On the media rights side, it includes a new radio deal with CBS that gave the Cubs the opportunity to market their product on various CBS radio platforms and to multiple age groups and audiences. The TV deal is the biggest game

---

1. For a list of legacy partners and sponsors, please see Appendix II.

changer and while it cannot begin until after the 2019 season it should be incredibly lucrative once the franchise finalizes a deal. That deal could bring in a haul in the billions.

Getting What They Wanted in Mesa

Kenney was also in charge of the Cubs' negotiations to build a new spring training facility in Mesa, Arizona. He had many in the Phoenix area–from the other teams in the Cactus League to politicians and local residents–furious with what they perceived to be Kenney's hardball tactics in holding Mesa over a barrel to get what he and the Ricketts family felt the Cubs needed to be successful.

Kenney was emphatic regarding what the Cubs wanted in a new year-round facility in Arizona and at first, Mesa and their city council refused to budge in what they were offering. Kenney not only asked for public funding to the tune of nearly $100 million but in the early stages of negotiations one proposal called for a surcharge on all tickets sold throughout the Cactus League to subsidize the Cubs facility.

That request was met with outrage from the other teams who call Arizona home in spring training and it opened Kenney and the Cubs up to tremendous criticism. Baseball commissioner Bud Selig met with the media at spring training in 2010 and was emphatic that there would be no "Cubs tax."

"It's in our hands, it's completely in our hands," Selig said. "We are going to find a situation we accept. If it involves a municipality, we're talking to them if there is a tax. We're looking for the right economic solution."

Selig's comments took away power from the Arizona lawmakers to pass legislation to raise a 10 percent tax on Cactus League tickets sold at all Arizona venues. "If it's not a tax from them [the legislature] then they're not in the picture," Selig said. "We're talking to everybody, including the lawmakers. And they've been very helpful, by the way."

Kenney however, responded to the criticism from the other teams in the Cactus League. "They're welcome to their opinion," Kenney said. "I think the legislators in Arizona and Mesa have one view, and others would like to use other [funding mechanisms], some that have been used already like [the Arizona Sports and Tourism Authority funds]. We're going to let the folks who do that for a living determine the best mechanism for financing the facility. We're happy that Mesa wants us to stay, and the [Ricketts] family is committed to trying to stay here."

The Cubs believed there was some misconception among fans about the so-called "Cubs tax," which Kenney said also would help fund future projects of Cactus League teams. Kenney said the surcharge was not the Cubs' idea. "We did not come up with the tax where we are the largest payer," he said.

When negotiations hit a snag early on in the process, rumors ran rampant that the Cubs were interested in moving to Naples, Florida, and in fact not only did negotiations begin but Kenney was even spotted in a helicopter touring the Naples area to scout potential spring training sites. "Naples went from a long shot to a very viable possibility in about three months. We had a site and we had a group of people in Naples who really wanted the Cubs there," Kenney said.

After the threat to move to Naples began to be taken seriously by those in charge of the Mesa end of the negotiations, things moved in a positive direction and it looked as though the Cubs would end up staying in Arizona, where the team had trained for every season since 1952, with the exception of 1966.

A public referendum was held in 2010, which if approved would give the Cubs $99 million of public financing to build a state-of-the-art facility. A facility that would not only be for spring training, but it would become a year-round home for the Chicago Cubs to train minor league players and to give major league players a place to train in the winter months when the Chicago climate makes training outdoors much more challenging.

Despite serious doubts that emerged throughout the process and despite many public pronouncements that the deal would never clear public and legislative approval, the funding for the facility received 63 percent voter approval, paving the way to keep the Chicago Cubs in Mesa in a facility that would be among the best in all of baseball. "The Cubs have been in Mesa for close to 50 years," Cubs Chairman Tom Ricketts said. "We'd like to stay in Mesa for another 50 years and we look forward to taking what is a truly great spring training experience and turning it into the most remarkable spring training experience ever."

The decisive victory ended more than a year of uncertainty, as the Cubs had entertained the bid for a new complex in Naples, Florida. The city's effort for statewide funding fell apart at the legislature in the spring of 2010, and the plan changed multiple times as Mesa struggled to find funding. Many times, supporters feared the effort was doomed and the Cactus League's most-attended team would bolt for Florida.

"It looked like sudden death," said Robert Brinton, immediate past president of the Cactus League as he spoke with reporters after the referendum results were announced. "We weren't going to win another one, we were out of the game, and here we won the World Series."

The Cubs generate $138 million a year statewide, according to a Mesa-commissioned study. The city acknowledges much of that leaves Mesa because of a lack of businesses around the current facilities, but says more of that will stay in the city with the new complex. The victory to build a new spring training facility was a big one for Kenney and his business team and meant the Cubs would have another big item checked off that was on Kenney's original checklist of things to do on the day that Tom Ricketts finalized the deal to buy the Cubs.

Not only that, once the astounding new facility was built, its positive effects for the Cubs—on the field and organizationally—could be felt throughout the franchise.

Upon arriving at the finished facility, Theo Epstein said, "We look forward to putting it to great use not just during spring training, but year round for our young players to be here and train. There have really been two things that all our baseball ops people have been saying since we walked into this facility for the first time a few days ago. One is, no more excuses. This place is as good as it gets, and the second is related to that, which is, if we can't get better here, we can't get better anywhere, so I promise you we will work extremely hard to get better...and to put that World Series flag on top of this complex to finish it off."

Tom Ricketts echoed those sentiments, adding, "I was here two or three weeks ago, and a player was working out, and he hops up off a weight bench and says, 'Mr. Ricketts, this place is *sick*,' and I'm like, 'You're right, this is sick. This is awesome.' So, anyway, it's a critical component of building the foundation of a team that's gonna be a consistent winner."

One of the key figures in getting a deal done to keep the Cubs out west was Mesa mayor Scott Smith who worked tirelessly to rally support for the Cubs' new spring training complex. "The new Cubs Park and adjoining Riverview Park will provide a spring training experience like no other in Major League Baseball," Smith said. "The two parks are connected by a palm tree–lined paseo with opportunities for retail, restaurant, and hotel development on either side. Mesa calls March our second Christmas when it comes to sales tax numbers, due to the influx of spring training spending. I can't think of a better way to support the economy than to build on our success and develop the parks into a destination for all to play and stay."

From a player's perspective the new spring training facilities were a game changer in helping players prepare for each season and for some it was the difference in them choosing the Cubs over another organization during free agency. "The new facilities in Arizona are huge for us," said Cubs All-Star first baseman Anthony Rizzo. "When you have a place to train that is as good as what we have built in Arizona it gives all of our guys a reason to get to spring training early or to spend a lot of their winter in Arizona. It helps us prepare for the season but it also brings a lot of guys closer together because they spend so much time together out of the season."

From a minor league perspective, being able to send players to the Cubs' home away from Chicago keeps them all together and helps the organization to monitor their progress as they develop. "Having all the players under one roof cannot be spoken lightly of," said Jason McLeod, the Cubs Senior Vice President of Scouting and Player Development. "We have a lot of staff in Arizona, we have outstanding facilities, and being able to keep our guys together helps them to develop a bond as they come through our system on their road to the major leagues."

Battling with the Rooftop Owners

Over the years, the Cubs have also had their battles with the rooftop owners (those who own the 16 buildings that surround Wrigley's iconic bleachers, selling rooftop seating to fans). As the rooftops became big business, the Cubs began the process of reclaiming their product from a group of businessmen who were, as the Cubs saw it, "profiting off the team without paying a dime for the ability to run their business."

That was initially rectified when the two sides agreed to a contract that was signed in 2003. The contract between the Cubs and the rooftop owners provided the team with a 17 percent royalty of the gross revenues of the rooftops, payments that each rooftop had to make to the Cubs to continue operating during Cubs home games.

The contract was put in force to not only provide the Cubs with a royalty payment but also to protect the rooftops, who wanted assurance they would be able to operate their highly successful businesses without fear of being sued by the Cubs and the City of Chicago.

However, after the sale of the Cubs to the Ricketts family in 2009 and the family's stated intention to completely remodel and overhaul the 100-year-old structure, that contract came under tremendous scrutiny. In fact, some of the language contained in the document was so vague that it gave Chicago mayor Rahm Emanuel an opportunity to allow the Ricketts family to renovate the ballpark and block some of the rooftop views for large video boards without fear of losing a lawsuit to the rooftop owners.

The boards are a staple at every other professional sports stadium in the United States and are a large source of revenue, but Wrigley Field had never had anything like them since it opened its doors to baseball in 1914. However, with Ricketts willing to fund the entire renovation project himself, without a dime of public money, Emanuel was quick to see the opportunity to trumpet a deal with the Cubs on several levels.

First, a deal that would cost the Chicago taxpayers nothing and would keep the Cubs in Chicago was a huge win for the mayor. Second, with the Cubs paying one of the largest amusement tax bills not only in the city of Chicago but in the state of Illinois, it was imperative to a cash-strapped municipality like Chicago to keep the Cubs within the city limits.

Additionally, allowing the Cubs to renovate their own stadium created a few thousand jobs in an economy that saw people struggling to find solid, well-paying jobs. A business that was going to help the local economy could only help a mayor who had seen his popularity plummet precipitously.

But how would the Cubs, in concert with the mayor's office, find a way around the 20-year contract that was signed between the Tribune Company and the rooftop owners in 2004? In a Comcast SportsNet exclusive, which I reported in 2014, it turned out that the answer lay in a flaw with the wording of the agreement, regarding how the Cubs were allowed to proceed with a renovation of Wrigley Field.

CSN Exclusive "Inside The Cubs Contract With The Rooftop Owners"

In a CSN exclusive, I have obtained a copy of the contract, I have had lawyers review the contract and I have the exact wording used in the deal.[2]

You can make your own judgement about who is in the right, who is in the wrong, and who might win a potential litigation, but one thing is for sure: This contract—signed in January of 2004, [which] at the time provided the Chicago Cubs with a new and significant revenue stream—has become a major nightmare for a team looking to jumpstart its business plan.

If it ends up in a legal proceeding, I believe the Cubs would win, but it won't be easy. It will be expensive and there is no sure thing. That's why I still feel a settlement is the best solution for both sides and I believe one will eventually happen sooner or later. Now, I am not a lawyer (although I did get accepted to law school way back when and my late father was a very successful attorney), but my opinion was sealed after talking with multiple attorneys who have reviewed parts of the contract at my request.

2. Please see Appendix III for a breakdown of the most important sections of the contract.

The agreement, which is dated January 27, 2004, runs until December 31, 2023, and says a number of very interesting things above and beyond giving the rooftops the right to run their businesses. Among them includes a provision that says the following:

> ***6.6*** *The Cubs shall not erect windscreens or other barriers to obstruct the views of the Rooftops, provided however that temporary items such as banners, flags and decorations for special occasions, shall not be considered as having been erected to obstruct views of the Rooftops. Any expansion of Wrigley Field approved by governmental authorities shall not be a violation of this agreement, including this section.*
>
> ***7.3*** *From time to time during each season, the Cubs shall authorize WGN-TV or other Cubs broadcasting partners to identify a phone number where fans can call to reserve Rooftop seating.*
>
> ***7.4*** *The Rooftops shall have the right to inform the public that they are endorsed by the Cubs.*
>
> ***7.5*** *The Cubs Director of Marketing shall meet with the Rooftops before the start of each Major League Baseball season to discuss opportunities for joint marketing.*
>
> ***7.6*** *The Cubs shall include a discussion about the Rooftops on their tour of Wrigley Field and shall include stories positive about the Rooftops in The Vine Line.*
>
> ***7.7*** *Each of the Rooftops may display broadcasts of Cubs games to patrons at its facility, including displaying such broadcasts on multiple television sets, without any infringement of any copyright owned by the Cubs or its assignees.*

The fact that the Rooftops were showing the game broadcasts on multiple televisions became an issue and one of the things that spurred both sides to agree on this deal back in 2004.

Now, looking at some of the above clauses in the contract, we find some very interesting things.

First, it appears to me that the Cubs were giving the rooftops an avenue to run their businesses in exchange for a significant amount of [money], which was a new [revenue] stream for the franchise.

Section 6.6, the main point of contention between the two sides, can be interpreted in different ways. I spoke with a noted attorney who reviewed the entire agreement for me. Here is what he said about this section of the contract:

"The last line of 6.6 is the one that an arbitrator might have to decide," he told me. "And let's be clear that unless both sides agree, the contract does not provide an avenue for a lawsuit in the typical sense of the word. Instead, it sends both parties before an arbitration panel. The arbitration process will keep everything in the litigation confidential, as opposed to a federal lawsuit, which becomes part of the public record.

"Now, in looking at 6.6, the question that will have to be decided is whether or not the word 'expansion' will apply to a sign or Jumbotron. Looking at the wording of the contract, **any expansion of Wrigley Field approved by governmental authorities shall not be a violation of this agreement, including this section**. Is a sign in right field or a Jumbotron in left field an expansion of Wrigley Field? Or is an expansion of Wrigley Field something that would have to include seating or making the ballpark bigger? This is no slam dunk win for the Cubs, although I think they would ultimately prevail, but I would say the same about the rooftops."

Now, with the Cubs looking to expand the outfield walls, the case can clearly be made that the project is an expansion of the ballpark rather than just putting in a Jumbotron and an outfield sign. Will an arbitration panel see it that way? That remains to be seen, but by building out the walls, the Cubs have clearly made a case that by the terms of the contract, they can proceed with their renovation plans **with governmental approval**.

Other observations that I have after reading and re-reading the entire contract multiple times includes the amount of promotional exposure the Cubs are supposed to provide the rooftops.

Consider that for a moment.

The very people that you are battling against so fervently are the same people that you are supposed to promote when the season begins? That is unbelievable.

Sources have confirmed to me that those marketing meetings have not been taking place for the past several years and that there is no joint marketing going on between the two sides.

Another very important part of the contract is **Section 6.2** which could be an integral part of any potential litigation:

> *6.2 If the Cubs expand the Wrigley Field bleacher seating and such expansion so impairs the view from any rooftop into Wrigley Field such that the Rooftop's business is no longer viable even if it were to increase its available seating to the maximum height permitted by law, and if such bleacher expansion is completed within eight years from the Effective Date (1/27/2004), then if such Rooftop elects to cease operations before the beginning of the next baseball season following completion of such expansion, the Cubs shall reimburse that Rooftop for 50 percent of the royalties paid by that Rooftop to the Cubs during the time between the Effective Date and the date of expansion of the Wrigley Field bleachers. The Cubs shall pay such reimbursement to the Rooftop within 30 days of receiving notice from the Rooftop it is no longer viable and has ceased operations. Any Rooftop receiving payment from the Cubs pursuant to this provision shall cease operations for the remainder of the term and shall not seek or accept any compensation or benefit related to activity on a Rooftop on a day of a game.*

The legal opinions on this clause look at the eight-year period that the Cubs are liable for potentially having to refund royalties and believe the Cubs could possibly win on an arbitrator's opinion of this section of the contract. Are the Cubs only liable for damages during the eight-year period that the agreement states? Or are they liable for the entire 20 years of the contract? It certainly seems that the Cubs have a solid chance to have an arbitration panel agree with them that the eight-year period (which expired on Jan. 27, 2012) was the only time in the contract that the Chicago Cubs were on the hook for a financial penalty or a return of royalties.

Finally, to wrap up everything that we have discussed and analyzed in this agreement, I turned back to one of the attorneys who I had review the contract and here is what he said:

"I can see this case from both sides of the argument. The Rooftops feel they signed a contract to run their businesses without having their views obstructed in any way for a period of 20 years from January 27, 2004, through December 31, 2023, and that they have paid the Chicago Cubs a significant amount of money for that right. Now, they feel the Cubs want to violate that contract because a significant renovation to the entire Wrigley Field campus threatens to impede their views and their ability to earn a living.

"From the Cubs' perspective, they believe that they have lived up to the contract and that the written agreement says that with governmental approval, **any expansion of Wrigley Field shall NOT be a violation of this agreement.** The Cubs also believe the eight-year period for returning royalties has expired, which means there is no avenue for damages. The Rooftops would proceed at their own risk, so to speak. The Cubs also have been careful to phrase everything that they have done to the park over the past several years as an expansion rather than as a renovation or remodeling of the park and the surrounding area.

"So, if the case goes to court and ends up in front of an arbitration panel, it could and most likely will hinge on the interpretation of the word 'expansion.' Is adding a Jumbotron, another outfield sign and moving the walls to limit the blockage to the Rooftops an expansion or is it simply a phrase being used to try to allow a Jumbotron and more outfield signage? This one could be tied up in court for a while and I think it is probably going to go the Cubs' way, but it is not a slam dunk. The fact though, that City Hall and Mayor Emanuel wants this to happen and that the Cubs will be bringing more jobs and more taxes into the city of Chicago [which desperately needs the revenue] leads me to believe both sides will be highly motivated and encouraged to settle this before it gets caught up in a lengthy court case that will cost millions of dollars for both sides in legal fees and will keep the Cubs from starting their renovation project. And, just to be clear, I understand why the Cubs don't want to start parts of the project without total approval. Should they begin digging and the case drags on, they will have no leverage at all to reach a settlement."

Finally, in doing significant research on this dispute, I was able to read the following public document which is the result of a City Council of Chicago meeting and subsequent vote on July 24, 2013, which passed 49–0 by the Chicago City Council:

> *"Specifically, but without limitation, Applicant shall have the right to expand the Wrigley Field bleachers to install (i) a new video board in left field, which may include an LED sign, a neon illuminated sign above it and two light towers to assist in outfield lighting; and (ii) a neon sign in right field, which signage has been approved by the Commission on Chicago Landmarks and, in addition to being part of the bleacher expansion, and along with all other signage contemplated by this Planned Development, is integral to the expansion and renovation of Wrigley Field and the development and redevelopment of the Property as contemplated herein."*

Thus, the argument can be made that the City of Chicago has granted the Cubs a permit to expand the bleachers, to add signage, lights, etc., and they have called it an expansion. Further, the economic protection period of eight years has lapsed.

The Cubs' position in the rooftop agreement appears to be as follows: The Rooftops pay the Cubs 17 percent for 20 years with no guarantees their views won't change. The Cubs feel they offered economic protection for the first eight years, which lapsed January 27, 2012. The Rooftops depended on the City never approving a change to the landmark ordinance or approval of a subsequent bleacher expansion. Both of those approvals came in July 2013.

Again, I go back to the lawyer that I had review the contract and this City Council document:

> *"After looking at the wording that the Cubs have used consistently and that the City Council of Chicago also used and approved by a 49–0 vote, I believe it strengthens the Cubs' position against the Rooftops in a potential lawsuit,"* he added. *"Again, no one can predict what an arbitration panel could decide,*

> *but it certainly seems the Cubs have done all they could do to demonstrate and prove that the entirety of the project—which includes a Jumbotron and signage—is indeed an expansion. If that is what it is and it ends up in front of an arbitration panel and they agree, then that will remove the roadblock standing in the way of the entire Wrigley renovation project."*

Chicago-based attorney Lester Munson, who has been a legal analyst at both ESPN and *Sports Illustrated* for the past 25 years, originally thought that the rooftop owners had a strong position as the Wrigley renovation debate raged on. However, after the CSN exclusive that I wrote was released, his interpretation of the dispute changed quickly.

"When I saw your story and the actual language of the contract that you released, my conclusion was, based on what you reported, that they [the Cubs] had all the leverage over the rooftop owners and their leverage had elapsed over the passage of time. I could see that the Ricketts family was in a very strong position against the rooftop owners due to the actual wording of the contract and no one had interpreted the contract that way until you researched it and wrote about it. In fact, given the leverage that Tom Ricketts had, I was somewhat incredulous that he was trying to settle with them rather than just crushing them in court. That tells me what a good person Tom Ricketts is that he tried to work with them to the degree that he did," Munson said.

After the CSN story broke, the Cubs received the governmental approval they needed to circumvent the contract and proceeded to plan out their four-to-five-year expansion, finally beginning construction in late 2014. A new 30,000-square-foot clubhouse, which is the second largest in baseball, was considered essential by Cubs baseball operations president Theo Epstein in luring free agents and opened in time for the 2016 season. It was met with rave reviews and it not only has every modern amenity that a baseball player would need but it also has state of the art features such as flotation pods that are soundproof and light proof and are filled with salt water to help players relax and decompress.

Another feature that the players have been taking full advantage of is a cryotherapy chamber which allows a player to enter a chamber for up to three minutes that is at -220 degrees. It helps to reduce inflammation and soreness which is prevalent during a 162-game season. "Our ownership has given us everything that we have asked for and more so that our players have all the tools to play their very best throughout the season," Jed Hoyer said.

The high-revenue video boards which were so controversial were put up in time for the 2015 season and were met with tremendous approval by the large majority of fans that attended games at Wrigley Field after their installation. Most of the rooftops found ways to work around any obstruction of their views but for one rooftop, the Skybox on Sheffield, they found underreporting their attendance and their revenues could land them in jail.

According to an indictment filed in 2015, the Skybox on Sheffield underreported the number of people that attended games on their rooftop and also failed to pay taxes on those revenues from 2008 to 2011. Skybox owner R. Marc Hamid went to trial in July 2016 and was convicted on all nine counts that he was charged with.

The scheme that Hamid was convicted of running accused him of underreporting attendance from 2008 to 2011 at the rooftop, which is located at 3627 N. Sheffield, almost directly down the first-base line at Wrigley Field. The falsified revenue and attendance reports that he submitted to the Cubs meant the

Tom Ricketts To Do List Upon Taking Control of the Chicago Cubs

1. Win the World Series
2. Renovate Wrigley Field for future generations to enjoy
3. New state-of-the-art spring training facility in Arizona
4. New state of the art Latin American training facility in the Dominican Republic
5. Best facilities top to bottom in MLB
6. Completely overhaul scouting department
7. Establish a Cubs Way of playing the game at every level
8. Improve controllable talent acquisition in all avenues (draft, international, free agency, and trades)
9. Portfolio of long-term commitments to existing impact major league players
10. Build and operate the best computer database in baseball for every facet of baseball operations
11. Greatly increase revenues from sponsorships and non-baseball events
12. Put every dollar after expenses back into the operation of the team

club did not receive as much as they should have in royalty payments under terms of the 2004 contract.

Prosecutors also were successful in proving that Hamid submitted false sales tax returns to the state of Illinois and amusement tax returns to Cook County and the City of Chicago for the same years, ultimately failing to report $1.5 million dollars in sales according to the indictment.

In January 2017, Hamid was sentenced to 18 months in prison.

Chicago Tribune baseball-writer Paul Sullivan, who has been a baseball beat writer on both sides of Chicago for the past 20-plus years, has seen the good and the bad during his lengthy career covering the Cubs and he marvels at what the Ricketts family has been able to accomplish in the seven years they have owned the Cubs.

"I thought that once Tom Ricketts was able to land Theo Epstein the chances of success were greatly increased. Before they landed Theo, I thought they would do what the Chicago Cubs always did. Sign a few free agents and hope for the best. Whether that was Milton Bradley, Alfonso Soriano, or some other established veteran."

On the business side, Sullivan is very impressed at what the Cubs have been able to accomplish but he believes that the business plan that has gone off fairly smoothly would not have worked nearly as well had the Cubs not been able to hire Epstein as the president of baseball operations.

"Getting Theo gave the Cubs the credibility they needed to overcome some of the missteps that they made at the start of the ownership change. They wanted public financing help to renovate Wrigley Field and that was a no-go. There are still things they want that they have been unable to get so far. They want to be able to close down the streets that border the ballpark and I believe they should be able to close down Waveland and Sheffield to have parties if they want.

"They haven't gotten everything they want with the plaza they are building but in time they will get what they want. Look at the night games they have gotten. They didn't get them right away but now they are basically like most other major league teams with the number of night games they are allowed to play at Wrigley Field. I know the Cubs want to be able to play weekend night games, especially Saturday night games and I believe those will happen in time as well," he said.

While Sullivan believes the hiring of Epstein played a key role in helping the Cubs advance their business agenda he also believes the Cubs finally learned to play the political game to get what they wanted. "It took them a while but they played the game. It took some arm twisting but they got friendly with Rahm Emanuel and once you're in with Rahm it helps tremendously despite the battles that they are still involved in with Chicago alderman Tom Tunney," he said.

However, despite all of the on-field and off-field successes the Cubs have had, most will judge the success of the Ricketts ownership on the Cubs winning the World Series. Sullivan though, doesn't agree with using that as the measuring stick when evaluating the ownership group.

"Maybe people will use that when they grade what the Ricketts have done as owners but I think that is wrong. They put the franchise in position to win the World Series and that is all they can do. Yes, they won but that is always going to be up to the team on the field. The family put the franchise in position to be successful and that is all they can do," he said.

"I've been a critic of Ricketts at times but there is no way you could say that he hasn't done everything he could to win the World Series here. He got Theo, revenues at Wrigley Field from the renovations, and the video boards are up, and while I think he wants to make money for himself like any owner does, he is obviously committed to winning. If they hadn't won it I don't think it would be fair to criticize him.

"He put them in position to win it and that is all that he can do. He can't go out there and play. But in the end, with the team winning the World Series and the way the ballpark is coming along I don't think that Tom and his family could be any happier with how things have gone so far."

Few know that Crane Kenney was set to leave the Cubs organization after the sale of the franchise and some related assets to the Ricketts family was completed in October 2009. "I was taking a job with some friends of mine and I was going to start after we closed the deal to transfer ownership from the Tribune Co. to the Ricketts family," Kenney said. "I gave Tom a list of things I thought he needed to consider as he began to overhaul the franchise and he asked me if I would stay on to try and implement them. I love being here and I wanted to see if we could accomplish what was necessary to move the Cubs franchise into the modern era.

"The family is the real heroes here," he said, "because what they did in showing the patience that they did in beginning this rebuild took a lot of guts."

5

Getting Theo

It was late in the 2010 season and the Chicago Cubs were struggling on the field. Manager Lou Piniella had resigned to spend time with his family and his ailing mother. With the Cubs business plan starting to take shape, it was time for Tom Ricketts to take a much closer look at the state of his entire baseball operations department.

At the major league level he saw a team headed in the wrong direction with an aging roster and very few long-term assets that could be part of a championship-caliber team. He also found a crumbling foundation throughout his minor league system. There were very few impact-caliber prospects and the Cubs most recent drafts had produced very little in the way of future stars.

In fact, the Cubs' first round draft picks dating back to 1998 would all struggle to be major contributors at the big league level for various reasons. From injuries to potential stars Mark Prior and Corey Patterson to picks that were complete busts, the Cubs' minor league system was one of the game's worst. This despite the fact that the team had picked in the top six of the draft an astounding five times in 11 draft classes.

Tom Ricketts commissioned a study of every franchise's minor league system and their draft records to find out who in Major League Baseball was making the most of acquiring young, controllable talent. He found several teams that had done a very good job but one team stood out above the rest in his evaluations.

The Boston Red Sox had built a perennial contender through multiple avenues of player acquisition including the draft, international free agency, trades, and major league free agency. In the same period where the Cubs had struggled, the Red Sox had hit pay dirt throughout the draft, which is as big a hit or miss proposition as there is in the sport.

To evaluate a player aged 18–21 (depending on if they were a high school prospect or a college player) and to project his level of success against the very best players in the world is at best an inexact science. However, the Red Sox had landed All-Stars at that time like Dustin Pedroia, Jacoby Ellsbury, Clay Buchholz, and future all stars like Anthony Rizzo, Mookie Betts, Xander Bogaerts, and several others who were making a major impact throughout baseball.

A productive farm system is the key to building a successful franchise because not only does it provide a pipeline of young talent but it is talent that is extremely inexpensive. MLB players are not allowed to test free agency until they have completed six full seasons in the big leagues. This system keeps them relatively cost-controlled, which allows franchises to spend bigger money on veterans who are free agents.

However, free agency is fraught with risks because teams are paying top dollar for a player who is almost always near or older than 30 or 31, which is when most players start to see a decline in their productivity. Players older than 30 are a big risk to sign to deals that are longer than three or four years because of the cost to acquire them and the chance that the back end of the deals will not see the productivity of the player to justify the large salary that they are almost always receiving.

Taking all of this into account, Tom Ricketts knew that he needed to hire a general manager who could rebuild the Cubs' substandard farm system. For far too long the Cubs had swung and missed in the upper rounds of the draft despite picking in the top ten on several occasions. Missing on a high pick can set a franchise back for years. Missing on multiple high picks can keep a team near the bottom of the standings for an extended period, which is just where the Cubs found themselves on multiple occasions including the 2010–14 seasons, after a poor draft record from 2000 to 2010.

"I knew what I was looking for after I made the decision to part ways with Jim Hendry. We needed to rebuild our farm system and start producing young talent that could make an impact at the major league level. I commissioned two of our front office guys to study every team in Major League Baseball and to see who was doing the best job in the draft and in each of the various ways that a team goes about acquiring talent.

"Every study that we did kept coming back to Theo and to the Red Sox. They did the best job at drafting and developing players who were making a big impact at the major league level. But until we made the decision to change our baseball operations hierarchy I had no idea who we were going to hire. In fact, until Jim's departure was announced in August I had not made one call or conducted one interview," Ricketts said.

However, all of that was about to change. There were rumblings in the industry that Epstein was unhappy in Boston and that his differences with Boston's ownership group could pave the way for his departure from the franchise possibly as soon as that fall.

Ricketts quietly went about his business talking with different baseball people who all gave him advice on what he should do with his suddenly vacant baseball operations post. He spoke with Oakland A's general manager Billy Beane, former Dodgers GM Dan Evans, and White Sox assistant GM Rick Hahn, among other qualified baseball men in the industry.

However, according to Ricketts, the only man that he ever formally interviewed for the post as the head of the Cubs baseball operations department was Theo Epstein. And the first person to recommend Theo Epstein to Tom Ricketts? That was none other than baseball commissioner Bud Selig, who knew that Epstein was looking for a fresh start and that the Red Sox were okay with him departing Boston.

"I knew the Cubs were making a change and I knew that Theo wanted out of Boston. That relationship had run its course and as the season was winding [down] I talked with Tom about what he was looking for in a new GM and I knew that Theo would be a perfect fit in Chicago. The Cubs got permission from the Red Sox to talk with Theo once the regular season ended and I knew that once they met it would be a perfect fit," Selig told me.

Ricketts considered interviewing several candidates for the Cubs general manager job until he learned of Epstein's availability and then he focused solely on interviewing him and gauging his level of interest in assuming the challenge of rebuilding the Cubs from the ground up.

"All of the other interviews that I did were informational or they were a chance for me to get to know someone better," said Ricketts. "However, Theo was the only guy that I specifically targeted. He was the only interview candidate that I ever met with. In fact, I chuckled at some of the reports that had me meeting with several different candidates, many of whom I have still never met. The report that seemed to get a lot of attention had me meeting with Pat Gillick. As we sit here today in June of 2016, I still have never met Pat Gillick."

But in Chicago, as word of Hendry's dismissal spread, people began to doubt Tom Ricketts' ability to land a proven general manager with a track record of success.

David Haugh, lead columnist for the *Chicago Tribune*, said, "When rumors started to circulate that the Cubs were going after Theo Epstein I remember thinking there was no way they could pull it off. I don't think confidence in Tom Ricketts at that point was very deep at all. I think that there was a sense that he was a novice. There was a sense that he was a fan who had made a lot of money and that he was a good businessman but he hadn't done anything yet to really earn the benefit of the doubt."

Cubs GM History, Since 1934
(source: 2016 Cubs Media Guide)

1934–40:	Charles Weber
1940–49:	James Gallagher
1950–56:	Wid Matthews
1957–75:	John Holland
1976:	E.R. Saltwell
1977–May 1981:	Bob Kennedy
May–Oct 1981:	Herman Franks
Oct 1981–Oct 1987:	Dallas Green
Nov 1987–Oct 1991:	Jim Frey
Nov 1991–Oct 1994:	Larry Himes
Oct 1994–Jul 2000:	Ed Lynch
July 2000–July 02:	Andy MacPhail
July 2002–Aug 2011:	Jim Hendry
Aug–Oct 2011:	Randy Bush
Nov 2011–Present:	Jed Hoyer

However, the rumors about Epstein and the Cubs persisted, and while Cubs fans salivated at the thought of a World Series–winning executive choosing to come to Chicago to accept maybe the toughest challenge in sports, no one truly believed it would happen. "When they had this opening after Jim Hendry was fired, people understood the need for major change but people didn't think that Tom Ricketts could pull it off because the Cubs were always about coming close and Ricketts at that point was just part of that and I don't think anyone really believed that he could get the guy recognized as the best mind in baseball," Haugh told me.

People have long wondered who was advising Tom Ricketts on baseball matters behind the scenes. Because it was not possible for a man who had never worked for a professional baseball team in any capacity let alone own one of the most scrutinized franchises in all of professional sports to know how to operate a franchise and make the correct decisions on building a baseball operations team that could accomplish what many believed to be nearly impossible.

While Ricketts talked to dozens of sharp baseball minds around the sport from other owners to former executives to media members to other current executives, Selig was always available to him for advice and guidance because he knew the inner workings of Major League Baseball better than most anyone else.

"Bud Selig was tremendous to me," Ricketts said. "He was always available to answer any question that I had and I called him a lot. As a former owner he knew things from that perspective and as the commissioner he had the respect of everyone around the game."

Selig remembers talking with Ricketts on a regular basis and found the new Cubs owner to be very inquisitive about every facet of owning an MLB team. "I spoke with Tom a lot as he navigated through the various issues he faced after buying the Cubs. He would call a lot and most of the questions and decisions he had to make I had seen many times during my time as an owner or as the commissioner. When he asked me about changing GMs he mentioned that he had compiled a list of names and that Theo Epstein was at the top of his list," Selig said.

"I told Tom that once he hired a GM he had to let the GM do the job he was hired for. I have always liked Jim Hendry but once Tom made the decision to make a change I told him he had to hire whoever he thought would be the best man for the job but then he had to let them do what they thought was necessary to improve the Cubs. I was in the great position for many years to evaluate talent and to evaluate GMs so the more I thought about it, understanding that Theo was about to leave Boston, it was critical to the Cubs to get Theo Epstein," Selig told me.

"The health of the Cubs franchise was very important to me and it was clearly in need of a lot of work," Selig added.

As the 2011 regular season wound down to its final eight weeks, the Boston Red Sox found themselves firmly in the AL playoff race and as the July 31 trade deadline came and went, Boston had the best record in the American League and was a robust 25 games over the .500 mark.

No one in New England could have seen the epic and ugly collapse that was to come in September as the Red Sox went from first place to out of the playoffs entirely. In fact, on September 1, 2011, the Red Sox still had the best record in the American League and they were 30 games over .500 with the New York Yankees hot on their heels and just a 1/2 game behind in the standings.

What happened over the next 30 days is still a sore subject among Red Sox faithful but in a haze of beer, fried chicken, and controversy, Boston had a collapse that was truly epic. No team has blown a bigger lead in September—a nine-game margin through September 3—and missed the playoffs. Boston went 6–18 after September 3 and did not win consecutive games at any point in September. When the regular season ended, the Red Sox were left to wonder just what had gone wrong, as not only did they not win their division, they missed the playoffs entirely.

"This is just maybe the worst situation that I ever have been involved in my whole career," designated hitter David Ortiz said. "It's going to stay in a lot of people's minds for a while. What we did this month, it was horrible. I have been in bad situations before, and believe me, when these things happen and you drop down like we did, it stays in your head for a long time."

What had happened was truly bizarre and unprecedented in baseball history. No team had seen their lead dissipate so quickly while their own players were reportedly drinking beer, eating fried chicken, and playing video games in the clubhouse during games.

"I just know that playing in Boston, you're required to play your tail off every day to try to win ballgames for this city," Red Sox star Dustin Pedroia said. "That's what hurt so much as a player, that we not only let each other down in the clubhouse but we let the city down."

The stunning collapse not only cast the Red Sox players in an extremely unfavorable light but it also made life difficult for then–Red Sox manager Terry Francona and then–Boston GM Theo Epstein.

"We take full responsibility for what happened, all of us, but collectively it was a failure, and I'm the general manager, so I take more responsibility than anybody. But I know we don't believe in scapegoats, and in particular no one blames Tito for what happened in September," Epstein said. "We all failed collectively."

As the controversy around the collapse raged in Boston, Cubs chairman Tom Ricketts found himself watching the final evening of the regular season at the bar in the lobby of the Omni Hotel in San Diego where the Cubs had just completed their regular season. "I always make sure that I go to wherever we are playing if our season ends on the road and I go through the clubhouse thanking everyone for their hard work and wish them a good winter. Some of the players and coaches won't be back and I want to make sure they hear from me how much we appreciate all of their efforts all season long," Ricketts told me.

"I decided to sit at the bar and eat dinner. I ordered a burger and all of the games were on TV along with all of the highlights from that day's action. I was sitting at the bar and I watched Boston blow a save and lose to Baltimore while Tampa Bay came back from 7–0 down after seven innings against the Yankees to win 8–7 on a walk-off home run. When I saw that the Red Sox had lost and that they were not going to play in the postseason I decided to wait a couple of days before I called [Boston owner] John Henry to ask him for permission to talk with Theo," Ricketts remembered.

Despite being stunned at the collapse of his powerhouse team, Epstein had known for a while that his time in Boston was coming to an end. "I thought I might have one more year there but I could feel that for me it was reaching a point of transition. It felt like 10 years would be it in Boston. It was starting to get really heavy there and I knew if I didn't leave after 10 years it might be hard to ever leave or leave on my own terms.

"One of the things I referenced in the editorial I wrote in the *Boston Globe*[1] when I spelled out my reasons for leaving was something that Bill Walsh believed. After 10 years in leadership it's a good idea to move on, both for the individual and for the organization because the individual needs new challenges and a new environment in order to grow and to stay challenged and motivated. Plus, the organization can benefit from a fresh perspective, new ideas, and a new energy with a new leader," he told me in the summer of 2016.

1. For Theo Epstein's October 25, 2011, farewell letter to Boston, please see Appendix IV.

While he didn't know what his next move was, he knew he wanted to stay in baseball. "I wasn't sure what I wanted to do but when the news came out that Jim Hendry was not going to be back as the general manager it definitely piqued my curiosity. However, I knew that it would be difficult for me to go to some random city just for the money or just to take a job after how wonderful my experience was in Boston and how that resonated with me. Naturally, I started to think about other places that would hold a similar meaning to me and the Cubs were just about the only place left that would. So I kind of always had in the back of my mind a dream of maybe coming here someday and trying to do what we did in Boston.

"Once Tom announced the change with Jim it started to move a little bit more to the forefront of my mind and I realized it might be something I would have to think about at the appropriate time when we were done playing. Then Tom reached out and I had a tough decision to make," Epstein said.

With the Red Sox season over so dramatically and filled with so much controversy, Epstein had a lot to think about. Did he want to leave his hometown and leave a job that had been his dream since he was a little boy cheering for his beloved Red Sox to move to a city he knew very little about?

But, did he want to stay in a situation that was not only dealing with the epic collapse but in a situation where his relationship with his bosses was fraying and was far from harmonious?

When Theo Epstein flew to New York City a few days after the 2011 regular season ended, he went to an apartment overlooking Central Park to meet with Tom Ricketts. "I remember walking into the apartment thinking, *Nice pad, 360-degree glass windows looking out on Central Park*. It was nice," Epstein joked. Then he got serious. "I think the longer you work in baseball and perhaps in any industry you realize how important relationships are and trust. Who you work with can go a long way in defining your happiness at work and your job satisfaction. I was really interested in meeting directly with Tom and I had heard great things about him. It wasn't like I had to leave the Red Sox, but I was just really curious with how he viewed the challenge that they had with the Cubs and what he was looking for out of the leader of his baseball operations department."

Epstein and Ricketts spent the evening eating dinner and watching the MLB playoffs while they discussed baseball and workplace philosophy. "I think Tom wanted to make sure I wasn't an asshole or at least that I could cover it up really well," Epstein chuckled. "I think he also wanted to make sure that I wasn't just coming to Chicago to cash in and just play out my career. That I was still motivated and that I was still hungry and still eager to find advantages and build a healthy organization and win. That I wasn't just going to coast somewhere off of my success in Boston. Which is the right thing to do. You don't want someone on the back side–even at a young age–if someone is mentally on the back side or checked out or not as hungry, no one would want that.

"From my end I wanted to see what he had to say. I saw it as a long-term project because of the talent deficit at the big league level and in the minor leagues and I wanted to make sure that he understood that and was good with it. I believe in building things from the bottom up to build a real healthy organization not just a big league team that might have a shot in a given year. I wanted to see if he would be supportive of that and have the patience for it and I was really happy to hear that was exactly what he was looking for. Plus, we had a really good time watching baseball and he had a chef there to cook us dinner and it was just a really good time. It was clear that evening that he was a really grounded, down-to-earth person and as I have gotten to know him he really is," Epstein told me.

As an executive, Theo Epstein is considered brilliant. So much so that many around the game believe he would be wildly successful no matter what business he chose to go into. "People like to work for Theo. I've had [other executives] tell me he could be running Morgan Stanley. He understands how to run a business," Hall of Fame baseball writer Peter Gammons said.

"He's clearly in charge but he gives people a lot of freedom and authority, and he wants to hear opinions contrary to his own. He's a natural leader who has a way of being able to relate to everybody, from the players in the clubhouse to the owners," Gammons added.

However, for all of the positives the Cubs job had going for it there was one factor that Epstein looked at as essential in getting him to consider the job and that was the Cubs' failure to win a World Series in 103 years, as of the end of the 2011 season.

"The Cubs job was intriguing to me for a number of reasons but had they won a World Series in their recent past I probably would not have taken the job. It would not have been intriguing at all. I would have probably stayed in Boston at that point. It was the challenge to accomplish something that hadn't been done in over 100 years. It was the challenge and the tremendously broad and deep impact that winning can have on so many people. In Boston it really made an impact on me," Epstein said.

So, on October 25, 2011, Theo Epstein accepted the challenge of running the Chicago Cubs and trying to end a drought unmatched in American professional sports. The Cubs had not won a World Series since 1908 and they hadn't even been to one since 1945. Their record of futility was the worst in sports and they were aptly nicknamed the "lovable losers," a moniker that made them a laughingstock around baseball.

"To me, baseball is better with tradition, baseball is better with history, baseball is better with fans who care, baseball is better in ballparks like this, baseball is better during the day. And baseball is best of all when you win," Epstein said during a standing-room-only Wrigley Field news conference.

"I firmly believe that we can preserve the things that make the Cubs so special and over time build a consistent winner, a team that will be playing baseball in October consistently, and a team that will ultimately win the World Series."

"I've waited a few weeks to say this, but it truly feels great to be a Cub today," Epstein said, having agreed to a five-year deal for a reported $18.5 million.

"I don't believe in curses, [and] I guess I played a small part in proving they don't exist, from a baseball standpoint," Epstein said. "I do think we can be honest and upfront that certain organizations haven't gotten the job done. That's the approach we took in Boston. We identified certain things that we hadn't been doing well, that might have gotten in the way of a World Series, and eradicated them. That's what we'll do here."

"When I got to Boston they hadn't won in 86 years. We didn't run from that challenge. We embraced it," Epstein said. "We decided the way to attack it was to build the best baseball operation that we could, to try to establish a winning culture, to work as hard as possible and to bring in players who care more about each other and more about winning than the people around them thought or the external expectations, the external mindset. That's something that is going to be important to us here as well.

"We're going to build the best baseball operation we can. We're going to change the culture. Our players are going to change the culture along with us in the major league clubhouse. We're going to make building a foundation for sustained success a priority. That will lead to playing October baseball more often than not. Once you get in in October there's a legitimate chance to win the World Series."

Epstein was also well aware that the Cubs massive fan base and the large media contingent that chronicles the team's every move would probably lose patience with him more quickly than the rebuild would probably take. "It might be in six months or it might be in two years but there will come a point in time that you will start to question the process. I'm okay with that because we believe in what we're doing and we will stay loyal to our plan," he told me the day he was introduced as the Cubs new president of baseball operations in 2011.

"I do believe that you can be honest and up front about the fact that a certain organization hasn't gotten the job done, hasn't won the World Series in a long time," Epstein said. "That's the approach we took in Boston. It wasn't a curse; just the fact that we hadn't gotten the job done. We identified several things that the franchise had done historically that probably had gotten in the way of winning a World Series and we went about trying to eradicate those. That'll be part of the process here," he said.

With the Cubs wait sitting at 108 years as the 2016 season began, fans of the Chicago Cubs were only able to dream about what a World Series title would look and feel like. However, Theo Epstein, with the perspective that he gained by first being a Boston Red Sox fan and then as their general manager, knows how profound the effect can be from winning a World Series.

"When you work in baseball you question yourself sometimes: *What are we really trying to accomplish?* My brother is a social worker and he saves kids' lives, literally. That has real meaning and he's making society better. I work in baseball. It's sports and entertainment. It's the bread and circus, it's not the most fundamental part of society.

"But, if you're lucky enough to be a small part of something like 2004, you could see the tangible impact that championship had on people's lives. People just about every day came up to me and shared a story about how much that championship meant to them personally or to their father or their mother or their grandparents who didn't live to see it but they felt at peace because they always wanted them to see it and they knew that they were experiencing it from above in some way. Just the magnitude of it and how it helped give people closure and brought families together.

Theo Epstein

- Born 12/29/1973 in NYC; raised in Brookline, MA
- Graduated from Yale (1995) and U. of San Diego Law School (2000)
- Joined Padres baseball operations department in 1996
- Red Sox Assistant GM: March–Nov. 2002
- Red Sox GM: Nov 2002–Oct 2011
- Cubs President, Baseball Operations: Oct 2011—Present

"The cathartic aspect of it all was on such a big scale that it was really rewarding to feel that I and the people I worked with played a small part in helping to add that kind of joy and happiness to people's lives. I knew that from afar that was possible here and that's really what made it appealing," he said.

Epstein knows that he has the backing of the Cubs' massive fan base and he also knows the pressure that comes with the job goes beyond just the grind of wins and losses that are a daily part of a baseball season. "This job is sort of a public trust. Anyone who is put in charge of a team that's important to people feels that way. It's a great motivator.

"It means that I feel a responsibility to always work my ass off. It means I feel a responsibility to always make decisions that are in the best interests of the Cubs and winning in the long haul.

Even if that makes me or other people uncomfortable, even if it's the hard thing for the short term. We have to do what's right for the long term for the Cubs. Every little decision we make can hopefully play a role in building an organization that's healthy enough to win the World Series.

"There are people counting on us and we can't snap our fingers and hand them a World Series trophy. But what we can do is work our ass off to build a healthy organization that's in a position to win it over a long period of time," Epstein said when we sat down and talked in August 2016. At the time, Epstein's Cubs were leading their division by double digits and they were the odds-on favorite to win the World Series. "That window started in 2015, when we won 97 games, and it is continuing in 2016 and hopefully for many years to come. We have to come through when it matters most and we have to get some breaks and we have to win 11 games in October."

At that point, Epstein could only dream about winning the World Series with the Cubs. He had no idea what was around the corner for his team in the fall of 2016. But that part of the story is not yet ready to be told. First, Theo Epstein has a franchise to build.

6

Building the Best Front Office in Baseball

No front office in baseball has more accomplished executives than the Chicago Cubs, who have two men working under team president Theo Epstein, in general manager Jed Hoyer and Senior Vice President Jason McLeod, who have both had multiple opportunities to run their own teams.

In fact, Hoyer left the GM job in San Diego, where he was the decision maker on all baseball operations decisions, to be the No. 2 man in Chicago because of the opportunity to work with Epstein and McLeod again. "I had a really good job in San Diego, but when Theo called me about going to Chicago with him, it didn't take very long for me to realize how special this opportunity is," Hoyer told me as we sat in his Wrigley Field office in May 2016.

However, whenever there is discussion on the Cubs hierarchy, the first name that people mention is Theo Epstein. So does being perceived as No. 2 on the Cubs pecking order bother Hoyer, who was the ultimate authority on all baseball decisions in San Diego? "No, it doesn't bother me," Hoyer said. "One of the first things we talked about when we did this was that this only is going to work if it's a total collaboration. No one knows who works on what deals or what contracts. Once you start getting into who deserves credit in a front office, it's a huge negative, and we've done what we can to avoid that," Hoyer told David Haugh of the *Chicago Tribune*.

The Cast:

	Title	**Previous Job**
Theo Epstein	Pres. Baseball Operations	BOS General Manager
Jed Hoyer	Executive VP, General Manager	SD General Manager
Jason McLeod	Sr. VP, Player Development & Amateur Scouting	SD Assistant General Manager
Shiraz Rehman	Assistant General Manager	ARI Director of Player Personnel
Jaron Madison	Director of Player Development	SD Scouting Director

Hoyer worked for and with Epstein in Boston when the two men not only won multiple World Series but grew as close as brothers. And it is that bond that brought the two men together again in Chicago. "I'm indebted to Theo for early on putting me in charge of things I probably shouldn't have been," Hoyer said.

When Hoyer left San Diego for Chicago, some in the game were surprised that he would leave to work for Epstein again rather than being in charge of his own team but those who know the two men weren't surprised. "That's a huge mistake that on the surface, people who don't know those two men could easily conclude," said Los Angeles Dodgers manager Dave Roberts, a former special assistant for San Diego's baseball operations under Hoyer in 2010. "But I don't think anybody in the game has more respect for Jed than Theo, and I don't think he would ever put him in position to just follow his orders. Jed is going to have the autonomy he needs to be successful."

"Before we got to Chicago," Hoyer said, "I remember having some really long conversations with Theo. I was still living in San Diego and he was still in Boston but we knew this [the Cubs job] was going to happen. We had a number of in-depth conversations about the Cubs job and then we took a few days without talking and we both evaluated the Cubs system, going through everything we could about the Cubs from top to bottom. Then we talked again and we both had come to the conclusion that it was a lot more barren than we had originally thought. The biggest thing was that the middle and upper levels of the minor leagues were not going to help us anytime soon. That was the conversation that I remember the most because that was when we really understood that this process was going to be a full rebuild and that this was going to take a while."

The perception of Epstein and Hoyer is that of computer geeks who allow technology to make every decision for them but that couldn't be further from the actual truth on how the two men run the Cubs. "Our family finds it sort of hilarious the way he's portrayed as this computer nerd or stats guy because while he was good in math, he was never particularly interested in it," said his mother Annie Hoyer, a psychiatric nurse practitioner at the Brody School of Medicine at East Carolina University, with a laugh. His father, Robert, is also on the faculty there and runs the Pediatric Outpatient Center. "He just loved baseball," she said.

In fact, on the glass wall in the Cubs baseball operations department is a series of mathematical equations that an observer would probably expect to see in a Theo Epstein/Jed Hoyer office. Except, as Epstein told Wright Thompson in an *ESPN the Magazine* article in September 2016, the numbers are meaningless.

Jed Hoyer

- Born 12/7/1973 in Plymouth, NH native; Wesleyan University graduate
- Worked in Scouting & Player Development for Red Sox: 2002–09
- Padres General Manager: 2010–11
- Named Cubs Executive VP and General Manager, Nov 1, 2011

"It is all fake numbers dressed up with sines and cosines," he told Thompson.

So when the Cubs dream team finally decided to accept the challenge that running the Cubs presented, they found the job much harder than even they had anticipated. They found a minor league system so devoid of prospects that Epstein and Hoyer were taken aback at how far away the Cubs were from even being competitive.

"Once we made the decision to come to Chicago, I remember sitting in our offices at Wrigley Field shortly after we started and mentally at that time we thought we were on a two-year timetable [2014] to be competitive. We were looking at the boards on the wall, one that listed every prospect in the organization and one that listed the upcoming free agent classes. Theo and I both said nothing is going to happen between now and 2014 that is going to allow us to be competitive. It was obvious that this was not going to be a two-year turnaround."

The Cubs new brain trust started to construct a plan to acquire as much young talent as they could in almost every deal that they made, hoping to jump start their plan with an infusion of prospects who could be core pieces of the Cubs' future. While Epstein and Hoyer dug their heels in for the lengthy overhaul ahead they also knew that they had a blank canvas to build their organization however they wanted it.

"In hindsight, when we were sitting there in November of 2011 there was no way we ever could have imagined that in the playoffs in 2015 that our 2013 first round pick would be our starting third baseman, that our 2014 first round pick would be our starting left fielder and that a lot of those things we had talked about would come together so quickly. I do think we had a number of things come together probably a year earlier than we thought they would," Hoyer said.

2015 Wild Card Game Starting Lineup and How Acquired

CF Dexter Fowler	Acquired from Astros via trade, January 2015
RF Kyle Schwarber	Drafted by Cubs, 2014
LF Kris Bryant	Drafted by Cubs, 2013
1B Anthony Rizzo	Acquired from Padres via trade, January 2012
3B Tommy La Stella	Acquired from Braves via trade, November 2014
2B Starlin Castro	Signed by Cubs as amateur free agent, 2006
C Miguel Montero	Acquired from Diamondbacks via trade, December 2014
SS Addison Russell	Acquired from Athletics via trade, July 2014
P Jake Arrieta	Acquired from Orioles via trade, July 2013

So how did the Cubs take a franchise that was exceptionally thin on impact talent and turn it into one of the most talented teams in baseball in just four years? "A few things happened that accelerated the process and made us much more competitive," Hoyer said. "We started to play better baseball towards the end of the 2014 season. Javy [Baez] came up and although he struggled he showed flashes and he was in the big leagues. Jorge Soler came up and he played well at the end of that season. Kris [Bryant] was crushing the minor leagues and Kyle [Hendricks] was pitching very well in the minors. We were able to acquire Addison Russell and Anthony [Rizzo] had started to come into his own. So a bunch of things happened that were all probably quicker than we would have imagined."

Between November of 2011 and the start of the 2015 season the Cubs were one of the worst teams in baseball and it led to a lot of long nights for Epstein, Hoyer, and McLeod as they racked their brains trying to come up with a way to bring more impact talent into the organization. The Cubs were going through the early stages of the revised business plan and with the struggles to get the Wrigley Field renovation plans approved which would bring a significant increase in revenue and a new TV deal still a long way away how would the baseball brain trust overhaul the baseball operations side of the business from top to bottom?

The answer was to build through the draft, make astute trades, and save money by not going crazy in free agency until the major league club was ready to compete for the postseason. That meant being willing to trade anyone at any time if the right deal presented itself.

Hoyer remembers going home after many losses during the early days of his time with the Cubs looking like he had seen a ghost and wondering how long it would take to see the rebuild start to show significant progress. After landing Kris Bryant in the 2013 draft with the No. 2 overall pick and trading for Addison Russell, Hoyer saw that progress that they were looking for late in the 2014 season.

Cubs Record by Year (2012–16)

2012: 61–101
2013: 66–96
2014: 73–89
2015: 97–65
2016: 103–58

"The most challenging moments emotionally that we had were 2012 and 2013," Hoyer told me. "In '12, we had Rizzo as a rookie, we had Castro and we had Baez in the minor leagues—of the guys that were performing. We signed Soler in the middle of that season—Bryant, Schwarber, and Russell weren't even in the organization yet. We weren't a destination at that point and we knew we had to become an appealing place to bring in free agents."

2012 Cubs Opening Day Lineup

RF	David DeJesus
2B	Darwin Barney
SS	Starlin Castro
LF	Alfonso Soriano
3B	Ian Stewart
1B	Jeff Baker
CF	Marlon Byrd
C	Geovany Soto
P	Ryan Dempster

Back in 2012 the Cubs brain trust knew they had a long rebuilding road ahead of them but they now admit the process was even tougher than they realized when they were considering coming to Chicago.

"If you think about where we were at the end of 2012, we thought that maybe that was the most painful season, which looking back on it, it was. But we knew we weren't going to add major free agents that off-season because it didn't make any sense. Our minor league system at that point, while it was getting better still wasn't any good. Those moments from 2012 were definitely the hardest," Hoyer told me.

Trading 40–60 percent of the starting rotation each season as they continued the rebuild became the norm and it was hard on the players, the manager and his coaches and certainly on a

Jason McLeod

- Born 11/30/1971 in Hawaii; raised in San Diego
- Pitched in the Astros system in 1991
- Worked for Padres in a variety of roles, including baseball operations, coaching & player development: 1994–2003; then as Assistant GM: 2010–11
- Worked for Red Sox in scouting: 2003–09
- Named Cubs Senior VP of Scouting & Player Development, Nov 1, 2011

fan base tired of losing. "Then we traded Paul Maholm to the Braves, worked on deals to trade Ryan Dempster, and we tried to trade Matt Garza but he ended up getting hurt," Hoyer told me.

The Garza fiasco is a very interesting story because most observers don't know that the Cubs had basically agreed to a trade to send Garza to Texas but in his final appearance as a Cub he pitched well in St. Louis before having to leave the game with an arm injury.

"On that Friday we had agreed to a deal to send Ryan Dempster to the Atlanta Braves for Randall Delgado, but the deal wasn't agreed to until after 5:00 PM and Ryan was supposed to pitch that night," Hoyer said. "I called Braves GM Frank Wren to tell him that we had a deal but that it was too late to scratch Dempster from that night's start. He was okay with Ryan pitching that night but over the next 24 to 48 hours it became clear that Ryan wasn't going to approve the deal, which was his right.

"The next day we agreed to a deal to send Garza to the Rangers after his start that day and I was in St. Louis watching him pitch. He struck out Matt Holliday on a 96 MPH fastball to end the third inning and shortly thereafter I got a call from our trainer to tell me that he had to come out of the game with an arm injury, so that trade was off as well. You want to talk about darker moments? That was a really dark moment because we needed to maximize the few opportunities we had to make deals and when Garza got injured that was a tough one."

Yet the Cubs front office soldiered on in their pursuit of impact talent as they scoured the world looking for players who could be part of the Cubs long-term future. They pursued the best international free agents, they explored every possible deal they could for the few marketable veterans the Cubs had and they saved their money for future free agent classes.

"I've given a number of talks to different companies about turnarounds and the one thing that I always look back on is the first time that we started to see light at the end of the tunnel was the middle to the end of the 2014 season," Hoyer said. "Probably shortly after the Russell trade because those guys were just killing the minor leagues. We would laugh about how well they were playing and we all said that we would never have a system like this again where every night you are looking up and it's Bryant, it's Russell, it's Schwarber, it's Soler, it's Baez, and these guys are just killing the minor leagues and it was in the upper levels of the minor leagues."

2014 Minor League Totals

Kris Bryant (AA/AAA)	138 games, .325/.438/.661, 43 HR, 110 RBI
Javier Baez (AAA)	104 games, .260/.323/.510, 23 HR, 80 RBI
Addison Russell (AA)	63 games, .302/.355/.529, 13 HR, 44 RBI
Jorge Soler (AA/AAA)	54 games, .331/.422/.709, 14 HR, 51 RBI

Hoyer added, "That was sort of the time that we all realized that our major league team was actually playing pretty well. Rizzo was playing well, Castro was playing well, and all of these guys that we were counting on weren't as far away as we probably would have imagined. We knew the transition to the big leagues would be difficult but I remember that time in the weeks after the Russell trade when we knew we had the organization on the right track."

Jason McLeod is considered one of the game's best talent evaluators and his role in the Cubs rebuild cannot be understated. He has presided over an influx of young talent unprecedented in recent baseball history with the 2016 Cubs 40-man major league roster fueled by 21 players that have spent time in the Cubs minor league system since McLeod's arrival with Hoyer and Epstein in 2011.

The way the Cubs had done business before the arrival of Epstein and Co. was to put most of their resources into the major league team and with division championships in 2003, 2007, and 2008 there weren't many complaints as the team challenged to win a World Series. But, underneath the limited major league successes was a crumbling foundation that guaranteed a bleak future as the major league roster aged.

"The Cubs hadn't spent a lot of their resources in the draft or in their minor league system," Hoyer said. "Instead, they pushed their money into the major league team. You have to remember the direction of the team was set by ownership and it was also dictated by the sale of the franchise. When we arrived Tom had green-lighted Jim Hendry in signing their big draft class in 2011 so we knew that we had to re-calibrate our spending in the international market, on the draft and on our front office, which at that time was the smallest front office in baseball."

McLeod said, "There were no illusions about how long it was going to take us to turn things around. We all knew that we weren't coming in and making a few moves and then ending up in the World Series in two years. The culture that we talked about was able to be instilled through the people that we put in the right positions on a day-to-day basis that could continue to keep driving that and enforcing it every day."

Baseball America Cubs Top 10 Prospect List Entering 2012
(From 11/11/2011)

1. Brett Jackson, OF
2. Javier Baez, SS
3. Matt Szczur, OF
4. Trey McNutt, RHP
5. Dillon Maples, RHP
6. Welington Castillo, C
7. Rafael Dolis, RHP
8. Junior Lake, SS
9. Josh Vitters, 3B
10. Dan Vogelbach, 1B

A key component in the Cubs' organizational ability to develop young talent is McLeod's ability to work with Epstein and Hoyer to create individualized player plans that are constantly updated as prospects move through the Cubs minor league system on their way to the big leagues. "We have a plan for each player and even when a prospect looks like he is ready to advance we stay true to our process. We want to give every player the best possible chance to make it to the big leagues," McLeod said.

Both Hoyer and McLeod are driven by a quest to have the best information possible to help them make the best decisions for the Cubs but McLeod says that desire starts at the top of the organization, with Theo Epstein. "In most rooms Theo walks into he is going to be the smartest guy in that room but he is also going to be the guy that is craving information and craving to see what you know and looking for ideas and constantly looking for ways to get better. That's what is so great about working with him. He is going to challenge you on pretty much everything but it is going to be in a constructive way. He is going to make you think about things and look at things in way that maybe you haven't looked at it yet."

McLeod added, "The Cubs' flat management structure allows for a free-flowing exchange of information because he is looking for ideas and he is never satisfied in terms of where we are and there is never a contentment to it. Theo comes in every day and he says to all of us in the office, 'We don't know shit!' He devours information and that has filtered down to all of us."

McLeod, who is the great grandnephew of Hall of Fame pitcher Carl Hubbell, has had numerous opportunities to leave the Cubs for a GM position and while that will probably happen at some point, he said he didn't want to leave Chicago before the Cubs achieved their goal of winning a World Series. "This has been the greatest challenge in the history of North American sports when you look at the championship drought. I think we all know, whether it's another team wanting to talk to Jed about a president of baseball operations job or someone asking me to interview for a general manager's job, we know how coveted those positions are," he said.

In fact, McLeod has had multiple teams express interest in hiring him as their GM, including his hometown San Diego Padres, but each time he has pulled his name from consideration. "Obviously very humbled and flattered the Padres were interested," McLeod said. "That's my hometown team. That's always been a dream job for me but as I got to sit and reflect and think about it, this is where I want to be right now."

Hoyer was thrilled when McLeod turned down the opportunity to interview with the Padres because he knows how important McLeod has been to helping to build the Cubs into the team that it is today. "I was mildly surprised he didn't want to interview but thrilled nonetheless," Hoyer said. "In this business there are only 30 of those jobs but it means a lot to us he wants to stay here. Jason loves what we're doing here. He's been such a huge part of what we want to build. He's been here for some short-term pain. I think he sees the picture coming into focus and wants to be a part of that."

McLeod also knows that with the solid foundation the Cubs have built the future is exceptionally bright for a team that finally accomplished what some believed was the impossible, to win the World Series. "We are in a special time and place with a very good young team that should be good for the foreseeable future," McLeod told me. "We've all gotten to play our small parts in putting this team and this organization together working for a great family like the Ricketts. It would be such a tough blow to go through those first three years especially and to know how much hard work went into this by so many people and then to have not been here when we won the World Series? I couldn't envision not being here when this team won and now that we have we want to win the World Series again."

7

Doubting the Plan

Everyone who has observed the Chicago Cubs either up close or from afar since Theo Epstein became the team's president of baseball operations knows all about the Cubs trade for Jake Arrieta or their drafting of Kris Bryant with the No. 2 overall selection.

However, there are many other moves that the Cubs front office has made since they arrived in Chicago in the fall of 2011 that have played a crucial role in the rising fortunes of the club. With a management philosophy based on transparency and aggressiveness, the Cubs made a series of moves that added impact talent to a franchise starving for it.

Shortly after accepting the job, Epstein and Hoyer made one of their first trades an important one when they traded the Cubs' highest upside starting pitcher, 25-year-old Andrew Cashner, to the San Diego Padres for 22-year-old minor league first baseman Anthony Rizzo.

Rizzo was originally drafted by the Boston Red Sox in 2007 and after battling cancer in 2008, he was traded to San Diego in 2010 in a deal for Padres star Adrian Gonzalez after Hoyer had become the Padres general manager. After tearing up the

MLB Worst Records (2012–14)

Team	W-L	Pct
Astros	176–310	.362
Cubs	200–286	.412
Twins	202–284	.416
Rockies	204–282	.420
Marlins	208–278	.428
White Sox	221–265	.455

minor leagues, he was promoted to the major leagues in 2011 but struggled mightily, hitting just .143 in 35 games. "To be candid, I don't think I did Anthony any favors when I was the GM of the Padres," Hoyer said.

Rizzo's struggles during his limited time with the Padres led San Diego to trade for Reds minor league standout Yonder Alonso making Rizzo expendable and the Cubs quickly pounced. "I got called up to the big leagues in 2011 and struggled a little bit," Rizzo said. "I wouldn't say some people wrote me off, but some people I guess lost some faith in me. For them to still have that faith, with everything they helped me through, it just shows me how loyal they are and I am so honored to play for them."

Rizzo started the 2012 season at Class AAA Iowa as the Cubs began the slow process of building a new culture and adding impact talent to their system. He made his Cubs debut on June 26, going 2-4 with a game-winning RBI double in a Cubs win over the New York Mets.

"I'm here to stay," Rizzo said before his Cubs debut. "I'm just going to work hard every day, learn, get better, go through the ups and down of a baseball player, the nicks and bruises, and that's about it." When reminded of that quote when we sat down in September 2016, Rizzo laughed but remembered the moment with crystal clear clarity.

"I remember how awesome all of the guys were when I was first called up by the Cubs in 2012," he said. "From Ryan Dempster to Alfonso Soriano to Reed Johnson to Jeff Baker, really all of the older guys in the clubhouse made me feel comfortable. They said they didn't care how old I was, they told me that I was here to help us win so just go out and do what you do. That was really comforting for me for older guys to say that and to make me feel so comfortable when I was new here."

Rizzo had a breakout season in 2012, hitting .285 with 15 home runs in 87 games after his recall from Class AAA Iowa. After the season, the Cubs approached him about a contract extension and Rizzo was happy to agree to a seven-year deal worth $41 million. If the Cubs exercise their option on two additional years of the deal, Rizzo will earn $14.5 million in both 2020 and 2021, bringing the total value of the deal to $73 million.

The 2013 season saw Rizzo struggle mightily at the plate, hitting just .233 and leading some fans and media to doubt his long-term viability as the Cubs first baseman of the future. However, after Dale Sveum was fired as manager following the 2013 season and was replaced by the lower key Rick Renteria,

Rizzo's Ascent

Anthony Rizzo's numbers with the San Diego Padres in 2011

G	PA	R	HR	RBI	BA	OBP	SLG	OPS
49	153	9	1	9	.141	.281	.242	.523

His numbers at Iowa (Cubs AAA) in 2012

G	PA	R	HR	RBI	BA	OBP	SLG	OPS
70	284	48	23	62	.342	.405	696	1.101

And his numbers in 2014, '15, and '16

G	PA	R	HR	RBI	BA	OBP	SLG	OPS
140	616	89	32	78	.286	.386	.527	.913
160	701	94	31	101	.278	.387	.512	.899
155	676	94	32	109	.292	.385	.544	.928

Rizzo rebounded nicely in 2014, posting a .286 average with 32 home runs and 78 RBIs.

The 2015 season saw Rizzo club 31 HRs and drive in 101 runs and hit .278, while also solidifying his status as the team's leader in the clubhouse and as one of the faces of the franchise. That role may have been cemented in July 2014 when Rizzo took exception with then-Cincinnati Reds closer Aroldis Chapman throwing high and tight twice to then Cubs outfielder Nate Schierholtz. "I was just trying to be a good teammate," Rizzo said of his actions in the ninth. "I have the utmost respect for this city and the Reds, but we as a team have to stick up for each other. Tempers flared. It happens. We're 50 men competing at the highest level and tempers are going to flare sometimes. Hopefully it's something that is resolved now."

Rizzo was furious at what he perceived to be unnecessarily dangerous pitches from the flame-throwing Chapman and when he went out to man his position at first base in the bottom half of that inning he went over to the Reds dugout and challenged them to a fight.

"Things were said–I don't really know what was said–and tempers flared," he said. "I don't think there's any bad blood. It's more about being competitive and standing up for your teammates."

Ironically, Rizzo and the man he had a problem with on that July day in 2014 were teammates as the Cubs won the franchise's first World Series in 108 years. "We were cool as soon as that game in 2014 ended," Rizzo told me. "I said what I had to say. Aroldis and I are cool and I am glad he pitches for us."

Now during the 2016 season, the Cubs veteran first baseman has put up MVP-caliber numbers while also helping a young roster to handle the increased pressure and expectations that come with playing on a Cubs team that legitimately believed all season that it could win the World Series.

Another trade made by the Epstein/Hoyer regime that has paid off handsomely was the Cubs trade of Ryan Dempster to the Texas Rangers for minor league right-handed starting pitcher Kyle Hendricks. However, as Epstein told me "you have to get lucky in this game," and the Cubs did just that after Dempster rejected a trade to the Atlanta Braves for pitcher Randall Delgado, who the Cubs scouts were very high on.

Dempster's refusal to go to Atlanta forced Epstein and Hoyer to engage in talks with several other clubs and after the Los Angeles Dodgers, which was Dempster's preferred destination, decided against dealing for the Cubs pitcher, the Texas Rangers stepped up and offered the Cubs a pitcher they had high grades on.

Kyle Hendricks, a talented starter who pitched at Dartmouth and had a very analytical approach to the game, was the pitcher the Rangers offered. However, Hendricks was not the kind of pitcher who lit up the radar guns and some scouts questioned his ability to succeed at the big league level.

Hendricks was a student of the art of pitching and Epstein, Hoyer, and McLeod all believed that if he was given a chance to develop, that his makeup, skillset, and ability to induce large numbers of ground balls from opposing hitters could be effective at Wrigley Field, where ground ball pitchers usually thrive.

Hendricks remembers the day he was traded and believes that the opportunity to come to the Cubs at a time when they were looking for young starting pitching was the biggest break of his career. "That was a wild day. I was in my first full year in pro ball, I was in High A, and usually as a young guy—especially in your first full year—I wasn't expecting to get traded at all. We showed up to the field on a road trip after a six-hour bus ride. I went out and played catch and they called me and Christian Villanueva into the manager's office and it was a whirlwind experience."

Getting traded for the first time can be a stunning and difficult thing to deal with for any player but it is especially shocking to a 22-year-old who was trying to find his way in the lower levels of minor league baseball. However, for the unusually mature Hendricks he saw that the move would provide a tremendous chance for him to get to the big leagues very quickly.

"I had family in town to watch me pitch and all of a sudden I have to pack and get to Daytona, Florida, to join the Cubs organization. However, it provided me with a huge opportunity and it opened up a lot of doors. A lot of the pitching coaches who have helped me develop and get to this point are in the Cubs organization. If I would have stayed with Texas who knows what that path would have looked like but getting the opportunity and getting traded over here and working my way up through AA and AAA with the resources we have over here, obviously worked out."

Hendricks also embraced the Cubs Way that Epstein was championing for the organization and he remembers the feeling of pride at being a member of the Chicago Cubs that was evident throughout the minor league system. "The Cubs Way, those words, they've always had phrases, sayings, things that really register with the young guys to keep them moving forward in the right way," Hendricks told me.

"It's always been team-oriented since I was traded to the Cubs organization. Usually in the minor leagues, guys are trying to make it as an individual player, but to create that team feel in the lower levels is very difficult to do. That's where I think the minor league personnel–not only the pitching coaches that I had, but the managers, the scouts in this organization top to bottom–everybody knows what they are doing and they all have one goal

Tom Ricketts talks about his family's new ownership of the Cubs during his introductory press conference at Wrigley Field on Friday, October 30, 2009. (Jim Prisching)

GM Jim Hendry (left), manager Mike Quade (center), and owner Tom Ricketts (right), talk during the press conference where it was announced that Quade, who replaced Lou Piniella for the final 37 games of the 2010 season, would be retained as manager. (M. Spencer Green)

Theo Epstein and Tom Ricketts shake hands as Epstein is introduced as the Cubs' President of Baseball Operations on October 25, 2011. (Charles Rex Arbogast)

Theo Epstein (center) and Jed Hoyer (right) listen to Jason McLeod (left), during the November 1, 2011, press conference to introduce Hoyer as the Cubs' new GM and McLeod as the new Senior Vice President of Scouting and Player Development. (Charles Rex Arbogast)

Fans enjoy a 2010 game from the rooftop bleachers along Waveland Avenue outside the left-field wall at Wrigley Field. The rooftop owners would battle the Cubs over renovations, including a jumbotron that would block the views and threaten their businesses. (Kiichiro Sato)

Wrigley renovation underway. Here, in October 2014, the work starts to take big bites out of Wrigley's outfield walls. (M. Spencer Green)

Anthony Rizzo strikes out with the bases loaded during his rough 2011 season with the Padres. One of the first moves the new-look Cubs made was acquiring Rizzo—who had connections to Epstein and Hoyer in Boston and San Diego—in a January 2012 trade with the Padres. (Ed Andrieski)

Jake Arrieta, here being pulled from a game and handing the ball to manager Buck Showalter, never reached his potential with the Orioles. The Cubs traded for Arrieta on July 2, 2013, and soon the right hander's results began to match his electric stuff. (Paul Sancya)

The Cubs would add to their rotation in a huge way when they surprised the baseball world by landing prized free agent Jon Lester, seen here greeting fans during the opening night of the 2015 Cubs Convention. (*Daily Herald*, Mark Welsh)

After officially being named manager of the Cubs, Joe Maddon offers to buy the assembled reporters a round of drinks at The Cubby Bear, a bar across the street from Wrigley Field. (M. Spencer Green)

Anthony Rizzo hugs Addison Russell after the shortstop ripped a game-winning double. The acquisition of Russell in the July 2014 Jeff Samardzija trade with Oakland added a huge piece to the Cubs roster of young stars. (Charles Rex Arbogast)

Kris Bryant, who the Cubs selected with the second overall pick of the 2013 draft, runs the bases after hitting a walk-off, two-run homer against the Rockies on July 27, 2015. (Andrew A. Nelles)

Kyle Schwarber, who the Cubs selected with the fourth overall pick of the 2014 draft, watches his monstrous home run in Game 4 of the NLDS fly toward the right-field scoreboard. (Warren Wimmer/Icon Sportswire)

in mind. When you are working together that well, then you see the product come together on the field.

"This plan was supposed to take a lot longer but with some of these young guys, these position players we have, winning 97 games last season, it just ramped up the process," he said. "Management saw that last year, they saw all the progress we made in the playoffs and how all of the young guys handled the experience, so coming into this year you saw all of the free agent acquisitions they made to bolster the team. They say: Here's your opportunity, so go for it this year. The guys feel all of the resources we have available to us and what we can accomplish with that."

Another under-the-radar move was the Rule 5 draft selection of closer Hector Rondon, who was left unprotected by the Cleveland Indians in the 2012 draft. The Cubs had scouted him extensively in Venezuela and Rondon appeared to be healthy after two major elbow surgeries. He underwent Tommy John surgery in 2010 and then fractured his elbow during rehab, and despite appearing to be healthy, the Indians chose to not promote him to their 40-man major league roster, thereby exposing him to the draft where the Cubs selected him with the second overall selection.

Epstein places great trust in his scouts and when they recommended that the Cubs use the second overall pick on a rehabbing reliever he put his faith in the men who he hired to evaluate talent. "Getting Rondon as a Rule 5 was a big one for us because we had a lack of power arms in our organization and he has turned out to be a big part of our bullpen," he said.

Addison Russell was far from an unknown commodity when the Cubs began talks with the Oakland A's for pitcher Jeff Samardzija in June 2014. The Cubs were already off the pace in the NL Central, while Oakland was in first place and was dreaming of winning the World Series. However, the A's had a starting pitching deficit and General Manager Billy Beane began calling around baseball looking for not only starting pitchers but high-level starters who could help lead his team throughout the rest of the season and in the postseason.

Ironically, he called the Boston Red Sox first about Jon Lester, who had rejected Boston's lowball contract extension offer in spring training of 2014. In June, Boston still had designs on the postseason, so they were unwilling to make Lester available in any deal. The Cubs were willing to move Samardzija at almost any point of the season but it had to be in the right deal. He had also rejected a contract extension proposal which all but sealed his fate as a trade candidate.

The Cubs engaged in talks with several teams and at one point the New York Yankees looked like the probable landing spot for the lanky right hander. But the Cubs were asking for New York reliever Dellin Betances and that was a no-go in the eyes of Yankees GM Brian Cashman. With a depleted farm system not able to provide high level-prospects, Cashman set his sights lower and asked for starter Jason Hammel, who was in his first year with the Cubs and was off to a strong start through the end of June.

However, Epstein and Hoyer had a plan to package both pitchers, Samardzija and Hammel, in the same deal if that was what it took to land the player or players they wanted in return. Cashman continued dialogue with the Cubs but was stunned when Epstein told him he believed he was close to a deal with Oakland for both pitchers.

"I think we were certainly in the arena. The fact that Theo was engaging me as much as he was, I know he likes our players. I know there's packages that had interested him for one or both combined that could have worked, but he always measured every conversation with me with 'There's a headliner player that if I can get, and I think I might be able to do so, it trumps every deal I could do in this game,'" Cashman said in an interview on WFAN radio in New York.

Epstein and Cashman spoke, according to the Yankees GM, at least seven times on the day the deal finally went down and when it was clear the A's were willing to include Addison Russell, Cashman knew he had no chance to top Oakland's offer. "I don't think [the Cubs] could've done a better deal than what they did in terms of that haul," Cashman said.

In fact, when Epstein finally agreed to the deal with the A's for Russell, outfield prospect Billy McKinney, and pitcher Dan Straily, Billy Beane told the Cubs brass, "Congratulations, you just traded for the next Barry Larkin [former Cincinnati Reds Hall of Fame shortstop]."

Looking back on the trade, Beane has no regrets about the deal because at the time Oakland was in first place and they were trying to solidify their team for a chance to win a World Series. "You always have to look at a trade in the context of the time it was made. Number one, there was not a belief that our pitching staff was good enough to hold onto a playoff spot and even after making the trades for Samardzija and Hammel and then acquiring Jon Lester from Boston we barely held onto a playoff spot as it was," Beane said.

"We also knew that the group of players that we had was not going to be sustainable. There was going to be a downward trend line in our team's performance. So this was the third year of a playoff-caliber team and our feeling was we might have one more shot at this for a while so we have to do everything we can to try to win.

"We weren't unaware of the consequences and we were under no illusion that Addison wasn't exactly who he was going to become," Beane told me. "That's the perils of having this job in any market but particularly in a small market. When you add players you have to give something up. In our marketplace we don't have the advantage of very often adding a player by just using cash. To us, minor league players are our currency. We knew darn well what we were giving up. We also knew that if we did not add more than one pitcher that we were not going to make the postseason and we were going to probably have to go through a cycle where we were down anyway. It was really trying to take advantage of the opportunity we had at that time knowing what the risk and reward was."

Another trade that received very little fanfare when it was consummated in January 2015 saw the Cubs send third baseman Luis Valbuena and pitcher Dan Straily to the Houston Astros for outfielder Dexter Fowler. The deal gave the Cubs a leadoff hitter with speed and power and he fit seamlessly into the Cubs clubhouse and was a big part of the culture change that Epstein and Hoyer were seeking.

Epstein also consummated a deal early in his tenure that saw the Cubs, knowing they were nowhere close to winning, trade set-up man Sean Marshall, a very solid left-handed specialist, to the Cincinnati Reds for prospects Travis Wood, a left-handed pitcher and a minor league infielder. Getting Wood, who had five years of team control when the deal was made, for the veteran Marshall was a no-brainer for the Cubs. They received a valuable young pitcher who needed time to develop while the Reds, who were contending, landed the veteran they needed for their bullpen.

Add in the deal the Cubs made with the Texas Rangers for starter Matt Garza that netted Chicago pitchers Justin Grimm and Carl Edwards, Jr. and two other players who are no longer in the organization and you start to see why the Cubs were able to rebuild their talent-deficient franchise so quickly.

Epstein and Hoyer were more than willing to trade anyone at any time if they felt the deal made the Cubs better in the long-term. They didn't worry about waiting until the July 31st deadline if they were offered a deal that they felt made sense. They operated with that mindset when they traded Scott Feldman for Jake Arrieta and they employed that same strategy when they acquired Addison Russell.

In the draft, the Cubs have made some astute choices that have been a big part of the rebuilding process. Kris Bryant was chosen with the No. 2 overall selection in the 2013 MLB First Year Player Draft and Epstein is quick to admit the Cubs got lucky when the Houston Astros decided against taking Bryant and instead chose pitcher Mark Appel of Stanford, who was from the Houston area. "You have to get some breaks and we got one when Kris was on the board for us at No. 2. He is a tremendous player and he was exactly what we needed," he said.

Bryant was thrilled when the Cubs chose him and he said that as soon as he heard his name called he knew all about the tradition and what would be expected of him by the Cubs hierarchy. "For me, the Cubs Way is all about being ready and playing hard every minute of every game. You see the history of the franchise, the ballpark, the ivy, the whole city and the neighborhood around the ballpark and you don't really need to be told, you just understand who the Chicago Cubs are and how special it is to play here."

Kyle Schwarber was the Cubs first round pick in the 2014 draft and the No. 4 selection overall and while his selection was a shocker to many around the game, McLeod, who ran the draft, and Epstein and Hoyer were holding their breath during the first three picks until they were sure Schwarber would be on the board for the Cubs. "We met with Kyle when his Indiana University team was playing in Arizona and we had a chance to sit down with him and we were blown away," McLeod said. "I laugh at Theo because he fell in love in the first five minutes of our first meeting with Kyle. We already knew he could hit but after the meeting we realized his makeup was off the charts."

Epstein was indeed enthralled by the slugging catcher, believing in a player that many scouts around baseball said had no chance at playing a position other than designated hitter. "We told Jon Lester when we were recruiting him, we have this kid Kyle Schwarber and he will be hitting 30 or more bombs a season for us," Epstein told me. "I fully believe that he will be one of the best left-handed hitters in baseball and despite his setback this season with his knee injury he proved in the World Series that he is close to being back to 100 percent. I am confident he will be all the way back in 2017 and he will be better than ever."

The other two first round draft picks that the Epstein/Hoyer/McLeod regime selected were Albert Almora and Ian Happ. Almora, a high school outfielder, was chosen with the sixth overall selection in 2012. He's risen through the Cubs system quickly and made his major league debut in 2016. He was also on the Cubs roster throughout the team's postseason run in 2016, playing a key role as a pinch runner in the 10th inning of the Cubs Game 7 victory over the Cleveland Indians. He is considered the team's center fielder of the future.

In 2015, the Cubs chose IF/OF Ian Happ, who starred at the University of Cincinnati and he has emerged as a Top 100 prospect in Major League Baseball. Happ is currently playing at Class AA Tennessee and, after starting his professional career in the outfield at the lower levels of the Cubs system, he is also being developed as a second baseman. Happ is only 22 years of age but he is on a rapid track to the big leagues and he should be knocking on the door of the Cubs major league roster soon. His successful development gives the Cubs another key piece to call up to the big leagues or to use in trade talks.

Notable Moves Under Theo Epstein

Via Trades, Free Agents, Draft Choices, and Contract Extensions

2011

November 30—Signed free agent OF David DeJesus to a 2 yr contract

December 8—Traded OF Tyler Colvin and D.J. LeMahieu to Colorado for 3B Ian Stewart

December 21—Traded P Sean Marshall to Cincinnati for P Travis Wood, OF Dave Sappelt, and IF Ronald Torreyes

2012

January 6—Traded P Andrew Cashner and Kyung-Min Na to San Diego for 1B Anthony Rizzo and P Zach Cates

February 2—Signed Cuban free agent P Gerardo Concepcion to $7 mil contract

April 4—Claimed 3B Luis Valbuena on waivers from Toronto

June 4—Selected OF Albert Almora in the MLB First Year Player Draft

June 30—Signed International free agent OF Jorge Soler to a 9 yr/$30 mil contract

July 31—Traded P Ryan Dempster to Texas for P Kyle Hendricks and IF Christian Villanueva

November 27—Signed P Scott Feldman to a 1 yr/$6 mil contract

December 6—Selected P Hector Rondon from the Cleveland Indians in the MLB Rule 5 Draft

2013

January 2—Signed P Edwin Jackson to a 4 yr/$52 mil contract

May 13—Signed 1B Anthony Rizzo to a 7 yr/$41 mil contract

June 6—Selected 3B Kris Bryant in the MLB First Year Player Draft

July 2—Signed International free agent IF Gleyber Torres to a $1.7 mil contract

July 2—Traded P Scott Feldman and C Steve Clevenger to Baltimore for P Jake Arrieta and P Pedro Strop

July 22—Traded P Matt Garza to the Texas Rangers for P C.J. Edwards, P Justin Grimm, IF Mike Olt, and P Neil Ramirez

August 1—Signed International free agent OF Eloy Jimenez to a $2.8 mil contract

2014

January 15—Signed OF Chris Coghlan to a 1 yr/$800,000 contract

February 13—Signed P Jason Hammel to a 1 yr/$6 mil contract

June 5—Selected C/OF Kyle Schwarber in the MLB First Year Player Draft

July 5—Traded P Jeff Samardzija and P Jason Hammel to Oakland for IF Addison Russell, OF Billy McKinney, and P Dan Straily

November 16—Traded P Arodys Vizcaino to Atlanta for IF Tommy La Stella

December 8—Signed P Jason Hammel to a 2 yr/$20 mil contract

December 9—Traded P Zack Godley and P Jeferson Mejia to Arizona for C Miguel Montero

December 10—Signed P Jon Lester to a 6 yr/$155 mil contract

December 19—Signed C David Ross to a 2 yr/$5 mil contract

2015

January 19—Traded IF Luis Valbuena and P Dan Straily to Houston for OF Dexter Fowler

August 18—Signed P Trevor Cahill to a minor league deal

October 19—Signed International free agent OF Eddy Julio Martinez to a $3 mil contract

December 4—Signed P John Lackey to a 2 yr/$32 mil contract

December 7—Re-signed P Trevor Cahill to a 1 yr/$4.25 mil contract
December 8—Traded IF Starlin Castro to New York (AL) for P Adam Warren and IF Brendan Ryan
December 8—Signed IF Ben Zobrist to a 4 yr/$56 mil deal
December 11—Signed OF Jason Heyward to an 8 yr/$184 mil contract

2016

February 25—Signed OF Dexter Fowler to a 1 yr/$13 mil contract
February 25—Traded OF Chris Coghlan to Oakland for P Aaron Brooks
June 9—Traded IF Arismendy Alcantara to Oakland for OF Chris Coghlan
July 20—Traded 1B Dan Vogelbach and P Paul Blackburn to Seattle for P Mike Montgomery and P Jordan Pries
July 25—Traded IF Gleyber Torres, OF Billy McKinney, P Adam Warren, OF Rashad Crawford to New York (AL) for P Aroldis Chapman
August 1—Traded P Jesus Castillo to Los Angeles (AL) for P Joe Smith
(OF Matt Szczur, IF Javier Baez + C Willson Contreras were acquired by Cubs before Epstein, Hoyer, McLeod joined organization)

When Theo Epstein and Jed Hoyer decided to replace their first managerial hire, Dale Sveum, after the 2013 season, the press conference to announce the move saw a media contingent that was openly questioning the direction of the franchise under the Cubs new baseball operations regime.

That day, Epstein was more than a little chapped at the perception that the Cubs were not on solid ground and that the franchise was not headed in the right direction and he made sure the assembled media knew it.

"I remember when we let Dale go after the 2013 season and we had a press conference at Wrigley Field. I knew there would be criticism because it was a tough decision and I felt horrible that we had to do it because Dale deserved better in a lot of ways, but I also knew why we were doing it. I knew where we were headed and I thought it made sense or otherwise we wouldn't have done it." he told me.

However, the media in attendance looked at the firing of Sveum as a sign that the Cubs were failing in their effort to rebuild the franchise and that the Epstein/Hoyer regime was starting over after a failed managerial hire.

However, a look back shows just how wrong those who doubted the plan were.[1] Those doubters failed to realize the talent upgrade that was going on in the system and focused only on wins and losses at the major league level in 2012 and 2013.

That bothered Epstein and he bristled at the tone and substance of many of the questions. "I was expecting some tough questions but I felt like the whole first part of the Q and A, almost every question was asked with a preamble of: this move demonstrates that this organization is failing or that this rebuild isn't going well or that you guys are starting over," he said.

However, around baseball the perception of the Chicago Cubs was radically different than the narrative being spun by the Chicago media. That perception that was felt in the other 29 front offices was also felt throughout the Cubs organization and it bothered Epstein and Hoyer that the people who were covering the team and saw them the most didn't seem to see just what was going on as the rebuild progressed.

"Deep down, I think all of us on the inside felt the opposite of what the perception was out in the public. We believed we were getting close and we kept saying, 'Holy smokes, we just acquired a lot talent. In the previous four months we had drafted Kris Bryant, traded for Jake Arrieta, traded for Kyle Hendricks, and we knew how good Anthony was going to be, so we felt we

---

1. For a fun look at those who doubted the plan, check out the tweets collected at Doubting Theo (doubtingtheo.tumblr.com)

were definitely on the right track," Epstein said.

It was during that press conference that Epstein finally put his foot down and told the assembled media just what was on his mind and just what he believed was going on in the revamped organization of the Chicago Cubs.

"We were starting to feel really good about the young talent that we had and how things were going in the minor leagues. For the first time we could see the road map for how they could get up to the big leagues and start to make a difference. I remember saying to everyone at the press conference, 'Look there's a real dichotomy between how you guys in the media are viewing this organization right now and how it's being viewed around baseball. And around baseball, the people who follow these things are looking at us and saying the Cubs are coming. They are coming fast and they are coming strong.'"

MLB Best Records (2015–16)

Team	W-L	Pct
Cubs	200–123	.619
Cardinals	186–138	.574
Dodgers	183–141	.565
Rangers	183–141	.565
Blue Jays	182–142	.562
Nationals	178–146	.549

That quote became a mantra that Cubs fans latched onto. It gave them hope that a bright future was not far away. However, Epstein wasn't done in his response to the packed news conference announcing the managerial move.

"That's what we felt and we felt that the morale in the organization was great. We knew we had to figure out the last piece and we had to get the environment at the big league level the right way. But we knew there was a lot of talent in the organization and it's starting to come and everyone is starting to feel really good about being Cubs. You guys are looking at it in the exact opposite way, so I just want to let you know that things are getting better around here. That was the first time that I had to really question the critics. Because we knew things were going really well and I wanted everyone else to know as well."

While everyone inside the game knew the Cubs' plan was going off exceptionally well, the Epstein/Hoyer regime was a frequent target of local critics who believed that the rebuild could have been done differently and much more quickly. They opined on signings the Cubs should have made, such as Prince Fielder, who inked a deal in excess of $200 million with the Detroit Tigers, or Albert Pujols, who left the Cubs archrival, the St. Louis Cardinals, to sign a deal with the Los Angeles Angels of Anaheim for $254 million.

Had the Cubs done either one of those deals, Anthony Rizzo would never have been acquired because the Cubs would have had no need for a young first baseman with the position locked up on a long-term deal for the foreseeable future. A look at how these two players have turned out since they signed their megadeals sees Pujols playing solidly for the Angels (though primarily at DH) while Fielder is out of baseball after suffering a career-ending neck injury while playing for the Texas Rangers, who acquired him in a trade with Detroit after the 2013 season.

Chicago Sun-Times columnist Rick Morrissey grew up in Chicago and has spent the bulk of his career writing about Chicago sports at both the *Chicago Tribune* and the *Sun-Times*. He was not one of the early believers in "The Plan" to strip the Cubs down to their foundation and to rebuild them from the ground up. "I think they did exactly what they said they were going to do but that's never been my bone of contention with them. My argument was, just because you did the right thing and built up the minor league system it didn't logically follow that you had to lose so badly at the major league level. You could have had a better major league product to offer fans for three or four years of horrendous losing," Morrissey said.

However, a look at the free agent market from 2012 to '14 shows high salaried players such as Pujols, Fielder, Yu Darvish, Zach Greinke, and Robinson Cano that the Cubs could not have afforded and most people around baseball believe that most if not all of those players would not have been interested in playing for the Cubs as they struggled on the field and had not yet improved their substandard facilities at Wrigley Field.

"In the moment, not looking back like that it's a philosophy," Morrissey said. "It's not a what-would-you-have-done type of situation. There were other players besides those huge-ticket free agents that a billionaire family could have purchased. They could have put more money into the major league payroll and at least been competitive instead of tanking for three seasons, even though they will never call it that."

However, when one examines the state of the Cubs upon Epstein's arrival in the fall of 2011, it is obvious that the Cubs talent level and overall infrastructure was far worse than anyone realized or was willing to admit. A look at the top players in the minor league system as well as a look at the Cubs major league roster shows a franchise so devoid of high level talent that most professional observers of the team now admit that the Cubs had to be rebuilt from the ground up to have any chance of building a foundation for sustained success.

"To try to patch together to achieve some level of respectability would have been foolish. The Cubs were so far away that it would have been throwing good money on a bad team that had no chance to compete and it would have slowed the rebuilding process," a former major league general manager told me.

Oakland A's GM Billy Beane is renowned in the industry for his ability to craft together competitive teams despite having to do it on one of the smallest budgets in all of baseball. Beane uses a mixture of analytical data and old-school scouting much like the Cubs do under Theo Epstein, but he believes that the Cubs' ability to stay disciplined to their long-term plan was one of the biggest keys in their eventual turnaround into a championship team.

"It was clear to me what they were trying to do," Beane said. "It comes down to not just trying to win once or make the playoffs once but that they were putting something together that was sustainable and could be good or great for a long time. The hard thing is finding a situation where you have the backing of the owner to stay the course as you go through a long rebuild. Theo had that with Tom and that is why their plan worked."

Morrissey has felt the wrath of some Cubs fans who believe that he did not understand or accept the Cubs plan under Epstein but he says that he has been misunderstood.

"I understood the plan. However, my only argument was that I believe the Cubs could have rebuilt the minor league system and spent money to put a major league product on the field at the same time. But what is the phrase? The winner gets to write the story? He gets to write the history. I just believe that Theo could have gotten you some more victories without damaging what he was trying to build for the long-term future of the Cubs."

So did the Cubs purposely tank multiple seasons to give themselves the best path to acquiring high-level talent? While the Cubs have never called what they did tanking, they do admit that they employed a strategy to use their available assets to acquire as much young talent as they could. Hoyer told me, "Once we saw how talent deficient the franchise was, we made the decision as a staff to make acquiring young talent a part of every deal we made. We needed to add as much talent as we could so we used the veteran assets that we had to do that and to jump-start our building process throughout our system."

From Epstein's perspective, the Cubs had a number of issues that had to be addressed when he arrived from a struggling major league team to a low-rated minor league system to substandard facilities, but one problem stood out above all others to the team president.

"We just didn't have enough talent. When I originally met with Tom Ricketts about the job, I saw the Cubs as a long-term project because of the talent deficit at the big league level and in the minor leagues and I wanted to make sure that Tom understood that and that he was good with that approach. I believe in building things from the bottom up to build a real healthy organization, not just a big league team that might have a shot in a given year," Epstein said.

Epstein and Hoyer also knew they needed to acquire a lot of pitching, but where would they find high-level starting pitching when it was the toughest commodity to find in the game? Little did they know a struggling pitcher who was bouncing back and forth from the big leagues to the minor leagues and back again was going to be perhaps the best trade in Cubs history.

8

The Arrieta Trade

The trade that gets heralded more than any other was the Cubs deal in July 2013 for Baltimore Orioles starter Jake Arrieta, who had been back and forth between Baltimore and Class AAA while struggling mightily in the early part of the 2013 season. In fact, when the deal was announced, the Cubs assigned Arrieta to their Class AAA Iowa affiliate, where he pitched briefly before being recalled by the Cubs. "I remember taking my wife and family away for a few days before I had to report to Class AAA with the Orioles. I knew I had good stuff and I knew I was a better pitcher than I had shown but I couldn't put it all together," he said.

In fact, Arrieta told me that his second career no-hitter, in Cincinnati on April 21, 2016, in a 16–0 Cubs victory, came exactly three years to the day that he was sent back to the minor leagues by the Orioles. "I remember being in the car with my family and I said to my wife that maybe I should give up baseball. I knew I had good stuff and I knew I could be a successful pitcher but for whatever reason it wasn't happening. It was very frustrating."

In Arrieta's last start before being demoted in 2013, he lasted only four innings against the Los Angeles Dodgers and needed 91 pitches to get through those innings. Despite allowing only two hits, he walked five, and was charged with five runs. At the time of his demotion he was 1–1 with a 6.63 ERA and had walked 16 batters in just 19 innings of work.

So what did the Cubs, under Epstein and Hoyer, see that not many others saw in 2013? First, the Cubs front office does an extensive postseason analysis that every one of their scouts and front office personnel fills out. It asks among other things, who around baseball is a player that we should look at that needs a change of scenery for any reason?

Many answered Jake Arrieta. He had tremendous stuff but was obviously struggling with his command and even more so, the mental side of the game. In fact, after announcing his demotion, Orioles manager Buck Showalter said, "The thing he's got to solve is the mental side of it. He knows he can help this club win. We know he can."

While many in the Cubs organization liked Arrieta from afar, many had also heard from friends around the game that Arrieta needed a fresh start but that he had tremendous talent. Ex-Cub (and 1996 National League Rookie of the Year) Todd Hollandsworth told me, "I have a lot of friends around baseball and I host a radio show on the MLB Network and they all tell me that Jake Arrieta is the most uncomfortable at-bat in the game today. And that was something that guys have been saying for a long time, well before he became the Jake Arrieta of today."

Cubs pitching coach Chris Bosio, a huge influence on the Cubs pitching philosophy under the Epstein/Hoyer regime, has been in baseball as a pitching coach for many years after his 11-year playing career ended. During his time as a coach with Cincinnati he remembers seeing Arrieta face the Reds in spring training and handling them with ease.

"I watched him punch out eight guys in three innings against us and I remember writing him up because it was against a pretty good Cincinnati Reds minor league club that was filled with guys who went on to play in the big leagues and he went through us like it was nothing. I still have the scouting report I wrote up on him, thinking that the last guy I had seen dominate like that was a Division 2 college pitcher I scouted named Jordan Zimmerman, who is now a star with the Detroit Tigers—that's how impressive he was that day," Bosio said.

Veteran baseball writer Tom Verducci wrote a great piece about Arrieta's transformation after sitting down with him in spring training of 2016, in which Arrieta opened up and looked back on his struggles to make it in the big leagues.

"There were so many things in Baltimore not many people know about," Arrieta [told Verducci]. "I had struggles with my pitching coach. A lot of guys did. Three or four guys—[Chris] Tillman, [Brian] Matusz, [Zach] Britton—were just really uncomfortable in their own skins at the time, trying to be the guys they weren't. You can attest how difficult it is to try to reinvent your mechanics against the best competition in the world.

"I feel like I was playing a constant tug-of-war, trying to make the adjustments I was being told to make and knowing in the back of my mind that I can do things differently and be better. It was such a tremendous struggle for me because as a second- and third-year player, you want to be coachable. I knew I got [to the majors] for a reason, and I was confused about why I was changing that now. You feel everybody has your best interests in mind, but you come to find out that's not necessarily the case."

Verducci has watched Arrieta dating back to his rookie season with the Orioles and has an interesting take on what makes the

Worst ERA in Baltimore Orioles History
(since franchise moved from St.Louis to Baltimore, 1954–Present, min 50 starts)

5.46	Jake Arrieta
5.05	Daniel Cabrera
5.02	Jose Mercedes
5.00	Rick Sutcliffe

2015 Cy Young winner tick. "Jake was considered an underachiever. His performance didn't measure up to the quality of his stuff. So it was a surprise. There were a lot of reasons why he struggled, but because his stuff was so good a lot of people thought it was just a matter of time and as it turned out a change of scenery. I remember one game when Buck Showalter told me, 'Wouldn't it be good to be Jake Arrieta? Young, good athlete, good looking, good arm.... Life is good.' I don't see Jake as someone who is ever content. He's a restless soul when it comes to finding incremental improvements. I got the feeling that Jake knew all along he was this good. Now he wants to find the limits to his greatness," Verducci told me.

Arrieta heard that and agreed wholeheartedly with what Verducci said. "That's just the philosophy of trying to grow and continue to develop regardless of where I am at in my career or in my life as a father, a husband, a son, a friend. There is always room for improvement in relationships or in between the lines. There is always something you can do to better yourself or the people around you. That's my motivating factors. Not only do I want to be at my best for myself but for the other 24 guys in that clubhouse because each and every one of us counts on each other."

In addition, as Verducci researched his story he found many people who couldn't understand why Arrieta was struggling so mightily to make it in the big leagues. Baltimore star first baseman Chris Davis remembers former Chicago White Sox star Paul Konerko telling him in April 2012, "That's the nastiest guy I've faced in the past five years," when they were talking about Arrieta. Dodgers catcher A.J. Ellis felt the same way, remarking, "I remember, in 2013, I faced Matt Harvey, the late Jose Fernandez, and most of the nastiest pitchers you could think of. The guy with the best stuff of all was Jake Arrieta."

Best ERA in Cubs History
(1920–Present, min 50 starts)

2.52	Jake Arrieta
2.84	Lon Warneke
2.89	Jon Lester
2.92	Kyle Hendricks

So why was this incredibly talented pitcher, in a sport where pitching is so hard to come by, struggling so mightily? Why couldn't the Baltimore Orioles unlock his abilities and why would they give up on him for the rental of a journeyman pitcher? The answer might lie in the Orioles organizational pitching philosophy at that time and Arrieta's struggles to succeed under it.

Arrieta is known as a crossfire pitcher and in Baltimore he experimented with several different variations of his windup but could never find any consistency in his approach. A crossfire pitcher throws across his body and some organizations frown upon that approach because some in the game believe that it leads to more arm injuries.

Under then–Orioles pitching coach Rick Adair, Arrieta was told to scrap the crossfire delivery as well as one of his favorite pitches, the cutter, despite the success he showed as he rose through Baltimore's system. Baltimore management felt that the cutter had a cumulative effect in decreasing fastball velocity, so it was banned throughout the organization. Arrieta also suffered from the Orioles changing pitching coaches after Mark Connor resigned and was replaced by Adair, who had a different pitching philosophy.

Bosio, himself a longtime major league pitcher, also employed a crossfire delivery and he remembers the first time he spoke with Arrieta shortly after the Cubs acquired him from the Orioles. "I told Jake that we wanted him to be himself. I remember that first conversation because Jake was very direct with me. I could tell how upset he was with how his career was going by the tone of his voice and the verbiage he used to deliver the message. The frustration was evident by how he spoke and I knew he was upset with himself because he knew he had talent and he was not achieving his potential," Bosio told me.

Arrieta said, "I remember getting a call from Dan Duquette and he told me we've decided to make a trade and we've traded you to the Chicago Cubs. It was something that I knew was in the process of happening. I didn't know where I was going to get traded to but I was pretty well aware a trade was looming and so it wasn't that much of a surprise. It was just a moment for me where I knew I had a chance to start over again and to go back to simplifying some things for myself. It was a chance to just go out there and pitch and to make pitching fun again."

What many people don't remember is that Arrieta did not immediately report to Chicago but instead he was assigned to Class AAA Iowa to give him a chance to pitch in a low-pressure environment. It was also a chance to give him an opportunity to go back to pitching the way he was comfortable and that was as a crossfire pitcher.

"I told him that we were sending him to Class AAA Iowa and that all I wanted him to do was to be yourself and pitch," Bosio said. "I told him that we wanted him to relax and to just get stretched out and that when he got to Chicago then he and I would go to work. I told him I knew that he wasn't enjoying himself. But we stressed to him to just have fun, be yourself, and pitch. That's it."

For many players a return to the minor leagues, especially after being a club's Opening Day starter would be very hard to deal with, but Arrieta relished the chance to reinvent himself. "I went to Iowa and I got back to who I was. I redefined myself and it took off from there. The relationships I made in this organization had a lot to do with that too. The coaches, the instructors, and the people I work with on a day-to-day basis and at spring training there are just a lot of good people throughout this organization."

The Cubs history is littered with bad teams and famous collapses and of course every sports fan knows that the Chicago Cubs hadn't won a World Series from 1908 until 2016 and they hadn't played in one before the '16 season since 1945.

But one particular trade made in 1964 stands out as perhaps the worst trade in baseball history. The Cubs, needing starting pitching, acquired 28-year-old veteran Ernie Broglio, who had won 18 games for the St. Louis Cardinals in 1963, for 25-year-old outfielder Lou Brock, had been erratic during his time with the Cubs but had shown flashes of real promise. The rest is history as Brock went onto a Hall of Fame career and Broglio, plagued by a sore arm, won seven more games the rest of his career and was out of baseball at age 30.

So when the Cubs traded Scott Feldman, who was off to a solid start to the 2013 season, along with backup catcher Steve Clevenger to the Orioles for a struggling minor league pitcher in Arrieta and a reliever in Pedro Strop who had an ERA north of 7.00, some openly questioned the move. One of those who ripped the trade was then–Cubs starting pitcher Jeff Samardzija, who told the Chicago media of his displeasure.

"I don't think this team improves by trading Scott Feldman," Samardzija said. "He was one of our better pitchers. He's thrown a lot of innings, a solid dude, a solid guy in the clubhouse. It's a shame to see him go, and the same with Clevenger. A great dude to have around, a great teammate who played the game hard and played the game the right way. It's unfortunate. Just hope the guys they get in return are comparable and bring the same attitude to the field every day that those guys brought."

When the Cubs recalled Jake Arrieta from Class AAA Iowa on July 30, 2013, he had made five starts and posted a 1–2 record with a 4.03 ERA in 22.1 innings of work with the Cubs' top minor league affiliate. After being acquired by the Cubs on July 2, his debut was a success as he pitched six innings and allowed just one run on two hits, picking up a no decision along the way. However, he was promptly sent back to the minor leagues and was not back in Chicago until he was recalled on August 16, and it was then that he was finally in the big leagues to stay.

The fresh start paid dividends and he quickly showed improvement under the tutelage of Bosio, who is one of the top pitching coaches in baseball. But the tweaks that Bosio and Arrieta made together were not as major as one might expect when you look at the dramatic turnaround that came fairly quickly with the Cubs.

"We changed Jake's pregame warmup routine. Every guy that we have, there is a sequence that complements the style of pitcher that he is. At that time, Jake was trying to be what we call a far-side guy. That meant that we wanted him to throw more arm side than so far across his body to complement what his approach was and that was something that we thought would allow him to keep his head and his shoulders a little quieter," Bosio told me.

"And to Jake's credit he bought into it. So he basically flipped the script and it got him to the other side of the plate and he started working different sequences to maximize what he did. It wasn't easy and it was a struggle at the start. I remember getting a call from one of our coaches down at AAA and he was concerned that Jake's pitch counts were so high early in the game. But obviously I couldn't do anything until we got him to Chicago, so we kept telling him to relax and just pitch and keep having fun.

"Then once we got him to Chicago I was able to get my hands on him and that's when our relationship took off. And to Jake's credit he tried a lot of different things and a lot of it took, but he also trusted me and that was a huge part of it and it was interesting to watch him grow because of the trust and his willingness to do that."

While Arrieta is now a household name around the game, most don't know about the 2013 conversations with his wife, Brittany, about giving up the game and putting his college degree in marketing to use in a career change. But then, he would snap back to reality and realize how much he loved playing baseball, until the next outing when he would struggle again or the next time he was sent back to the minor leagues. Then the doubts would creep right back into his mind.

Then the trade to the Cubs gave him a new lease on his baseball life and the rest they say is history. "Working with Bos [Chris Bosio] has really been seamless. We go over certain things but we don't try to change my delivery completely. We try to look at small things we can adjust to be more consistent and that's where it ends. He has a lot of insight and a lot of experience from his career that he can pass on to us in a very positive way and that is what's happened over the past couple of years," Arrieta said.

The relationship that Bosio and Arrieta have is especially close, considering the lack of success that Arrieta had in Baltimore, the struggles that he had with his last pitching coach with the Orioles, and how his career has turned around since he began working with Bosio after the trade that sent him to the Cubs.

"Our relationship is so strong because from day one we had the same goal in mind," Arrieta said. "We're on the same side, the same team and we are trying to accomplish the same goals. If you can say those things about your pitching coach and the player, if those things are aligned in the relationship, it's going to work out really well.

"You can't guarantee results but you can work in a positive manner and make progress from a work standpoint and that's what we've done since I've been here. We are always trying to evolve and make progress and be better from it. Once you think you've figured everything out in this game a humbling experience is right around the corner. That's something that will never go away for any player."

Today, after all of the success, the Cy Young Award, and the increased paydays, Bosio says their relationship has only gotten stronger. "Our relationship is one that he can say anything to me and I can say anything to him, which is not an easy thing to do in this day and age with these guys. There are certain things I will say to him that he understands that are unique to him that I probably wouldn't say to anyone else. This is a unique guy with unique stuff but once it clicked it was dominant and it was overpowering. But the biggest thing was the freedom that he had mentally to change because this guy was so talented physically."

However, even Bosio admits that he did not see a Cy Young and one of the best in the game status in Arrieta's future when the Cubs acquired him in 2013. "I thought he could be a number two or number three starter. At that time, we didn't have a lot of pitching and we were just trying to acquire guys. That was Theo and Jed's plan all along, to acquire as many arms as we could. We had very little pitching in our system so we needed to increase our inventory of arms.

"We also had Jeff Samardzija and it was fun transferring him from a power-throwing reliever to a starter. We had Ryan Dempster, Matt Garza, and Paul Maholm, but that was about it. Jake's stuff was so electric and so violent that once he started to understand the mechanical part of it and trusting it and he started tweaking his workout regimen, it was spectacular to watch, not only for me but I think for the rest of Cubs Nation. It was special, it was absolutely special.

"But, I agree with Theo, there was no way that you could forecast picking up a guy like that [who] had some of the struggles that he had that we saw on video to say that this guy is going to win a Cy Young," Bosio went on. "Any time you make a trade and you acquire a player that is an underachieving starter, plus a struggling reliever in Pedro Strop, for a pitcher that was pretty hot at the time in Feldman and you give up Clevenger as well, there is no way you think you are getting a Cy Young guy down the road. But, once I got my eyes on him we knew we had something pretty special. We started to do some tweaks and we saw the movement on the pitches and once we saw the movement, then we saw the command and we knew we had something special. I remember that like it was yesterday and I thought, *Holy cow! This guy is unbelievable.* Then, once the command became more consistent and he was able to duplicate and then the feel and the verbiage and the terminology that he started using with me it was huge.

"Then he started to be able to sequence stuff and then he was able to take those sequences to game action and it was awesome to watch. Then, the big thing was he started to be able to repeat it from start to start. He'd have one good start, then he'd have another good start, then he'd have one with a few walks and he'd have a high pitch count and he'd struggle a little bit so he had to learn to be more pitch efficient. We were trying to challenge him to get more early contact and once he started grasping early contact that's when he started getting deeper into games. It was at the tail end of 2014 when we started to see it all come together," Bosio said.

There aren't many pitchers who have dominated for an extended stretch like Jake Arrieta has over the past two seasons, but Bosio sees a striking similarity between Arrieta and another former pupil of his, Hall of Famer Randy Johnson. "With Randy, I would hear from Hall of Fame hitters who were right handed that Randy was almost impossible to hit. I can understand a left-handed hitter saying that about Randy but these were right-handed hitters.

"I am hearing the same thing about Jake from hitters who are both right handed and left handed," Bosio continued. "You never know where the ball is going or he throws that pitch that everyone calls a slider but [it's] really a 91 MPH cutter at you that breaks so much it ends up coming from off the plate and it ends up at your kneecaps. He throws across his body, it is uncomfortable for a hitter and again, I was very similar because I threw across my body and I understood where Jake was coming from.

"When you throw that way you are constantly told that you have to get more in line and I heard that all the time. There were things that we did and things that I did because of how I was taught that I tried to pass the torch that Pete Vukovich [former MLB pitcher] taught me and I tried to pass those things along to Jake, who is a guy who was much more talented than I was as a pitcher.

"This guy is throwing mid-90s, a 91 MPH cutter, then we got command of the curveball and the change up and then the thing that we tried to work on was pitching to both sides of the plate and as a right-handed batter he throws so far behind them that you get that front hip to open up and that's where you take the sting out of their bat," Bosio said.

"I don't look back on my struggles with regret," Arrieta told me. "All of the experiences that we go through, the good and the bad, make us the person that we are currently. I hang on to a lot of the negative experiences that I have had in the past from a career standpoint because they motivate me and they keep me hungry to get better and better."

One look at the Cubs pitching staff and any observer can see Chris Bosio's fingerprints all over most every guy who now pitches for the Cubs. From Arrieta to Kyle Hendricks to Pedro Strop to Hector Rondon to Travis Wood and on and on, Bosio is the guru the Cubs have been looking for, for a very long time.

"The players deserve the credit. It's special to me, I'm not going to lie. It's fun and I'm so happy for the players because they deserve a lot of the credit. They could have quite frankly, turned their head the other way and said I'm going to keep doing it my way, but they trusted me and our staff and our organization. They trusted our other pitching coaches Mike Borzello and Lester Strode and they trusted our defense. The organization has done a great job acquiring really good players in trades and through the draft and they have been able to put players around these guys to complement the players that we already had," Bosio told me.

But no matter how good coaches such as Chris Bosio are, he understands that the players are the ones that have to perform on the field and that fact will never be forgotten by him. "The players are the ones that have to go out there and apply it and they've done that. Some of these guys have had big paydays and hopefully more of these guys will but it's been a lot of fun to be a part of and it's something that I'll never forget in my coaching career."

"From talking with him and people who played with and against him, you learn a lot about his demeanor and competitiveness, his will to win," Arrieta said. "He's a guy who didn't put up with much. He was a tough guy back in the day. Still is. But that fire he had, he instills a lot of that in these guys here and he has a lot of credibility because he did this in the same game we're playing and he did it for a long time. Any time you can have a mentor or instructor who has those credentials, it really helps guys to be able to latch on to him and use that information to the best of their ability."

Epstein has several key moments that he recalls from his tenure running the Cubs but he knows that the Arrieta trade was one of the watershed moments of his administration. "The Arrieta trade was a big one for us and it has been huge for us but what we're seeing now is obviously a best-case scenario. No one saw him going from where he was to Cy Young. No one. We thought he had a chance to be a solid part of a rotation or a high-level reliever, but this has worked out far beyond what we projected," Epstein told me.

For Arrieta, he knows just how fortunate he was to be traded to the Cubs and how close he came to never realizing his immense potential. "I knew I had this ability in me. I really did, because I always looked at the guys who were doing this at the highest level and I knew I could do this. Even in flashes I pitched like a number one, like a dominant starter in the big leagues, so it was just about finding the consistency. That was the struggle, it was figuring out how to put it all together as consistently as I could every five days. Not go out and throw a shutout every start or go out and throw eight innings and only give up one run.

"How could I at least keep the team in the game?" Arrieta said. "If I only go five or six innings can I limit it to three runs? Can I keep my team in it? Are we still in the game in the seventh or eighth inning? Is it a one-run game or did I give up seven runs and put the thing out of reach for my guys to climb out of the hole? Those are the motivating factors even on days where you don't have your stuff. Do whatever it takes and give your best effort to keep the team in the game."

To look at Arrieta now with a Cy Young Award, a $10.7 million payday for the 2016 season and talk of a $200-plus million contract when he reaches free agency after the 2017 season, it is hard to believe that he actually contemplated quitting the game just three years ago. But he says those awful struggles in Baltimore are experiences that he cherishes today because those times are what makes him the pitcher and person he is now is.

"Those tough times have taught me to be humble and not getting too high or too low. Finding a way to stay even-keeled, focusing on the task at hand for that day and knowing that when I get out onto the mound I've prepared as well as I possibly could, which creates confidence.

"Preparation simply leads to confidence. You can have false confidence but at the end of the day internally you're going to know whether or not that confidence is real or fake," he told me.

Arrieta is also known for his incredible workout regimen that has turned his 6'4" frame into a sculpted physique not commonly seen in a major league clubhouse. Despite questions from those who don't know him about how he has developed his body to this degree, Arrieta has always been a fitness freak. "I have always been this way. It's just been magnified because of the success that I have had over the past couple of seasons.

"With everything I have done in terms of health and wellness, people are more intrigued by it because of all of the coverage due to my success and it's been broadcast a lot more. But since I was a little kid I had a passion and an interest for health and wellness and strength, conditioning, and nutrition. Those things go hand in hand to be in the best possible shape you can be. And with what I do for a living it's vitally important that I am able to understand and have a grasp of how I can use those components [strength and conditioning combined with nutrition] to have the health, the longevity in my career, and the success to play this game as long as I can," Arrieta told me.

Pilates, weight training, a strict diet combined with multiple hours a day of stretching, and a mental approach that is hyper focused have all contributed to making Arrieta one of the toughest pitchers to get a hit off. His OBA (Opponents' Batting Average) is the best in baseball over the past two seasons and have put him in the team photo of the best pitchers in all of baseball. It's hard to believe that this is the same guy that considered walking away from the game just three seasons ago as he struggled with an ERA of 7.23 and multiple trips back to the minors.

"There were times in my career, like obviously when I thought about walking away from the game, those weren't the happiest times in my life, specifically my career. Having kids makes it way easier to deal with the successes or failures on the field because when you get home they don't care. They want to enjoy your company. They want to run around the house and play hide and seek. Things that really help me get away from it at times and I'm just tremendously lucky to have the family that I do that's been so supportive through everything–my wife, Brittany, specifically.

"Regardless of where we've been she's been on my side and she's been my ultimate supporter. She's basically been the key component of helping me get through this as well as we did. Because some of the things that we went through were tough. It's hard not to be happy in this environment with these guys we're playing with, in this city. The happiness is at an all-time high for sure," he said.

Family has been the bedrock that has helped bring Jake Arrieta back from the baseball dead. The place in his mind where he actually considered quitting the sport because he was struggling so much but deep down he knew he had so much more talent than he had showed.

"We've had moments where my wife [Brittany] has rolled over and looked at me in bed and she'll just smile, like after a really good outing or after the no-hitters and I'll know exactly what she's thinking. So yeah, some of the things that I've been able to do recently in my career, it's hard to think that certain things are possible. But to finally do some of these things and experience it and experience it as a family and as a team, it's tough to put into words how meaningful it is," Arrieta said.

9

The Odd Arrival of Joe Maddon

Rick Renteria was the man to lead the Cubs in 2015. Until he suddenly wasn't.

Prior to the Cubs final series of 2014, as the Cubs played the Brewers in Milwaukee, Theo Epstein was asked if Renteria would be back as the Cubs manager for the 2015 season. "Yeah, absolutely," he responded when he was questioned by a throng of Chicago media who were there to cover the end of the Cubs season.

Sure, Renteria was signed through 2016, with team options in 2017 and 2018. But this was year three of the Epstein regime, and the Cubs were 71–88 to that point in the season. After all, the first managerial hire this front office made was Dale Sveum, and he only made it through two years of his three-year contract.

And with a minor league system full of talent that was about to make the jump to the major leagues, the questions about

Renteria were legitimate. Was he the man to manage all of the Cubs' top prospects as they made their way to the major leagues?

The Cubs would only get one chance to make a first impression on players making their major league debuts and they had to make the transition from the minor league system to the pressures of playing at Wrigley Field as smooth as possible. Players like Anthony Rizzo, Kris Bryant, Addison Russell, Kyle Schwarber, Jorge Soler, and Javier Baez were the backbone of the Cubs youth movement. Add in veterans like Starlin Castro, Jake Arrieta, and others, and it was essential that whoever was going to manage the Chicago Cubs in 2015 knew how to handle a clubhouse and could command the respect of a collection of extremely diverse personalities and backgrounds.

But no one saw what was about to happen in Tampa, Florida. Not even then–Tampa Bay Rays manager Joe Maddon, until Rays president Mathew Silverman called him in early October to inform him that he had a clause in his contract that granted him a 14-day window to talk to other teams if his previous boss, Andrew Friedman, ever left the organization.

Silverman had just been promoted after Friedman resigned to accept a position with the Los Angeles Dodgers as the head of their baseball operations department. The last thing he wanted to do was to replace his field manager but he had an obligation to inform Maddon of the clause in the manager's contract.

Maddon knew nothing about the clause and called his agent, Alan Nero (who ironically is based in Chicago), and the two men had a lengthy discussion about Maddon's options. Maddon was on a road trip in his 42' RV that he nicknamed "Cousin Eddie," driving from Tampa to his hometown of Hazleton, Pennsylvania, with a friend, and told his agent to continue contract discussions with the Rays.

However, his head started spinning with the possibility of being a free agent for the first time in his life. "I thought, 'You have two weeks to become a free agent for the first time in your life. You're an idiot to not try, to not see what happens,'" he said. "And my intent was to do that while still negotiating with the Rays. That was my goal. We got to the point where it became obvious that I thought they did not want to negotiate much more," he told Scott Miller of Bleacher Report in December 2014.

"So we opted out, and I thought I'd find out what the rest of the world thought." He didn't have to wait long to find out, as Nero's phone rang and rang and kept ringing. The agent had gone about the process of informing the other 29 teams in baseball of Maddon's availability and 10 teams expressed interest in hiring Maddon.

Then this headline hit the media on October 24, 2014: "Maddon Opts Out of Contract, Leaves Rays"

Then Matt Silverman issued this statement:

> *"Joe Maddon has exercised an opt-out in his current contract, a contract which was not scheduled to expire until after the 2015 season.... We tried diligently and aggressively to sign Joe to a third contract extension prior to his decision.*
>
> *"As of [Thursday] afternoon, Joe enabled himself to explore opportunities throughout Major League Baseball. He will not be managing the Rays in 2015. Joe has been our manager for nine seasons, and the foundation of success laid during his tenure endures. We thank him for all that he's meant to the organization."*

The Rays had just lost Andrew Friedman to the Dodgers. Now they would have to find a new manager as well. Matt Silverman made his feelings known:

"I'm surprised by it and disappointed.... I believed that Joe wanted to be the manager of the Rays long-term. That was my intention and Stu's [Tampa owner Stuart Sternberg] intention, and we dove headfirst into discussions about an extension. But it takes two parties to reach an agreement, and we weren't able to reach an agreement. And that's how we got to this day.

"In Joe's contract, he had the ability to opt out if certain events took place, and one of those was if Andrew Friedman wasn't an employee of the club.... And the last several days, we worked with Joe to try and figure out a contract extension. And we engaged and made many offers, and it became clear from his responses that it was not an exercise that was going to lead to an outcome, so he opted out yesterday. And we are turning the page to begin the process to look for a new manager."

Maddon offered an explanation for his sudden departure:

"I just hope they will understand that this was a unique opportunity for me and my family, and beyond that, the charities that I'm attached to.... There was nothing else that I was looking for before that. Up until Andrew left I did not have this kind of opportunity whatsoever. And then once Andrew left and this opportunity opened up, I had to consider it.

"And I really ask anybody if they really looked at it, if they will put themselves in my shoes, what would they have done? So it's not an easy decision, a very difficult decision. Talk about agonizing, that pain in the gut type of stuff, absolutely. But at the end of the day, I thought it was the right thing for me and my family...."

> *"I know that Matthew reached out and they came up with an offer.... It did not meet up to what I [wanted] and we came to an impasse. And that happens. There's no friction between me and him or me and [principal owner] Stu [Sternberg]. I had great conversations with Matthew and Stu, they were very candid and open. I felt good about it moving forward. I hope they don't feel betrayed, because I don't feel betrayed by the offer."*

Almost immediately, the Cubs were among the frontrunners to land the Hazleton native. Maddon, the 2008 and 2011 AL Manager of the Year, was heralded by many as one of the finest managers in the game. and he was well-known for his unconventional thinking. Some examples of his less-than-conventional thinking include walking then-Rangers slugger Josh Hamilton with the bases loaded while *leading* 7–3. The Rays went on to win 7–4.

Another memorable Maddon moment came with his Tampa Bay Rays team struggling. So what did the manager do? He employed what he called the "Tommy Tutone" lineup, after that group's popular song. His batting order went 8-6-7-5-3-0-9 (the 0 was his DH).

Maddon looked for any way he could think of to get his team to relax and to handle the rigors of a 162-game major league season. Sure, Major League Baseball was hard work and serious business but Joe Maddon was going to take every opportunity he could to inject some fun into his team and their clubhouse.

Organized, themed team trips became a staple of every season. Players had the "jersey" trip, where each player wore a jersey of their favorite team from another sport. Or the onesies trip, where every member of the Rays travel party flew back to Tampa at the end of a road trip in whatever one-piece sleep attire they chose.

Maddon invited celebrities and bizarre characters alike to visit the Rays clubhouse. A Seminole "medicine man" made an appearance. A magician took the players' minds off of a losing streak. Live penguins, pythons, and a collection of zoo animals were all welcome in the Tampa clubhouse. Some in baseball rolled their eyes at the New Age manager but the results were obvious. The Rays were playing inspired baseball.

Dress codes were out and fun was in—as long as the players played hard and respected the game. If a player wasn't sure if they should wear a particular piece of clothing all they had to do was follow Maddon's mantra. "If you think you look hot, wear it." Maddon's teams in Tampa played hard, won a lot of baseball games, and they had fun doing it.

Joe Maddon's Themed Trips and Other "Moments" of Levity with The Rays and the Cubs

Woodstock wardrobe to Seattle

Custom basketball warmups to Philadelphia

Pajama onesies home from Los Angeles (twice)

Zany suits trip to Miami

Short shorts trip (players who wear sandals must have their toenails painted)

College football jerseys to Oakland

"Accidental preppies" to Houston

Camouflage to Baltimore

Team letterman jackets to Boston

All-white attire to Miami

Nerd theme to Boston

Grunge look to Seattle

Hockey jerseys to Toronto

Johnny Cash (all black) to Toronto

Guests and Events

Simon the Magician performed in the Cubs Clubhouse

A Seminole "medicine man" to help the slumping team change its fortunes

A 20-foot long, 115-pound reticulated python

Four members of Tampa's Sol Caribe band played merengue, salsa, and other music

A pair of South African penguins, Cliff and Shelly, from the Florida Aquarium; a disc jockey; magician; and Mindy, the umbrella cockatoo

Had Brookfield Zoo in Chicago bring a collection of animals onto the field for pregame

Brought a mariachi band into the Cubs Clubhouse

Had a buffet breakfast during practice before Game 3 of the 2015 National League Division Series

That philosophy made Joe Maddon the perfect fit for the Chicago Cubs. He was exactly what Theo Epstein and Jed Hoyer were looking for. Like manna from heaven, he had suddenly become available. Now all they had to do was close the deal.

Of course, the most important thing on Joe Maddon's resume was the winning. In 2008, Maddon took a Tampa Bay franchise, which had previously never won more than 70 games in a season, to the World Series following a 97-win campaign. That was followed by several additional winning campaigns, including four more with 90-plus wins.

Indeed, Epstein and Hoyer were interested. Now they needed to act. Maddon was preparing to venture off from Tampa in "Cousin Eddie" when he received a call from his agent that the Cubs were interested. Maddon started to figure the best way to meet with Epstein and Hoyer, but with no reasonable locations to cross paths, Maddon decided the best thing to do was to remain in Florida and have the Cubs representatives come there. Theo Epstein and Jed Hoyer showed up with a $20 bottle of wine they got from the Publix across the street from the RV park.

"I gave them a tour of the RV, and we all had a beer," said Maddon. "Those big, thick Miller Lite wide-mouth bottles. We had some chips and salsa. We stood in the middle of the RV and BS'ed. Maybe for half an hour. Then we went outside and, seriously, there's this little micro beach right behind the RV. We had the only beach available in this RV park. It was available to that spot."

"It was weird," Hoyer said, chuckling "We flew to Pensacola, drove half an hour, got to this RV park on a tiny beach. The interview was on four beach chairs over three or four hours. It got kind of cold as the sun was going down."

Theo Epstein still laughs when he remembers that initial meeting after Maddon opted out of his Tampa Bay contract. "I tried to dress appropriately for an RV park and also was trying to stay incognito as I walked through O'Hare Airport [to fly out of Chicago]. I had on old, faded jeans, sneakers, untucked Nike polo shirt, and a Bears trucker cap. Jed, I think, had loafers, dressier jeans, and a tucked-in polo.

"I remember making that trip and what I thought it might mean for the future of the Chicago Cubs. The entire meeting had a relaxed, natural vibe, like old friends catching up and hanging out," Epstein said. "No pretenses whatsoever."

"It was very casual, as it should have been," Maddon said. "We're sitting on the beach talking philosophy. The water is right behind them. The sun's setting over my shoulder. You could see that they were tired from traveling. But they were great."

After their lengthy meeting in Florida with Maddon, Epstein and Hoyer made the decision to change managers once again. Thus, Rick Renteria's fate with the Cubs was sealed on Halloween 2014.

Theo Epstein's Statement:

"Today we made the difficult decision to replace Rick Renteria as manager of the Chicago Cubs. On behalf of Tom Ricketts and Jed Hoyer, I thank Rick for his dedication and commitment, and for making the Cubs a better organization.

"Rick's sterling reputation should only be enhanced by his season as Cubs manager. We challenged Rick to create an environment in which our young players could develop and thrive at the big league level, and he succeeded. Working with the youngest team in the league and an imperfect roster, Rick had the club playing hard and improving throughout the season. His passion, character, optimism, and work ethic showed up every single day.

"Rick deserved to come back for another season as Cubs manager, and we said as much when we announced that he would be returning in 2015. We met with Rick two weeks ago for a long end-of-season evaluation and discussed plans for next season. We praised Rick to the media and to our season-ticket holders. These actions were made in good faith.

"Last Thursday, we learned that Joe Maddon—who may be as well-suited as anyone in the industry to manage the challenges that lie ahead of us—had become a free agent. We confirmed the news with Major League Baseball, and it became public knowledge the next day. We saw it as a unique opportunity and faced a clear dilemma: be loyal to Rick or be loyal to the organization. In this business of trying to win a world championship for the first time in 107 years, the organization has priority over any one individual. We decided to pursue Joe.

"While there was no clear playbook for how to handle this type of situation, we knew we had to be transparent with Rick before engaging with Joe. Jed flew to San Diego last Friday and told Rick in person of our intention to talk to Joe about the managerial job. Subsequently, Jed and I provided updates to Rick via telephone and today informed him that we will indeed make a change.

"We offered Rick a choice of other positions with the Cubs, but he is of course free to leave the organization and pursue opportunities elsewhere. Armed with the experience of a successful season and all the qualities that made him our choice a year ago, Rick will no doubt make an excellent major league manager when given his next chance.

"Rick often said he was the beneficiary of the hard work of others who came before him. Now, in the young players he helped, we reap the benefits of his hard work as we move forward. He deserved better and we wish him nothing but the best.

"We have clung to two important ideals during our three years in Chicago. The first is to always be loyal to our mission of building the Cubs into a championship organization that can sustain success. The second is to be transparent with our fans. As painful as the last week was at times, we believe we stayed true to these two ideals in handling a sensitive situation. To our fans: we hope you understand, and we appreciate your continued support of the Cubs."

Renteria was officially out on a Friday. The press conference to hire Joe Maddon was the following Monday. That's how quickly the move to hire Maddon happened. But how big was the move for the Cubs? Did Maddon really play that big a role in changing the Cubs culture?

Cubs Recent Managerial History

2003–06	Dusty Baker	322–326 (.497)
2007–10	Lou Piniella	316–293 (.519)
2010–11	Mike Quade	95–104 (.477)
2012–13	Dale Sveum	127–197 (.392)
2014	Rick Renteria	73–89 (.451)
2015–Present	Joe Maddon	200–123 (.619)

"It was really important because Joe brings a unique environment to the big leagues with him," Epstein told me. "There were certain things we just got wrong during the rebuild and there were certain decisions that we would like back and certain challenges that just stayed with us. One thing that we were struggling to do was build an environment at the big league level that was as supportive of young players, as much fun, as special an atmosphere as we had in the minor leagues.

"We just couldn't do it. It's hard to do because of the grind of the big leagues, how much stress there is here, how hard it is to develop players at the major league level and how hard it is to win up here. We'd been through a couple of managers already and Joe really helped us solve that last problem," he said.

Maddon looked back on his initial meeting with the Cubs brain trust. "I remember our conversation in Florida behind my RV and they talked a lot about needing to improve the culture at the major league level. Hearing that kind of a comment from them, from my perspective I thought—and I told them—that's all workable and doable. I didn't know a whole lot about the Cubs and the situation. I can't tell you I knew a whole lot because I didn't. I was coming in there pretty cold because [of] being an American League guy for so many years. I just knew that I trusted Theo and Jed and that they had a lot of really good young players because we had played them that season at Wrigley Field. I knew they were going to be good.

"Culturally, not having been around the clubhouse, not understanding what they had in place, I didn't know. Honestly, I didn't know. I just told them what I liked to do and I talked to them about relationship building and trust and that from there you could have an open exchange of ideas. That's what I remember and I remember that I trusted them and I believed that they were going to be successful," Maddon told me.

Epstein has always spoken about how important the hiring of Maddon was to take the major league team to the next level. However, he also believes that the vibe he was looking for at the major league level was already developing rapidly throughout the Cubs minor league system.

"I think the turnaround in the organization, the morale improving, all that happened really organically from the bottom up and the guys in the minor leagues deserve a ton of credit for that. I felt the fun that we had in 2015 that the world could see really started in the minor leagues and in instructional league in Arizona in 2012, in my view. But, it would not have gotten that way at the big league level if not for Joe and it wouldn't have been that exact team had he not put his signature on it in the way that only he can," Epstein told me.

Having interviewed Maddon in Boston before hiring Terry Francona and having played against him for a number of years when he was in Tampa, Epstein and Hoyer knew Maddon was excellent at his craft. But, after working with him for the past two years they believe Maddon is even better than they thought.

"He's so good at getting players to trust him, respect him, admire, and want to be around him. There's something in the air around his teams where guys feel they can exhale and be themselves and have fun. That allows young players to adjust exponentially more quickly than when they look at the manager and the manager is tense or they feel that the next mistake they make they're going back down to the minor leagues. Looking back, I don't see how we would have created that type of feel up here without him. He's awesome at what he does and we wouldn't have gotten where we did last year and this year without him," Epstein told me.

Maddon loved his time in Tampa and says he never seriously thought about leaving the Rays until he learned that his boss, GM Andrew Friedman was leaving to take over the Los Angeles Dodgers baseball operations. "I'm serious, I wasn't thinking about leaving, but after Andrew left [and] I was told that I had a clause in my contract that allowed me to opt out of my deal, I decided to look around. And, after finding out that the Cubs had interest, I decided to accept their opportunity," he said.

He also knew that despite the team's subpar record in 2014 that the Cubs were on their way to a major turnaround. "The challenge is so outstanding, how could you not want to be in this seat?" he said to me in an interview on Comcast SportsNet after his introductory press conference outside Wrigley Field.

"I'm going to be talking playoffs next year, I'll tell you that right now. I can't go to spring training and say anything else. You have to set your goals high, because if you don't set them high enough you might hit your mark and that's not a good thing. We're going to talk World Series this year, and I'm going to believe it. It's in our future."

While Maddon hadn't thought about leaving Tampa until after Friedman resigned, he had actually thought about the Cubs job a couple of years earlier during a Rays road trip to Chicago. After having dinner one evening with Rays play-by-play voice Dave Wills, the two took a drive around Chicago and they specifically drove by Wrigley Field at Maddon's request. "I remember Joe telling me that whoever came to the Cubs and won the World Series would be remembered forever in Chicago and around baseball. He thought it was a fantastic opportunity to do something that so many had failed at doing and I could tell that it really intrigued him. I think he's the perfect fit for the job," Wills said.

Epstein and Hoyer had interviewed Maddon in 2003 for the Red Sox managerial vacancy when the then–Angels bench coach finished second to Terry Francona for the gig. "Comparing him to when we interviewed him a decade ago, he's got the confidence," Epstein said. "He's done it and he knows it works. All he has to do is be himself and he can win."

As Epstein said, while the Cubs pursued their next manager, Jed Hoyer flew to San Diego to meet with Rick Renteria so he could deliver the news face to face. The two men had a great working relationship dating back to Hoyer's time with the Padres, but when he arrived in San Diego, Renteria already knew why he was there, as news of Maddon's availability had broken in the media.

After being told that the Cubs were indeed pursuing Maddon, Renteria handled his departure with tremendous class, a trait that surprised no one who knew him. In fact, as the Cubs soared to 97 wins, Renteria chose not to speak with the media throughout the 2015 season despite multiple opportunities. His first public comments came in November of 2015, when he was named the bench coach of the Chicago White Sox.

"I am totally, completely happy with the opportunity that the Ricketts family, and Theo and Jed [Hoyer] and everybody from the organization extended to me to get on the field as a manager with the Chicago Cubs," Renteria said.

"It was a great experience. Obviously, anybody that has been in that arena knows that change sometimes occurs. As abruptly as it might have seemed, things happen and there are a lot of kids on that club this year and a lot of people I worked alongside of who deserve to have as much success as they possibly can."

Renteria had two years left on his Cubs contract and while the Cubs have never confirmed it, multiple sources told me that the club did indeed add money onto what they owed him as a thank you for his hard work.

Despite being disappointed at the sudden turn of events, Renteria, an extremely likable guy, took the high road no matter how he felt deep down inside. "You step away from it a little bit and you reflect, it's just a business. It's just baseball. And that doesn't take away from anything I believe I brought to the table at the time.

"It would be foolish for anybody who's doing something, who's giving themselves to a task, to not feel the wind blown out of you a little bit [but] you take a step back, you regroup," Renteria said. "I'm sure, quite frankly, there was no intent on anybody's side to create a difficult situation. It was what it was."

With the Cubs managerial job now open, the path was clear to seal the deal with Maddon. A five-year/$25 million contract brought the manager the Cubs had been searching for from Tampa to Chicago, and a new era in Cubs baseball was about to begin.

The future Cubs skipper had been taking notice of Theo's plan in action. "The two things that stood out this past summer were this cathedral across the street and then the groupings of players, youthful, talented, and really into the game. They never quit and it was beautiful to watch.

"I heard all about it, you see it, you read about it," Maddon said. "Then you see them firsthand. When I'm watching all this, the thing that strikes me is the player development program and the scouting. It has to be outstanding to get those guys out here. I was really impressed with all that from the other dugout."

Best Record in a Season by a Manager, Tampa Bay Rays History

2008	Joe Maddon	97–65 (.599)
2010	Joe Maddon	96–66 (.593)
2013	Joe Maddon	92–71 (.564)
2011	Joe Maddon	91–71 (.562)
2012	Joe Maddon	90–72 (.556)
2009	Joe Maddon	84–78 (.519)
2015	Kevin Cash	80–82 (.494)
2014	Joe Maddon	77–85 (.475)

The introductory press conference was electric as Maddon told stories and fired up the Cubs fan base with thoughts of contending right away. "Listen, for me, I'm going to be talking playoffs next year. Okay, I'm going to tell you that right now because I can't go to spring training and say another thing. I'm just incapable of doing that. Why would you even report? Why would you not want to accept this challenge in this city in that ballpark under these circumstances with this talent?" Maddon said. "It's an extraordinary moment."

The phrase that Maddon uttered at his first press conference announcing his hiring was one that still captivates Cubs fans today and it is splashed across the wall of the tunnel that leads from the Cubs state of the art clubhouse to the playing field at Wrigley. It says, simply, "Don't ever permit the pressure to exceed the pleasure."

As Maddon met the Chicago media and charmed the room like an entertainer, he maintained a tremendously positive outlook despite the fact that the Cubs had not finished over .500 since 2009 and they had more losses in the previous five seasons than every team in baseball other than the Houston Astros, who were also embarking on a teardown and rebuild much like the Cubs.

"It's always sunny in Chicago, right? I'm very optimistic about it. I'm not here to make any bold predictions, except that every spring I go to camp, I expect to go to the playoffs. I do not like playoff baseball beginning and I'm in the backyard cooking steaks. I hate that. I want everybody else cooking steaks while we're playing baseball in October."

But, the big question that I wanted answered now that the Cubs were champions was this: Did Joe Maddon really believe what he said at his introductory press conference in November 2014 that his team could go to the playoffs in his first season or was that false bravado designed to fire up the fan base?

"I knew we had a good veteran group with guys like Jon Lester, David Ross, Miguel Montero, and others, plus we had some good young players as well. I wasn't 100 percent sure but I knew the veterans we had would help the young kids. It wasn't like I was coming in and the coaching staff and I had to teach everyone how to win. Part of it was I had to coach my coaches so they knew what I wanted, but it was not false bravado. I knew we were talented and I thought we could be really good," he told me.

At the end of his first press conference as the Cubs manager, which was held at the Cubby Bear bar across the street from Wrigley Field with the iconic ballpark under construction, Maddon offered to buy everyone a round. "A shot and a beer," he said. "That's the Hazleton way."

The Cubs hiring of Joe Maddon sent shock waves throughout baseball. The "lovable losers" had a star-studded front office who had loaded the franchise with young talent and now they had one of the best managers in the sport piloting their club. Optimism ran high throughout the organization that the Cubs were finally ready to make a move in the standings.

Shortly after Maddon was hired, the Tampa Bay Rays requested an investigation by MLB into possible tampering on the part of the Cubs. The claim was that Maddon opted out of his contract only after learning what the Cubs had to offer. The Cubs could have been forced to compensate Tampa Bay with money, prospects, or draft picks if found guilty. However, in April 2015 the Cubs were officially cleared of any wrongdoing.

With Maddon officially onboard the Cubs felt that they were ready to take the next step towards contending for a World Series championship. However, Epstein knows that as good as Maddon is, no manager can be successful without a talented roster of players.

"Talent comes first," Epstein said. "We had a massive talent deficit. If Joe Maddon was managing the 2012 Cubs, it still doesn't go very well.

"The trades for Rizzo, Arrieta, Russell, and Hendricks, and the drafting of Bryant and Schwarber, etc., that stuff comes first for me. However, there's no champagne without Joe and what he's brought. He huge, invaluable to this organization."

With Joe Maddon now in charge and minor league stars like Kris Bryant, Addison Russell, and Kyle Schwarber ready to make the jump to the big leagues, the stage was set for a 2015 Cubs campaign beyond anyone's wildest dreams.

The atmosphere and culture at the major league level changed dramatically after Joe Maddon was hired in November 2014, and that culture was what Epstein and Hoyer knew had to get better for the franchise to take the next step in their massive rebuild. "Joe's a combination of everything we look for in a manager," Epstein said. "Everyone associates him with new school because they've used analytics in Tampa and he's so open-minded, but this is an old-school baseball guy with a wealth of knowledge. We were reminded of that [when] talking baseball [with Maddon]. It's hard to find old school and new school in the same package."

Epstein and Hoyer had experience with Maddon and after hiring him, Epstein believed his new manager was a perfect fit for the Cubs. "Comparing Joe now to when I interviewed him a decade ago, his confidence has reached a new level because he has done it, and it has worked," Epstein continued. "He knows he can connect. He knows all he has to do is be himself and he can lead and he can win. That's why we feel he's our long-term fit as a leader."

Maddon brought a new direction and a sense of camaraderie that had previously been missing for several years and his new team responded immediately to his laid-back demeanor and colorful approach.

"I want us to play the game the same way, whether it's March 15 or July 15 or October 15," he said. "When you build that mindset, when you get to the end of the season, a playoff situation, you don't change your game. I think that's the trap that a lot of groups fall into, that, 'I got to try harder. I got to do more. I got to step up.' I really don't like that phrase, 'step up,' at all. That insinuates that you have not been trying prior to that.

"If we could build a thought process where you come to play every day regardless of the date, don't apply any more weight to any game, by the time we get to the playoffs, the game feels the same, and I don't think it will be intimidating at that moment in any way, shape, or form."

Maddon remembered with crystal clear clarity when he had to get everyone's attention that the way the Chicago Cubs had played the game was changing and changing dramatically. "That first spring training we were going through drills and I didn't like them. I didn't like the way we were going through drills, I didn't like the attitude about them and I didn't like the attention to detail. So it became very obvious to me right there that we have to change that. It's not going to work that way. We are not just going to go through the motions and we are not just going to attempt to get this right kinda. It had to be done right, properly. So, I got really upset and I cut off a relay drill one day. I don't know if that laid the groundwork or not but I'm really big on fundamentals. I think everybody is, but at some point you have to draw the line. To me that was totally unacceptable what I saw that day and that really stands out in my mind. I did not like the way the group was going through team drills and I thought that had to change," Maddon told me.

Maddon is not a big team meeting guy and he told me that meetings are very overrated. "I try to have three meetings a year. That's it. We meet at the start of the season, when we come back after the All-Star break and if we are playing in the postseason, right before the playoffs start. Meetings are really overrated because I want our guys to handle the day-to-day situations themselves. I don't have to meet with them about every different thing that comes up," Maddon told me.

However, Maddon does meet with the media twice a day throughout the season. Before and after every game he sits and answers questions from the large following of beat writers and broadcasters who cover each game and every move the team makes both at home and away.

"I have a team meeting every day when I meet with the press because I know that my players will watch everything, they will read everything, and they will see everything on Twitter. So any time I talk publicly it's like having a team meeting. I can use phrases like 'Embrace the target' as often as I like and I don't have to sit them down directly, but indirectly I know they're going to read it. It's like anything else: the more they read it, the more they see things working, the more they are going to embrace the phraseology and I know that. So in my mind when I talk to the press every day I'm having a mini team meeting. I know whatever I say, whether they hear it directly or indirectly through their parents, their agent, their girlfriend, or their buddies, they are going to hear whatever I said. I'm almost always never negative in public because I believe you praise publicly and criticize privately," Maddon told me.

However, his interactions with his team in the clubhouse are legendary and his players appreciate his candor and his style in how he communicates with his players in a group setting. "They are monumentally different from other managers," starter Jake Arrieta said. "Not because other managers aren't great managers. It's just that Joe communicates to the players in a significantly different manner, and it really resonates throughout the entire team. He expresses his desires to be great as a team, and how he really regards relationships. It's really special to see how everybody gets on board so quickly with messages that he provides."

Cubs All-Star first baseman Anthony Rizzo is one of only two players that was with the team when they lost 101 games in 2012 and is still with the team when they won 103 games in 2016 (Travis Wood is the other) and he is a big fan of Maddon's unique style in how he treats his players and how he deals with them. "They sink in because Joe is so personable, especially [after] having a couple of years of a relationship with him now," he said. "Everything he says now most of us know has already been said. But everyone is excited about playing for him."

Cubs All-Star second baseman, Ben Zobrist, played for Maddon in Tampa and despite having had several different managers in his career he says that Maddon always keeps things fun and interesting, especially when it comes to the tedious days of spring training.

"He does it every year. It's interesting. You usually go through these long days and your kind of like, 'All right, ho-hum, we have to do the same things we've always done,' and we hear the same things.

"With him you know it's always going to be something original and different. And he kind of keeps it light and fun. You know it's going to be a new season, with a different group. He always wants to find a way to make it better than last year."

Maddon is a stickler for detail and he is fanatical about his players not making mental mistakes, such as missing signs or fundamental miscues. "I will never be hyper-critical about physical mistakes ever. Those things are going to happen and there is nothing you can do about them, it's part of the game. I don't like the mental mistakes which are created by a lack of preparation, not caring enough, not understanding, or being willing to dig deep enough. Those are the things that upset me," Maddon said.

But, perhaps Maddon's boss Theo Epstein put it best when he had this to say about his manager's role in the Cubs turnaround. "Joe was really the finishing piece in our rebuild. Our scouting and player development departments were humming. We had acquired a ton of elite young talent. Morale was great in the minor leagues and in the front office. But the losing had taken a toll at the big league level and we were having a really difficult time establishing an environment in the major league clubhouse that would allow young players to thrive.

"The tone instantly changed upon Joe's arrival. He creates a world within a world in that clubhouse where young players can relax, be themselves, and have fun. Young players are rewarded for showing their personalities as long as they prioritize winning. Veterans are empowered to lead, and everyone starts walking around with confidence and swagger. Our on-field personality developed out of this vibe, and there's no way we win 200 games the last two years without it."

10

Jon Lester Takes a Leap of Faith

On the first day of free agency in November 2014, Jon Lester received a package via FedEx at his home in suburban Atlanta. The return address was 1060 W. Addison Street in Chicago, the home of the Chicago Cubs. The same Cubs who had not won a World Series in 106 years at that point and hadn't even played in the Fall Classic in 69 years. In short, one of the losingest franchises in American professional sports wanted in on the Jon Lester sweepstakes.

Outside of those in the know in the world of Major League Baseball, the Cubs were looked at as the "lovable losers" and a franchise that was mired in a rebuilding process that held no guarantee of success. However, inside the offices of the Chicago Cubs, Theo Epstein knew he and his organization were on the verge of exploding onto the national scene with a treasure trove of outstanding prospects in the club's minor league system.

In 2013, after his club had concluded another awful season with a record of 66–96, Epstein appeared in studio on Comcast

SportsNet's *Sports Talk Live* TV program. It was there that he again uttered one of his more memorable quotes that had the Cubs fan base excited at the possibilities the future might hold for their downtrodden franchise.

"Throughout our organization the morale is high and while our record at the major league level this past season might not show it, ask around the game. Because the word around baseball is, the Cubs are coming fast and the Cubs are coming strong."

It was with this mindset and after a 2014 season that saw the Cubs finish 73–89, but start to show improvement in the second half of the season, that Epstein and Jed Hoyer set their sights on one of the biggest prizes in that winter's free agent class. The Cubs needed a front-line starter and that winter's player market had a handful of candidates that fit the bill perfectly. However, while Max Scherzer and James Shields might have been more attractive to others, only Jon Lester knew Epstein and Hoyer and much of the Cubs front office intimately well.

He was drafted by the Boston Red Sox, rose through the Boston minor league system while Epstein was the Red Sox general manager, and came to the big leagues with Epstein in charge. He had also battled cancer during his time as a member of the Red Sox and he, Epstein, and Hoyer had developed a tremendously close bond. They had laughed together, cried together, and they had won together.

Lester believed in the Cubs brain trust and he was confident that in time the Cubs would be winners. His big question though, was just how soon they would be contending. He had won two World Series rings with the Red Sox and he wanted more. "I said it the day I signed here. I did not come to Chicago to rebuild. I came here to win and that meant win right away. Now, did I see us winning 97 games in 2015 when the season started? No, I probably didn't. But once I got to Arizona and I saw how much talent we had I knew we would be pretty good right away."

Lester is also a consummate family man. He is most comfortable at home with his wife, Farrah, and his children or sitting in a duck blind, hunting. He eschews the glitz and glamour that some athletes revel in. "I like being at home and being with my family. I just don't like to go out running the streets. That's just not me. I also like to be comfortable in my surroundings and it took some time to get used to a new city, a new team, a new ballpark, and all that goes with it. My family and I had no idea what living in Chicago would be like but it really has been great for all of us. It has a small-town feel and we love it here."

The Lester signing was probably the biggest watershed moment for the Epstein/Hoyer regime and that fact was not lost on Jon Lester, both during the Cubs recruitment of him and when he thinks back on the process today. "Look, I was going to get paid ridiculous money no matter who I signed with. I knew that going in, so I knew that I had to trust the people I was going to play for and I had to believe that the team I was going to was going to have a good chance to contend and to win.

"Theo and Jed kept telling me that [the Cubs could contend] throughout the process and they kept telling me that if we get you here it is going to change the whole free agent market for us. It is going to make other people believe in what we are doing. Obviously, for me to sign here was a belief in what Theo had to say. I think the thing that helped me so much was the fact that I knew Theo, Jed, and Jason so well. Hell, three quarters of the front office are old Red Sox guys that I have known either in the minor leagues or in the big leagues. I knew I wasn't going to get the BS from those guys. I knew I could trust them," Lester told me one morning as we sat in the dugout at Wrigley Field.

Lester chuckled when he thought back on the courting process that helped to convince him to take a chance on the unproven Cubs, who were coming off another sub-.500 season. "This has been taken the wrong way when I've said it before but I love Theo's arrogance about his guys. He believes in his guys and that is huge for a guy like me when you are listening to someone tell you about a Kris Bryant, a Javy Baez, an Addison Russell, or any of our other young guys. He kept showing me video of these guys raking in the minor leagues and I kept thinking that's great, but it's the minor leagues. He and Jed kept saying this guy is going to do this and this guy is going to do that and they basically hit the nail on the head on all of them."

Another thing that attracted Jon Lester to the Cubs was his belief in the type of people that Theo Epstein was building around on the Cubs roster. "I told Tom Ricketts this recently, that the biggest thing that I have always loved about Theo is that he isn't scared to take a lesser player because he is a good person. He would rather have the good teammate, the good person on and off the field that may not be a 1A player than get the 1A player that is an asshole.

"That's what makes our team so special. We have some superstars but we don't have any egos on this team. People go out and do their job and we play as a group. He talked about that from Day One when they started recruiting me and it was very important to me and I definitely have seen it since I signed here."

For Lester to choose the Cubs over several other franchises who were all offering huge money and who all had a better track record of championship success, he had to believe in not only the prospects in the Cubs minor league system but in the promises of better facilities, increased spending on free agents, and of almost immediate success at the major league level. That brought him back again to his belief in Theo Epstein and his management team.

"If Theo wasn't here I am probably not sitting here with you today. It wasn't about the money. The relationship with Theo really helped that. It helped convince me to believe what he was saying. The same went for Jed and Jason.

"And it really went to the discussions I had with Tom Ricketts during the process. Tom was right there with Theo. I trusted him. He's a guy's guy. He looked me in the eye and there was no beating around the bush. They said they were getting a new clubhouse, they said these prospects will be successful, and they told me we would win quickly at the big league level. I told the media when I signed here that I wasn't coming here for a rebuild," Lester said.

"Last year we weren't expected to do anything. With KB coming up, with Addy coming up, and with Jake having the year he had, and Rizzo having the year that he had, we had guys really buying in. That, plus the leadership of guys like David Ross and everyone on our team contributing is why we won 97 games."

However, signing Lester to a $155 million deal was not without risk, even if the Cubs front office knew the person and the player as well as any star they had ever gone after. Yes, he was a model citizen and a tremendous teammate in the clubhouse. And yes, he was an outstanding pitcher who had been a part of two World Series championship teams. But when you spend that much money on someone's arm it is not without some risk.

A medical exam is standard operating procedure before a player signs a free agent contract and a look at Jon Lester's elbow by the Cubs doctors revealed a bone chip. That is not a major deal compared to the myriad other injuries that could have been found but it was still an issue nonetheless and an issue that Epstein had to make sure he was okay with.

In Jeff Passan's outstanding book *The Arm*, he dedicates an entire chapter to the Cubs' pursuit of Lester after the 2014 season. Passan was given exclusive, inside access to Lester's free agent decision-making process and he paints an amazing picture of what Theo Epstein and Jed Hoyer are like when they chase a player who they envision as a key piece of their future.

"I had never let someone in the media get that close to me," Lester said, "but Jeff has a great reputation and he pitched me on letting him chronicle my free agency with the assurance that everything would stay confidential until after I made my decision on who I was signing with. It was great to have someone who had no vested interest in who I signed with to bounce things off of."

Passan is one of the best baseball writers in the sport and he remembers all of the conversations with Lester as the free agent process played itself out over a 2 month period in the fall of 2014. "Jon was great to deal with and he was really open and honest with me during a very stressful time in his life. It was a unique opportunity for me to see someone in one of the most important times in their life," Passan said.

"It's difficult to feel badly for someone who's about to make $150 million-plus, but the decision legitimately ate at him. His heart was in Boston. His head was in San Francisco. His gut was in Chicago. And, in the end, Theo Epstein and Jed Hoyer made him believe. Which, in hindsight, looks awfully damn smart of Lester."

Epstein and Jed Hoyer pulled out all the stops as they pursued Jon Lester because while they knew that his pitching abilities would be huge for their young Cubs team, his professionalism and winning attitude would be almost as important as they attempted to build a winning culture in the Cubs clubhouse.

On the day free agency began in 2014, when the DVD arrived at the Lester family home in suburban Atlanta, the Chicago Cubs began their all-out assault on Jon Lester, his family and his agents and they began to show him why the Chicago Cubs were a perfect fit for all of them.

"It was an object lesson in confidence," Passan said. "Epstein and Hoyer understood what they'd built, and now was something arguably more difficult: convincing others to join. Which took prior relationships and immense amounts of trust and an incredible level of conviction. And perhaps more than anything, that stood out—they needed to make Jon Lester believe every bit as much as they did."

As the Winter Meetings approached, Theo Epstein and Jed Hoyer went into full recruiter mode in trying to persuade Jon Lester to choose a Cubs team that had posted a 73–89 record in 2014. But it was a Cubs team that had played very well in the last third of the season and had people around baseball expecting them to take a major step forward in 2015.

Theo Epstein sent letters, e-mails, texts, and care packages as he wooed a man that he had grown very close to during the time they shared in Boston. When Jon Lester and his wife, Farrah, flew to Chicago for their initial recruiting visit they were at ease as they listened to the Cubs pitch because, as Jon Lester told me, "we trusted Theo and Jed so we were at ease as soon as we sat down with them."

The Lesters, their agents—Sam and Seth Levinson—and a contingent from the Cubs front office spent a good portion of their day in Chicago meeting at Wrigley Field and listening to the picture of the future that Theo Epstein painted. Tom Ricketts joined the group when everyone met for dinner at one of Chicago's most popular restaurants, RPM Steak, and the Cubs used the opportunity to let Jon know just how important he was to the future of the franchise.

He heard about all of the improvements in the organization and the improved facilities that were just a year away. He and

Farrah were promised that a decision to choose the Cubs would be a decision that would be about more than baseball. The Cubs under Epstein and Hoyer are a family and that means the Cubs look out for their players and their families all day and every day.

There is a doctor and a nurse on call 24/7, so that if a player's family needs medical care in the middle of the night or if the team is on the road and a player's family has an emergency there is someone to turn to at all times. A team nutritionist makes sure that there is a diet plan for each and every player that needs one and that the food in the clubhouse is the best in baseball before and after every game. A team psychologist is always available and the Cubs medical staff is very well respected around the game.

The new 25,000-square-foot clubhouse is the second biggest in baseball (behind only the New York Yankees) and has more amenities than one can imagine. A state-of-the-art weight training center keeps players strong and healthy and a cryotherapy chamber helps handle the bumps and bruises of a long season.

A players' lounge that is complete with every video game known to man gives the Cubs a respite from the media onslaught that is prevalent at every home game. That onslaught starts 3 hours before first pitch, when the clubhouse is open to reporters, and doesn't end until well after a game has gone final.

There is also a party room, complete with strobe lights and a smoke machine, where the Cubs celebrate each and every home victory for 30 minutes. A practice that is a Joe Maddon staple because, as the Cubs manager says, "I believe in celebrating every win because we all know how hard it is to win a Major League Baseball game."

The Cubs also made sure Lester knew they had a first-class media relations staff led by former Red Sox media relations man Peter Chase and his assistants Jason Carr, Safdar Kahn, and Alex Wilcox, to manage the player's media obligations. Those

Jake Arrieta and David Ross hug after the final out of Arrieta's April 2016 no-hitter against the Reds in Cincinnati. (John Minchillo)

Javy Baez exalts as umpire Mike Muchlinski calls out Denard Span, caught trying to steal second during Game 4 of the 2016 NLDS against the Giants. (Marcio Jose Sanchez)

A fan holds up a sign with the hopes of all Cubs fans, as Kyle Hendricks walks off the field in Game 6 of the 2016 NLCS against the Dodgers. (Patrick Gorski/ Icon Sportswire)

Aroldis Chapman and Willson Contreras celebrate after Chapman closed out a 3–2 victory in Game 5 of the World Series to cut the Indians lead down to three games to two. (Nam Y. Huh)

Jason Heyward hangs on Wrigley's right-field wall to make an amazing catch on a fly ball hit by the Indians' Trevor Bauer during the third inning of Game 5 of the World Series. (Charles Rex Arbogast)

Dexter Fowler and the whole Cubs dugout celebrate Fowler's leadoff home run, which began a World Series Game 7 considered one of the greatest games ever played. (AP Photo/Charlie Riedel)

Ben Zobrist holds the World Series MVP trophy after the Cubs' epic 8–7 extra-inning victory over the Indians. (David J. Phillip)

Kris Bryant hugs the Commissioner's Trophy during the Game 7 postgame celebration. Bryant, in just two short years, has been the NL Rookie of the Year, a two-time All-Star, the NL MVP, and the best player on a Cubs team that won the organization's first title in 108 years. (David J. Phillip)

Jake Arrieta (center right, with a finger in the air) and Kyle Schwarber (far left) wave to fans outside Wrigley Field during the parade. (Paul Beaty)

Cubs fans fill every available space as they celebrate the team that finally brought a championship to the franchise. (Kiichiro Sato)

Tom Ricketts holds up the World Series final-out ball given to him by Anthony Rizzo during the Grant Park rally. (Charles Rex Arbogast)

responsibilities can be overwhelming at times in a town with a fan base as rabid as the Cubs. In fact, Chase even made a presentation to Lester when he made his visit to Chicago. Chase had come to the Cubs from the Red Sox in 2006 and the two men had crossed paths briefly in Boston. Chase laid out what Lester could expect from the Chicago media, a horde perhaps larger than Boston's but maybe not as vicious at times. He also made sure Lester knew that Chase and his staff would be there for him at every turn whether that was at Wrigley Field, on the road or even in the off-season.

Plus, traveling secretary Vijay Tekchandani is very well respected by the players because of his uncanny ability to handle all of the team's travel arrangements, which can change on a moment's notice, while also taking care of myriad special requests for every player like a Las Vegas concierge.

Each and every aspect of life as a Chicago Cub was laid out for Jon Lester so that he and Farrah would know how comfortable they would be if they chose to move their family to Chicago. And comfort was very important to Jon Lester, as he likes his routine and he does not like a lot of change. Having Epstein, Hoyer, and McLeod gave the Cubs a major advantage over the other teams pursuing Lester.

The Cubs organization makes sure that there is no stone left unturned in any area of a player's life, with the belief that if a player can relax because their family is comfortable they will be able to relax and concentrate on baseball. "We try to do everything first class for our players because we want to have the best possible environment for them and their families if they choose to play here," GM Jed Hoyer told me.

Hoyer saw how important it was to go the extra mile when he worked with Epstein in Boston and he believes that treating the players and their families in a first-class manner goes a long way in multiple areas for the organization. "First, we want our guys to know how special it is to be a Chicago Cub. We want them to feel that they are treated better here than anywhere else. That mentality helps us in free agency and it helps throughout a long season when the players have to grind through 162 games and hopefully all the way to a World Series championship," he said.

Jon Lester is not a rah-rah type of leader. Instead, he leads by example, demonstrating a work ethic that others strive to live up to. He treats everyone with class and respect and he is considered a leader wherever he plays because of how he goes about his business. And on a very young and unproven Cubs team at the time Epstein and Hoyer were chasing him, Jon Lester was a must-have. If he chose the Chicago Cubs, it would send shock waves around the rest of Major League Baseball that the rebuilding Cubs were a force to be reckoned with on any player they chose to pursue.

In other words, convincing Lester to sign with the Cubs would be a watershed moment in the Epstein/Hoyer regime and a clear indication to the fan base that the Cubs were indeed back and ready to contend. "Theo said that signing me was very important to them because he felt people would see that the Cubs were ready to take the next step. I wasn't as sure about that as he and Jed were, but I understood their point." Lester told me in June 2016.

The Cubs' initial offer to Jon Lester was for six years and $135 million, an offer that Theo Epstein did not know at the time but was the highest on the table at the start of the process. Before Lester's camp even had responded to the offer, Epstein upped it to show Lester how much he was wanted in Chicago.

According to Passan, the Detroit Tigers had a five-year, $100 million deal on the table, with Toronto at five years and $125 million. Atlanta, a dark horse in the Lester derby, was at six years, $120 million, and the Boston Red Sox were also at six years, $120 million after an embarrassingly low offer of just $70 million in the spring of 2014. That offer led to Lester being traded to the Oakland A's in July 2014 and that trade really was the impetus for Lester deciding to test free agency.

"If I hadn't been traded to the A's I'm not sure if I would have ever left Boston. Being traded opened up my eyes to the possibility of playing somewhere else. It was an experience that I didn't expect but it also gave me a different perspective. In fact, I talked about what it was like to play for the Cubs with Jeff Samardzija, who had also been traded to the A's and he told me how much he loved playing for the Cubs," Lester told me.

As the free agency recruiting continued through November and into early December, Jon Lester heard from additional teams as the San Francisco Giants entered the derby as did the Los Angeles Dodgers, who asked for time to put together a serious offer.

The Cubs tried to seal the deal just before Thanksgiving but Jon Lester was not ready to make his choice. He had yet to meet with the Giants, who were flying to see Lester and they were bringing their All-Star catcher, Buster Posey, with them as part of their contingent. They had won World Series in 2010, 2012, and 2014, and they had money to spend as well. In fact, their final offer was actually higher than the Cubs' final offer.

In the end, however, Jon Lester made his choice between going back to Boston or taking a leap of faith on the unproven roster of the Chicago Cubs. A roster that was loaded with young talent and a roster constructed by two men he trusted more than most anyone in baseball, Theo Epstein and Jed Hoyer. "If Theo and Jed weren't running the Cubs I am probably not here. I trust them and they convinced me that being part of the chase for a championship with the Cubs and trying to do what hasn't been done in 108 years would be a great step in my career," Lester told me.

"From the start," Passan said, "I thought the Cubs were the favorite, if only because of the relationship the front office forged with him in Boston. And Jon Lester is a really smart baseball mind. Even though he understood prospects come with an inherent risk, the sheer volume the Cubs had made it such that even if a few failed, the overwhelming likelihood was their lineup still would be stacked. Turns out the kids are even better than Lester could've imagined."

For the foreseeable future, Jon Lester will spend his seasons on the North Side of Chicago; he and his wife and two sons are looking at this chapter in their lives as part of "the Lester Family Adventure."

"We loved our time in Boston," Lester said. "It was a great chapter in our lives. And hopefully in five years we can look back on our time in Chicago as another great adventure for me, my wife, and our kids."

11

The Three-Headed Monster

Theo Epstein's management philosophy shows a very self-confident executive who manages a very large staff under him with what he likes to call a "flat management structure." Epstein doesn't want yes men around him, preferring to have people who feel empowered to speak their minds and to provide honest opinions rather than what they believe the boss wants to hear.

Epstein is also someone with an unquenchable thirst for information and knowledge. He and those around him live by a very simple mantra that followed them from their time in Boston. "We don't know shit" is the way Epstein starts each and every day when he goes to work.

"Theo is almost always the smartest person in whatever room he walks into," Jason McLeod told me. "However, he always wants to ask the most questions and he strives to learn whatever he can from anyone he talks to. He challenges everyone around him to look at things from a different perspective than maybe you had before and he looks at information as the most important thing that he can get his hands on."

For Epstein, he believes that good, old-fashioned hard work can overcome a lot and that a great work ethic combined with information gleaned through many different sources can give the Cubs an advantage over the other 29 teams in Major League Baseball.

"There is a mindset too that's associated with that, that I think is important and I think when we are at our best we are able to embody that mindset and hopefully cultivate it here," Epstein told me. "That includes leaving no stone unturned, being extremely thorough, and being very detail-oriented. Understanding that pushing and digging and working your ass off and making sure that even the smallest detail, getting it just a little bit more right than maybe our other 29 counterparts with the other teams can ultimately lead to winning. It might impact one player or it might impact 100 players but it might impact one player and it might change his life.

"Or it might just make him better in one small area that might show up every day or it might show up one time, in one playoff game, in one situation where he's feeling a little bit more confident or he's better prepared or he's better at some aspect physically, or mentally or fundamentally than he would have been otherwise. And that is going to win us a baseball game and that might win us a series and that might win us the World Series.

"So we are trying to build a culture where everyone feels that same mindset or adopts it," Epstein continued. "Players, coaches, managers, scouts, front office, GMs, and interns. Everyone adopts that mindset looking to come to work to make the organization better in some small way."

While the Cubs were building their philosophy after hiring Epstein and Co., they were also changing their infrastructure throughout the organization. McLeod though believes that no matter what changes were discussed, the most important thing that Epstein brought to the Cubs was a desire to build a healthy organization. "It's one thing to have these catchphrases and monikers of sorts but it's another thing altogether to really build a culture, defining: Who are we and what are our beliefs? What are we going to be? So as we were having this conversation on plate discipline or pitching philosophy it all fell under this umbrella of culture and finding the right people, the right teachers to implement our philosophy and what our expectations were going to be. That starts with Theo and Jed and me but it works down through the staff to really live this way every single day," he said.

Perhaps no term best describes the Ricketts/Epstein partnership better than "transparency," which was evident from the day Theo Epstein started running the Chicago Cubs. The new regime pulled no punches when describing what the immediate future would look like shortly after taking the job in November 2011.

That transparency continues to this day with Epstein and Hoyer extremely honest with the media in their press conferences and meetings on the field at Wrigley throughout the season. When the media and the fan base wanted the Cubs to sign Albert Pujols or Prince Fielder, Epstein and Hoyer were honest in saying moves like that were not in the offing.

"We're not trying to hide the ball. We're being honest with our fans. There might be another trading deadline in our future when we trade away 40 percent of a really good rotation. You do that because there's going to be a day when you acquire two starting pitchers at the deadline to cement your club and go on a run in the postseason," Epstein said.

Epstein was also asked if he noticed Chicago is a two-team city with an intense rivalry between the Cubs and their South Side rivals, the White Sox. "Obviously, I've noticed it," he replied. "There's a choice. You can say we're going to Band-Aid this thing and try to polish it up the best we can and make it as presentable as possible to try to squeeze every last fan through the gates this year and we'll deal with next year next year. Or we can say we want to make this thing right, no matter how tough the road is. We're taking the second path, so it doesn't matter how many teams are in the city, we're going to take the path we feel is right."

Epstein knew accepting the challenge of running the Chicago Cubs would not be an easy job. He also knew there would be no short-term fixes to make the team competitive rapidly. However, he also never hid the fact that building a franchise was a lengthy and sometimes painful process from his massive fan base.

"I didn't use the word rebuilding, and I won't," he said. "Scouting and player development is the key to year-in and year-out success, not the occasional lucky hit. There are no definitive answers in this game, no shortcuts. When you think you've got it all figured out, you can get humbled very quickly."

And when the Cubs began to contend in 2015 the Cubs front office was quick to tell people that the following off-season would be spent trying to address the few weaknesses the team had. Whether it was after a tough season or a good season, Epstein, Hoyer and even their bosses in the Ricketts family were honest with the media and in turn their fan base by telling them the truth and not what they wanted to hear.

"We don't tell you guys everything but we do try to be honest when we are asked a question so that everyone understands what we are doing. It was not in the best interests of the organization to sign an older free agent when we first arrived here and we knew that so we tried to be as honest as we could," Epstein said.

"Everyone in the organization has to be treated with that respect no matter what role you play in the organization. That's why I believe so strongly in having a flat organization and to not overly rely on hierarchy or reporting structure. Sometimes you need reporting structure but as a front office we have kind of a boiler room, physically and figuratively.

But, our management philosophy and structure is flat. I've worked in organizations where if the player development assistant has an idea or a question he cannot walk into the GM's office. He can only take it to his boss and hopefully it works its way up. Here we've tried to create an environment where we are just talking baseball. Asking questions is a good thing. People are encouraged to walk into my office or Jed's office if they have an idea, a critique, or a question and vice versa. Jed and I will walk through the cubicles and ask questions, does anyone have a solution to this problem? It's great. That kind of dialogue and give-and-take is huge in generating good ideas," Epstein told me.

Jed Hoyer put it best when he talked about how their front office began to change the way the Cubs did business from the day that they started. "No disrespect to anyone that came before us, but the way the Cubs were run was different than the way Tom and his family want them run now. The Ricketts family will spend whatever it takes to make sure that our players are treated first class in every area of the franchise. Having an owner that wants to run a franchise that way and is willing to spend the money to do things like that is huge. It allows us to do whatever we need to do in every area of the organization," Hoyer said.

One example of how the Cubs are run differently under the Ricketts family ownership is in how even their minor league prospects are taken care of on and off the field. The facilities in Arizona, which is the Cubs' winter home, are perhaps the best in the game. Not only are there opportunities to work on the field but the Cubs strength training facility, their medical and training staffs, and their psychological departments are all considered as good as any franchise or better around baseball. That's a far cry from the days of Andy MacPhail ordering Cubs staff to ship the Wrigley Field weight equipment to Arizona and back each and every year rather than stocking a weight room in Arizona with its own set of equipment.

A former MLB executive told me, "It's really not that hard to figure out why the Cubs hadn't been successful. They were not run as well as they could be because they didn't put enough emphasis on their minor league system and they were well behind the curve when it came to analytics. Add in that they were run like a mom-and-pop business in a lot of areas and it all added up to them trying to catch lightning in a bottle every season. They almost succeeded a couple of times but there was no chance to establish a run of sustained success."

Before the Ricketts/Epstein partnership began in late 2011, the Cubs minor league system was among the worst in the game. Sure, the Cubs had produced a handful of solid prospects over the years but the player development plan and the depth of the farm system were far from where they needed to be to produce a steady stream of low-cost, high-reward talent to build a solid major league club.

"When we arrived in Chicago, Tom gave us a mandate to build a healthy organization no matter what the cost was," Jed Hoyer told me. "He didn't want a quick fix, he wanted us to build the franchise on a solid foundation."

In speaking with executives with other teams in baseball it quickly became apparent that the Cubs are spending money in ways that they never had before the sale of the franchise. Their reputation around the game now is that the Ricketts family will spend money not only on players but on the absolute best in every area of the organization. The end result is that the Cubs are first class in every way on and off the field.

While the Cubs front office did not want to get into specifics, major league sources told me that the Cubs upgraded just about every area of the organization, even going so far as to provide food for every minor league player on a daily basis that was far better than the organization had ever provided, spending in excess of half a million dollars more than they had previously just on food to feed their prospects.

"Look, we spend a lot of money on signing players and trying to train them to someday play at Wrigley Field," Hoyer told me. "Why wouldn't we want to make sure that our players are not eating fast food everyday but rather they are eating nutritious, healthy food as they train and develop their minds and bodies to someday play at the major league level? Tom has never said no to anything that we have wanted to do and Theo, Jason, and I believe that we need to give our players at every level of the organization the best of everything as they try to help us win a World Series. We want them to know how special it is to be a Chicago Cub."

Epstein, Hoyer, and McLeod have worked together in Boston and in Chicago and the three men are as close as brothers. It is that relationship that makes their unique professional dynamic work so well. Not many men would leave a job as the general manager of the San Diego Padres to become the number two man in Chicago. And in McLeod's case, he left the assistant general manager's post he held under Hoyer in San Diego to become the Senior Vice President of Scouting and Player Development with the Cubs.

However, when Epstein called late in the 2011 season to broach the possibility of reuniting the "Theo Trio" in Chicago, neither Hoyer nor McLeod had any reservations about saying yes.

"Look, I loved San Diego. The Padres were great to me and I felt we were building something special out there. But, my relationship with Theo is so strong and the chance to be a part of one of the greatest challenges in sports history in a great city like Chicago in a franchise that has such great tradition like the Cubs was something I could not say no to. Plus, getting to do it with Theo and Jason after all of the success we had in Boston and knowing how special what we accomplished was to so many people was what made it all the more appealing to me," Hoyer told me.

Epstein has always made it clear that had the Cubs won a World Series in their recent past he would not be working in Chicago today. He was intrigued by the challenge of trying to accomplish something that many believed to be impossible. But he also would not be running the Cubs if Jed Hoyer and Jason McLeod had not agreed to join him in the ultimate quest for baseball immortality on the North Side of the city of Chicago.

With so many baseball front offices employing a GM-only philosophy, the Cubs unique set up with a president of baseball operations plus a general manager had to have two men in virtual lockstep to make it work. "Trust and friendship is how we make our front office dynamic work. If you have any breakdown in trust even to the smallest degree or if one of the two in the tandem is out there looking for credit or is looking to deflect blame or is trying to be ambitious about their career or is trying to separate themselves from the other guy in any way, then it is the single worst front office structure imaginable," Epstein told me.

"It only works with complete and utter trust, buy in, teamwork, collaboration and mutual support. We've known each other since 2002 and we totally trust each other and we respect and admire each other in a lot of ways, so it was easy for us to make it work. I think we balance each other really well, we cross-check each other really well as far as pushing each other to make sure that we are looking issues and decisions the right way. These days it's a big job so we split up a lot of it like the time-consuming stuff such as staying in touch with other teams. I talk to the GMs that I have a good relationship with and Jed talks to the GMs that he has a good relationship with," Epstein added.

"When we do a deal with Texas, for example, Jon Daniels and I have worked very well together over the years so I'm the one talking to Texas. When we did a deal with Seattle this year, Jed and Jerry DiPoto have a great relationship, so he handles those discussions. The same thing applies to agents. I don't undermine Jed's authority in any way and he is not trying to grab mine in any way. It works. Ultimately, if there has to be a final call on the handful of decisions we have a year that we don't have a strong consensus, I have to make that call, but I would never do it without fulling flushing it out with Jed first," Epstein told me.

McLeod, who many around the game believe is qualified already to be a general manager, had ties to the San Diego Padres organization going back to his childhood growing up in Southern California. "My mom is a Padres season ticket holder and my family is from San Diego. However, when Theo called he told me and Jed that he would not take the Cubs job if we would not go with him. Jed and I talked and the challenge to accomplish something so special in Chicago plus the opportunity to have the three of together again was something that we all just couldn't pass up," McLeod told me.

Epstein and Hoyer both know how important McLeod is to the organization and his skills are crucial to the overall health of the franchise because it is his department that is responsible for the pipeline of young talent that the Cubs rely on to feed their major league team, as well as to provide Epstein and Hoyer with players that can be used in trades to acquire additional talent. "Jason is the best in the game at what he does and I would not have taken the Cubs job if he hadn't agreed to come with me and Jed. He knows how to evaluate talent, he is a tremendous people person, and he is someone that I have 100 percent trust in," Epstein said.

So, how are three very talented executives who are all good enough to run their own franchises able to put their egos in check and work together for a common goal? Simply put, they work toward building a consensus on every major decision that has to be made.

"Theo is the best at valuing everyone's opinion and then discussing a decision until we reach a consensus that everyone is completely comfortable with. We are all so close and we all trust each other completely and that makes our management structure work very well. We have to have trust and loyalty and the three of us do. Jed could be a president of baseball operations and I have had some calls about being a GM but we are all so lucky to be here, all of us together accomplishing something that has meant so much to so many people," McLeod said.

As for the sales and marketing side, the Cubs know they have a rock star in Theo Epstein and they will utilize his star power to help close a deal when necessary. And Epstein is more than willing to help out when asked. But the business side of the game is something that holds no appeal to the Cubs baseball boss.

"It's not my favorite thing. I've never been attracted at all to the business side of baseball or the business side of anything really. I mock all of my friends who work in finance. I just don't understand what they do. I don't get making money off of money. It's not my favorite part of the game but I also understand that we have an obligation to help them out because they help us out.

"I always tell our business guys if there is something we can do that will move the needle, just let us know. We try to always be there for them. We try to be transparent with them on our plans and we ask for the same thing in return and it's gotten to a really good place. I really like the business guys that we work with and I think there's a really good trust going both ways which is nice," Epstein told me.

Epstein also doesn't allow many people to get too close to him and that certainly applies to members of the large media contingent that follows the Cubs every move. So why does a man who is so wildly popular have one personality for the public and an entirely different one for those he works with and is closest to?

Epstein laughed as we looked out on the playing field at Wrigley in August 2016 and I posed that very question to him. "To a certain extent it's by design. For me it makes more sense to act one way publicly and then be myself behind closed doors. I've never fully come to terms with the public aspects of the job and being a little local celebrity and having local fame. I just feel like–and I learned this by getting the job in Boston at such a young age–that there was a lot of interest in me at that time.

"There were a lot of opportunities to do things such as late night talk shows, national stuff as well, and I said no to all of that stuff. I learned from some good people that once you thrust yourself out there, something might seem really fun and appealing, such as wouldn't it be great to be on the cover of this magazine or wouldn't it be great to share this part of your life. However, once you put yourself out there it's really hard, almost impossible, to then say no. To say, 'Hey guys, this part of my life is off-limits,' or 'This is just for me and my family.' So it's not worth it.

"There is nothing truly rewarding that comes from attention, publicity, and praise. Because the other side of praise is criticism and they're both going to come. One doesn't come without the other. So if I were to attach a lot of meaning to that in my life—even the praise—if I were to allow that to make me feel really good about myself then I would have to attach meaning to the criticism and I would let people who don't even know me get me down about myself and that doesn't make sense.

"I want my private life to be private and I don't want to be influenced by this weird public element that's part of my job. So I'm going to be pretty by-the-book publicly and pretty boring and just do my job. Then I'll be myself behind closed doors because once you put yourself out there it's really hard to get it back. It's hypocritical to try to get it back. If I was to sit here and tell you all of these stories about myself, what I'm like away from the field or what my favorite flavor of ice cream is that no one really cares about but someone might try to write a story about, it would be hypocritical of me to try to draw the line if you asked a question about my son or my family. So why even go there? Instead I'll give you guys in the media what you need because I respect you but I'll keep the real stuff to my friends and family."

Another aspect of Epstein's management style involves how much he and Hoyer have to do with the day-to-day decisions regarding each day's lineup and day-to-day game strategy plans. Many around baseball believe that Epstein, Hoyer, and the Cubs analytical system, nicknamed "Ivy," have tremendous involvement in manager Joe Maddon's decisions. However, Epstein says that is tremendously overstated.

"We're involved but never in a way that takes autonomy and authority away from the manager and the coaches. We want our manager and our coaches to be really effective and in order to be really effective they need to be respected by the players. If we are making those decisions for them they're not going to be respected by the players and they are not going to be effective. Also, we hired them because they are really good at what they do and we want them to make decisions based on their knowledge, their instinct, and their decision making, and to make good decisions.

"Our job is to help share our perspective and provide information and if we have a good idea to run it by them and to explain why it might be worth considering and then we all go from there. Joe is the most open-minded manager I've ever been around and he wants that information, so it's all transparent. We dedicated one analytics guy almost exclusively to Joe so he could be there to answer questions and that role also involves creating a lineup matrix on any given night that shows by the numbers what an optimal lineup might be or what optimal matchups might be.

"Joe usually wants to put that into play because he believes in certain objective truths about the game. However, Joe will also deviate from it when he has a reason to, based on personality reasons or based on his own eye or based on certain things that go on in a clubhouse behind the scenes," Epstein told me. "The good thing is we are just transparent about it, so Joe can always say I want to do this for this reason and we can always say you should maybe consider this for this reason and it's just an open exchange of ideas. In the end, it's his call."

12

2015—The Kids Are Ahead of Schedule

On the heels of a 73–89 season, there was an awful lot of hope. And hype. Hope and hype that people outside the Cubs organization didn't truly understand. Sure, the Cubs had some highly touted prospects but were they worth all of the hoopla that was surrounding the Cubs after five miserable seasons?

There was a new manager (Joe Maddon) and a new ace (Jon Lester), and that loaded farm system looked ready to produce some quality players. But how quickly would they adjust to the major leagues? Some of those questions were answered quickly, as Kris Bryant led all major leaguers in spring training with nine home runs (in only 14 games). But as electric as the Las Vegas–native Bryant was, the Cubs weren't rolling the dice on Bryant quite yet.

The decision was made on March 30 to send Bryant to Iowa (AAA) to begin the season. The MLBPA (Major League Baseball Players Association) knocked the decision, as did Bryant's high-powered agent, Scott Boras, himself a former Cubs minor leaguer. "You are damaging the ethics and brand of Major League Baseball," Boras told *USA TODAY*. "Kris Bryant has extraordinary skills. Kris Bryant is a superstar. He has distinguished himself from all players at every level he's played.

"Everybody in baseball is saying he's a major league player ready for the big leagues. I have players call me. Executives call me. The Cubs people want him there. Everyone says, 'They cannot send this guy down.' It's too obvious. This isn't a system choice. This isn't a mandate. This is a flat ownership decision. Do they really want to win here?"

Boras was irate at the Cubs' decision to return Bryant to the minor leagues simply because by delaying his major league debut the Cubs could control his time before free agency for an extra full season. Players must complete six major league seasons before they are eligible for free agent status. By missing the season's first eight games it would leave Bryant short of the necessary number of days that he must be on the major league roster for 2015 to qualify as a full season. Boras believed it was unfair and violated the spirit of the MLB collective bargaining agreement.

"The fact that this player is so talented that you're worried about what you're going to do with him seven years from now," Boras said, "gives you an idea about his value to the team. So stop saying this is the system. If this was a losing team, okay, it's not prudent to bring him up. But Tom Ricketts talks about this team being ready to win now. And if you're ready to win, you've got to give them every resource to do it," Boras railed.

Epstein talked openly at his disagreement with how Boras saw the situation and he too was loud and passionate in his defense of what the Cubs were doing with their top prospect. "Ownership doesn't have anything to do with it," Epstein told *USA Today*. "We're making an organizational decision. And I'll be the one, as president of baseball operations, making the decision.

Kris Bryant's Performance by Level

Year	League	Games	HR	RBI	BA	OBP	SLG
2013	Rookie AZ	2	0	2	.167	.143	.333
2013	Low-A Boise	18	4	16	.354	.416	.692
2013	Hi-A Daytona	16	5	14	.333	.387	.719
2013	AZ Fall Mesa	20	6	17	.364	.457	.727
2014	AA TN	68	22	58	.355	.458	.702
2014	AAA Iowa	70	21	52	.295	.418	.619
2015	AAA Iowa	7	3	10	.321	.364	.679

"You never have a second chance to promote somebody the first time. You want to make sure they're in the right place. In Kris' case, we know he's ready offensively, we just want to get him in a good rhythm defensively. We do a better job at player development than we do strategizing on how to save a few dollars here and there. That's what we want to be all about. We don't think we screwed him up and we don't think we're going to," Epstein said.

Boras continued to speak loudly and passionately to anyone with a microphone or a newspaper column and he refused to back down. "What this spring has illustrated is that he should have been in the big leagues last September. He could have gotten his seasoning then. Major League Baseball fans missed something. They missed the opportunity to see this man perform, and the Cubs missed the opportunity to get him acclimated and established for 2015. The Cubs haven't had a pennant since 1945, so why worry about something six years from now? Other owners, when given the choice, have done this. Why not give yourself a chance to win, too? He certainly believes he should have been in the big leagues last September," Boras said, "and he certainly believes that if his spring performance is among the best 25 players, he should be in the big leagues now."

"Today is a bad day for baseball," the MLBPA said in a statement. "I think we all know that even if Kris Bryant were a combination of the greatest players to play our game, and perhaps he will be before it's all said and done, the Cubs still would have made the decision they made today. This decision, and other similar decisions made by clubs, will be addressed in litigation, bargaining, or both."

Still, Epstein remained undaunted in making the decision that he and his front office team felt was best for the Cubs and Kris Bryant. "When we talked after the [2014] season," Epstein said, "he was really happy how he held up physically, but he's an honest kid, and he said that he was a little mentally drained from the grind of the long season. I think it was the right thing, to let a guy go through his first full season, and feel good about the numbers he put up.

"Now, with a full year under his belt, we think he's really close to the big leagues. We think it will happen this year. We just don't know when. I thought he played very well at third after he came back from missing a bit of time with the arm issue," Epstein said. "I thought he moved very well. I think he's on his way to being a very good third baseman and he will continue to work on it."

However, everyone around the game knew that the underlying issue was service time. By waiting only nine days, the Cubs would gain an extra year of club control of Bryant. Instead, the Cubs starting third baseman for the April 4 season opener at Wrigley Field was Mike Olt, a player who hit .160 with 100 strikeouts in 258 plate appearances in 2014, and who would be designated for assignment by the end of August.

2015 Cubs Opening Day Lineup

CF Dexter Fowler

RF Jorge Soler

1B Anthony Rizzo

SS Starlin Castro

LF Chris Coghlan

3B Mike Olt

C David Ross

P Jon Lester

2B Tommy La Stella

As the season began on *Sunday Night Baseball* against the archrival Cardinals, the biggest story wasn't Bryant, nor was it starting pitcher Jon Lester, who made his Cubs debut after signing a team-record (at the time) 6-year, $155 million deal during the off-season.

The 3–0 loss to the despised Cardinals was overshadowed by horror stories of endless bathroom lines and fans resorting to urinating in plastic cups (and discarding those cups throughout the concourse) instead of waiting in line for an inning and a half or more.

As Jed Hoyer said later that week, "Hopefully, our team is what you want to talk about–not bathroom lines or porta-potties."

However, things would get better and they would get better very quickly.

All the commotion over Kris Bryant's service time ended up being over only eight games (during which the Cubs went 5–3 anyway). Bryant finally made his MLB debut on April 17 at Wrigley Field against the San Diego Padres. He went 0-for-4 with three strikeouts, which was followed by a 2-for-3 performance with three walks. Bryant walked 16 times in his first 16 games, even if the power wasn't there...quite yet.

Through the end of April, the Cubs posted a solid record of 12–8, which was their first winning record entering May since 2008. The surprise team leaders in home runs were catcher Miguel Montero and outfielder Chris Coghlan, who had three apiece. Pitcher Jon Lester, the Cubs key off-season addition, struggled in his first month as a National League pitcher to the tune of a 6.23 ERA in four starts. However, some of his early-season struggles can be traced back to an arm problem that he dealt with towards the end of spring training.

The month of May started with a 1–0 win over the Brewers at Wrigley Field, courtesy of the first career home run of a highly touted Cubs prospect. And it wasn't Kris Bryant. It was Addison Russell, the main prize from the Jeff Samardzija trade (back on July 5, 2014).

Cubs in Baseball America's Top 100 Prospects (Entering 2015)

1	Kris Bryant
3	Addison Russell
12	Jorge Soler
19	Kyle Schwarber
38	Carl Edwards Jr.
83	Billy McKinney

Russell debuted April 21 at Pittsburgh with three strikeouts, much like Bryant, but he quickly showed why the baseball world was so shocked when the Cubs were able to pry him away from the Oakland A's in the 2014 trade for Jeff Samardzija and Jason Hammel.

Bryant finally went deep on May 9 in Milwaukee off Kyle Lohse (in his 92nd career plate appearance). Bryant and Rizzo, the slugging duo eventually known as "Bryzzo" by the fan base and eventually in an MLB ad campaign, each posted seven homers and 20-plus RBI in May, giving Cubs fans a taste of things to come, even if the 14–14 record for the month was a step back from their impressive April.

A few other highlights from the season's second month:

On May 15, the Cubs won a wild 12-inning affair with the Pirates, winning 11–10 on a Matt Szczur single which looked to be an easy pop fly to shallow right field, until Pirates outfielder Gregory Polanco tripped and fell, which allowed the winning run to score. From that game forward, the Cubs would go 21–9 (and a rain-shortened tie) against the Pirates through the end of the 2016 season.

Less than a week later, Kyle Hendricks gave everyone a glimpse of his future excellence with the first Cubs complete game shutout of the season (the first of Hendricks' career) in San Diego. The righty entered that start with a 5.15 season ERA, and he struggled with inconsistency from start to start, finishing the 2015 season with a mediocre 3.95 ERA. Jon Lester bounced back from his rough start to post a 1.76 ERA in six May starts and started to show why Epstein and Hoyer were so driven to land him in free agency.

Entering June, the Cubs hovered a handful of games over .500 (26–22) but they were six games in back of the front-running St. Louis Cardinals and a game ahead of the Pittsburgh Pirates in the National League's Central division.

Starlin Castro, still only 25 years old, remained an enigma though. After starting his career in eye-popping fashion back in 2010, when he hit a home run and a triple and drove in six runs in his major league debut, the Cubs shortstop remained wildly inconsistent in the field and at the plate.

Fans were still holding out hope though for the young shortstop who was extremely popular in and around Chicago. He had finished 2014 with a .388/.417/.524 slash line over 27 games from August 1 until an injury ended his season on September 2. He started the 2015 season red hot with a .325 average in April but he then plummeted down to .262 in mid-June. However, he had his moments when he recaptured the imagination of the Wrigley faithful just as he did when he collected walk-off hits in consecutive games June 13 and 14 against the Reds. But the frustrating cycle of ups and downs for Castro would continue throughout the season and eventually would cost him his starting spot at shortstop.

June 16 was a notable day for the Cubs for two reasons. Jake Arrieta allowed four runs in five innings, walking six in a disappointing 6–0 loss to the Indians at Wrigley Field. That game though would end up being the last time during the 2015 season that he turned in a non-quality start.

The second memorable moment for the Cubs came in the ninth inning of that day's game against the Cleveland Indians. Coming in to catch reliever Zac Rosscup in the top of the ninth was Kyle Schwarber. The fourth overall pick out of Indiana University in the 2014 MLB Draft was pounding Double-A pitching to the tune of a .320/.438/.579 slash line with 13 home runs in 58 Games. The stocky 22-year-old struck out looking against Marc Rzepczynski, but by season's end, Schwarber would make hitting major league pitching look easier than spelling Rzepczynski.

Schwarber would be heard from the next day in a 17–0 win over the Indians in a game packed with oddities. The contest saw the 6'0" 235 lb. Schwarber crack a triple for his first major league hit (oddly enough, Anthony Rizzo also tripled for his first major league hit back in 2011). The 41,000-plus fans in attendance at Wrigley Field that day saw Kris Bryant's first career grand slam, which came off outfielder David Murphy, who was pressed into pitching duty in the blowout.

Another first for Bryant came five days later. It was his first multi–home run game, with the first of the pair coming courtesy of All-Star Clayton Kershaw. His second multi-homer effort followed on July 4.

Kyle Schwarber was sent to Class AAA Iowa a few days after his first taste of major league action, but he returned for good on July 17 and picked up right where he left off as he continued to mash big league pitching. In what many refer to as "the Schwarber Game" on July 21 in Cincinnati, the big rookie hit a game-tying two-run home run in the ninth, and capped it off with a game-winning blast in the 13th.

Perhaps, however, the most notable moment of July was the history the Cubs made in a loss to Philadelphia.

Phillies star Cole Hamels, who was making his final start before he was traded to the Texas Rangers at the 2015 trade deadline, went out in style, no-hitting the Cubs in a 5–0 victory at Wrigley Field. Before Hamels spun his gem on a warm and sunny Saturday afternoon, the last pitcher to throw a no-hitter against the Cubs had been Sandy Koufax, who tossed a perfect game on September 9, 1965. From that point forward, the Cubs would play a remarkable 7,920 games in between no-hitters.

On the losing end of that game was Jake Arrieta, who fell behind early after surrendering a three-run home run to Ryan Howard in the third inning of the loss. Little did anyone know at that point that the next regular season game the Cubs would lose with Arrieta on the mound would be the following season at the end of May. Arrieta's second half of the 2015 season would not only be outstanding, it would be historic.

The Cubs as a team took off in late July. On Monday, July 27, they were one out away from an 8–7 loss that would have been especially painful because their bullpen allowed four runs to the Colorado Rockies in the top of the ninth inning. However, Kris Bryant turned a demoralizing loss into a walk-off win by crushing a John Axford pitch deep into the Wrigley Field bleachers. From that game forward, the Cubs went 46–19 through the end of the 2015 season.

Success aside, the Cubs were still looking to improve. Edwin Jackson, a big free agent signing from 2013 who never lived up to expectations as a rotation mainstay, was designated for assignment at the end of July (and released a week later), making room for veteran reliever Rafael Soriano, who the Cubs signed after a tryout.

At the trade deadline, Dan Haren was added in a trade with the Marlins with a pair of minor leaguers heading to Miami. Also joining the mix was reliever Tommy Hunter, who came over from Baltimore for outfielder Junior Lake. Clayton Richard, picked up for an occasional spot start in early July, joined the bullpen for the final two months. Reliever Trevor Cahill, who had been released by the Atlanta Braves, was signed to a contract and added to the roster in mid-August.

Maddon wasn't opposed to a shakeup among the position players, either. On August 7, Addison Russell took over as the starting shortstop, supplanting the struggling Starlin Castro, who saw his slash line fall to .236/.271/.304 on the season (including .170/.194/.202 in July). Maddon met with Castro and informed him that going forward, Addison Russell was the starting shortstop.

"Schwarber is obviously swinging the bat really well and so is Coghlan," Maddon said. "Just trying to be creative keeping the bats in the lineup right now. I told Starlin it's not a day off. I want him to understand that up front.

"It's something that's going to be considered daily. I did not give him any promises regarding how he's going to be utilized other than just to stay ready off the bench. I didn't want to give him any kind of false promises whatsoever.

"He can be playing tomorrow. I'm not sure yet. I want to see how it plays today, but I wanted to be up front with him and let him know it's not a day off."

"Schwarber is the impetus regarding this maneuver right now," Maddon said. "More than Starlin. We have to include Kyle right now. Then the next guy you have to include is Coghlan. You've got to get those guys in there based on their performance and our lack of offense."

The move however, ended up being permanent. Schwarber, who was hitting .342/.429/.633 with six home runs and 18 RBI (in 25 games) at the time, was too good an option to have sitting on the bench and he settled in quickly, playing primarily in left field with occasional time at catcher, and Russell hasn't played any other position than shortstop since the change was made. After spending some time on the bench, Castro played second base the remainder of the season and played it throughout the 2015 postseason.

Jason Hammel was another player whom Joe Maddon kept an eye on down the stretch. After leaving a July 8 start with a hamstring injury, Hammel was on a very short leash, averaging 85 pitches per start with only two quality starts in his 14 starts after the All-Star break (5.10 ERA). Arrieta and Lester were strong at the top of the rotation, but with an inconsistent Hendricks and an ineffective Haren (6.31 ERA in five August starts), Hammel's slide was a legitimate concern.

One player Maddon did not have to worry about was Jake Arrieta. From the All-Star break heading into his August 30 start in Los Angeles, the bearded right hander posted a 1.20 ERA in eight trips to the mound. And the ERA dipped even lower after he tossed the first Cubs no-hitter since Carlos Zambrano no hit the Houston Astros in 2008. Arrieta went on to post a 0.75 ERA–a Major League record for a season after the All-Star break. The Cubs won each of his last 13 starts after the Cole Hamels no-hit loss on July 25.

In August, the Cubs kicked it up a notch, going 19–9 including a season-long nine-game winning streak from August 6 to 15 (which started with a four-game sweep of the defending champion Giants at Wrigley Field). Kris Bryant posted a .330 average and 1.042 OPS with 7 HR, Schwarber led the team with 9 HR and 24 RBI and Arrieta was 6–0 with an incredible 0.43 ERA in six starts (he would be even better in September and October, with a 0.39 ERA to finish the regular season).

The Cubs clinched a wild-card berth and their first postseason appearance since 2008 when the Giants lost to the A's on September 25, but there was little doubt the Cubs would make the postseason. There were also a few stretch run surprises along the way. Starlin Castro finished strong after his move to second base with a .369/.400/.655 slash line and 21 RBI from September 1 on. Dan Haren rebounded to post a solid September (2.20 ERA in six starts).

When the dust cleared, the three best records in baseball resided in the NL Central.

Best Records in Baseball 2015

Team	W–L	Pct.
Cardinals	100–62	.617
Pirates	98–64	.605
Cubs	97–65	.599
Royals	95–67	.586
Blue Jays	93–69	.574

The National League Wild Card Game was October 7 in Pittsburgh, pitting two teams with 97-plus wins. It would be Jake Arrieta for the Cubs against Pittsburgh-ace Gerrit Cole, and Arrieta was outstanding. He shut out the Pirates with a complete-game performance for the ages allowing just four hits with 11 strikeouts and no walks. It was the first postseason shutout in MLB history with 10-plus strikeouts and zero walks.

While his performance devastated the Pirates and their loyal fans it came as no surprise to the Cubs who expected such a performance from their ace. In fact, in early September, Arrieta spoke to the team on a flight home from a road trip guaranteeing them he would defeat the Pirates in the Wild Card Game.

The 100-win Cardinals awaited the Cubs in the Division Series. Future-Cub John Lackey, at the time the Cardinals ace, tossed seven scoreless innings and the NLDS started the same way the regular season did, with a Cardinals shutout of the Cubs. However, that victory was all St. Louis would achieve in the series. The Cubs roared back with a 6–3 win in Game 2, keyed by a five-run second inning that was capped off by a Jorge Soler home run to center field.

Game 3 was an 8–6 Cubs win that saw the North Siders set a postseason record with six home runs—and they were hit by players hitting number one through six in the batting order. Jorge Soler's home run made it nine straight plate appearances reaching base to start his postseason career. Game 4 was a 6–4 win that saw Javier Baez take Lackey deep with his three-run home run giving the Cubs an early 4–2 lead. The Cardinals tied the game 4–4 before Anthony Rizzo smacked a home run in the sixth to give the Cubs a lead they would not relinquish. Kyle Schwarber added the exclamation point in the victory with a towering home run which landed on top of the right-field video board at Wrigley Field. A home run that was so majestic the Cubs encased the ball in a plastic case atop the video board for the remainder of their 2015 playoff run.

The Game 4 win clinched the Division Series and sent Wrigley Field into a state of bedlam. In fact, the clinching game was the first postseason clincher in the history of Wrigley Field which opened in 1914. Tens of thousands of fans who couldn't get a ticket to the decisive game jammed the area around the ballpark so that they could bask in the emotion of the evening.

The victory over the Cardinals opened everyone's eyes around baseball to the Chicago Cubs. Suddenly, the team known as the "lovable losers" had a new image as winners. Memories of the painful rebuild were a thing of the past as fans looked forward to a bright future with their young and talented team.

The 2015 NLCS paired the Cubs and one of their archrivals, the New York Mets, who had defeated the Los Angeles Dodgers in the other National League Division Series. Chicago appeared to have the upper hand going into the matchup, having swept all seven regular season games between the two teams.

Unfortunately, this time the exact opposite happened. The Mets, backed by dominant starting pitching, eliminated the Cubs in a four-game sweep. Four single runs in the first, fifth, sixth, and seventh innings were enough for the Mets to post a 4–2 win over Jon Lester in Game 1. The New Yorkers jumped in front with three runs in the first inning in Game 2, in a battle that saw Noah Syndergaard outduel a to-that-point-invincible Jake Arrieta, who would later admit to being tired and having run out of gas after throwing 92 more innings in a season than he ever had before in his career.

Game 3 was close until the Mets finally figured out the Cubs bullpen late in the game, scoring twice in the seventh inning to give them a 5–2 victory. The win gave the Mets a commanding 3–0 lead in the best-of-seven series and stoked the fears of a Cubs fan base thinking again of billy goats and curses and that elusive World Series.

Game 4 was a disaster from the beginning, with Jason Hammel coughing up four runs in the first and another one in the second on the way to an 8–3 Cubs loss. The sweep at the hands of one of the Cubs' most hated rivals was a bitter pill for the Cubs and their fan base to swallow and it put a damper on what had been an amazing breakout season for the Cubs' young and talented team.

The series MVP was New York second baseman Daniel Murphy, who homered in all four games in the series and tormented Cubs pitching to the tune of a .529 batting average. The Mets, who built their young team around a rotation of power arms while the Cubs were building through a collection of offensive stars, saw their pitchers dominate Cubs hitters. In fact, the domination was so thorough that some experts around baseball began to wonder if the Cubs' approach would have the staying power to get past the Mets and their loaded pitching staff in the near future.

There was plenty to accomplish before the start of the 2016 season and Theo Epstein and Jed Hoyer went right to work. They needed to add pitching, better situational hitting, and they needed to tighten up their defense. They had big plans and they believed a World Series championship was within their grasp but they needed a major increase in their budget, an increase that ownership had not yet approved.

13

2016—That Magical Year

The Cubs' 2016 season actually began the day after they were eliminated by the New York Mets in the 2015 National League Championship Series. The 4–0 sweep at the hands of one of their most bitter rivals was a tough pill to swallow for Theo Epstein and Jed Hoyer as well as the Cubs fan base. Again, the Cubs were denied entrance at the door of the World Series but while fans were disappointed, Epstein and his staff knew the Cubs were close to breaking through and that the outstanding 2015 season may have come a year ahead of schedule.

The baseball operations staff headed to Arizona, where Epstein and Hoyer's staff would participate in a critical self-analysis of what the Cubs needed to take the next step in their pursuit of a World Series championship. They also needed to evaluate their entire system from top to bottom as they did every off-season to prepare for the upcoming General Manager's meetings and the December Winter Meetings, where most of the off-season activity, including extensive trade talks, took place.

As their organizational meetings took place in the fall of 2015, several priorities emerged from the four days at the Cubs' opulent winter home. First, they had to add more starting pitching and they had to improve their team defense. In addition, Epstein, Hoyer, and Joe Maddon wanted to know what the Cubs' depth was going to look like. Over a 162-game season, depth can play a crucial role, perhaps more so than signing one star to a multimillion-dollar contract.

"Depth is one of the most underrated strengths a team can possess. You cannot try to put together an All-Star team in the winter and neglect the bench pieces that can be the difference between winning and losing during a long season," GM Jed Hoyer told me. "It is vitally important that you have players that can fill a role when the invariable injuries and slip in performance happens over 162 games."

One decision the Cubs had to make–and make fairly quickly–was on the future of Starlin Castro in a Cubs uniform. Castro had long been a popular player with the Cubs fan base and he had compiled gaudy numbers over his first six seasons in the big leagues, with many believing he would be a long-term fixture on the North Side.

However, inside the Cubs executive offices there was little doubt in the belief that Castro was not the long-term answer at second base. Yes, he had a solid bat and he was a well-liked teammate, but his attention to detail and his lapses in concentration were not in line with what Epstein and Hoyer saw for their young, rising team. They wanted a more consistent player and a player who was more versatile.

Starlin Castro was what the old Cubs *were.* He was a popular player but he wasn't considered a winning type of player. In December 2016, the free agent class had a player in it that was a winning type of player, a player who was as consistent as they came in the game of baseball. He had won a World Series, he played multiple positions, and he had a work ethic that was off the charts. In addition, he played for Joe Maddon in Tampa and their relationship was excellent. And he was interested in reuniting with his old manager on the North Side of Chicago. His name was Ben Zobrist and he was coming off of a World Series championship with the Kansas City Royals. He had been acquired by the Royals during the 2015 season, which meant he would not cost the Cubs a draft pick as compensation for signing him.

But before the Cubs could sign Zobrist they had to find a taker for Castro and that taker had to also assume his long-term contract, which still had a minimum of $38 million guaranteed left on it. By moving Castro and his contract it would not only open up second base but the payroll flexibility to sign Zobrist, who Epstein, Hoyer, and Maddon looked at as a critical addition for the Cubs.

Maddon loved what Zobrist could bring to his team not only on the playing field but in the clubhouse, where his young but talented team was ready to take the next step in challenging to win the World Series. The talented youngsters needed a role model who could teach them the ins and outs of professional baseball. And someone who could show them what type of work ethic it takes to win a championship. Plus, the Cubs lineup needed someone who could get on base at a high rate. Ben Zobrist checked all of the boxes and then some.

Then on December 8, the Cubs made a series of moves that signaled that they were going for it and that a World Series was what they believed was attainable if they could fine tune their roster to address their few weaknesses. Long rumored to be on the trade block, Castro was finally dealt to the Yankees for Adam Warren and a player to be named later (Brendan Ryan). Meanwhile, Zobrist, was inked to a four-year, $56 million deal to take over as the Cubs second baseman. And an earlier-agreed-to deal with veteran righty John Lackey (who, with the Cardinals, handed the Cubs their lone loss of the 2015 NLDS) was finalized for two years and $32 million.

Joe Maddon was ecstatic at landing Zobrist, who he felt was a crucial piece if his Cubs were going to take the next step in their journey to win a World Series. "Preparation is the key to who Ben Zobrist is," Maddon told me. "This guy prepares daily as well as anybody I've ever been around. He takes care of himself as well as anyone I've ever seen. You can't care any more than he cares. He has one agenda. He has one agenda every day, that's it, and that's to win. He doesn't care if he gets to hit or he doesn't get to hit. He'll take his walks to help a team score runs. He'll see pitches to help his teammates and he'll play a variety of positions. He knows that by him moving around that we're better everywhere else. He is the consummate teammate. He gets it. He got it from the first time I met him. In a day and age where everything is about a particular person it's never been about him. The world's never rotated around him ever. He is an altruistic person in his whole life and when it comes to baseball he definitely demonstrates that and the other guys feel it."

Just a few days later the Cubs made even bigger news, stunning the baseball world when a franchise-record $184 million contract (over eight years) was handed to St. Louis Cardinals Gold Glove right fielder Jason Heyward. Not only did this give the Cubs an elite outfielder (31.1 WAR over his first six major league seasons), but it deprived the Cardinals of their top two players in 2015, when measured by the highly popular analytical stat WAR (Wins Above Replacement).

2015 Cardinals WAR (baseball-reference.com) Leaders

6.5 Jason Heyward (now with Cubs)

5.6 John Lackey (now with Cubs)

3.9 Matt Carpenter

3.9 Carlos Martinez

3.9 Jaime Garcia

After factoring in the savings gained by trading Castro to the Yankees, the moves added $234 million to the Cubs payroll and sent shock waves throughout baseball. The Cubs were obviously pushing all of their chips into the middle of the table. They were all in using a poker metaphor. Epstein and Hoyer had decided the time was right to take a shot at winning the World Series. "We looked at next year's free agent class and decided we liked what was available to us now so we used some of next year's budget to add to our club now," Epstein said.

The expectations were off the charts when pitchers and catchers started arriving at Camp Maddon in early February 2016. With the additions of Heyward, Zobrist, and Lackey piled on top of a 97-win season in 2015, the media was predicting a championship and the Vegas oddsmakers agreed, installing the Cubs as the clear favorites to win the World Series. That meant when the full squad arrived at spring training on February 15 the pressure and the scrutiny would be unlike anything many of them had ever seen in their baseball careers. Joe Maddon decided to meet that pressure head on.

He adopted a team mantra, "Embrace the Target," and he encouraged open dialogue about the dream of winning a World Series. Anthony Rizzo told me, "For sure we talked about it. As soon as we got to spring training guys were talking about it. Everyone else was, so why wouldn't we? We knew we were talented enough and we knew we had great chemistry. So yes, everyone talked about it from spring training on."

So who counseled Maddon on dealing with the off-the-charts attention, expectations, and intense pressure that his team would have to deal with from the moment they showed up at spring training until the end of the 2016 season? "My counsel was Tom Clancy in the book *Clear and Present Danger*. That was my counsel. The character in the book, Jack Ryan, was working within the White House as an advisor and the president was receiving counsel to deny that he knew someone who had run afoul of the law. Jack Ryan disagreed and told the president to admit that he was friends with the person and to run towards the controversy instead of away from it because it was true. I took that and applied it to our team.

"For us to deny everything that was out there would be disingenuous. It's there. Of course it's there. Of course the word 'pressure' is there, of course the word 'expectation' is there. Of course they are. So why run away from it? Why not use it to our advantage? But to use it to your advantage you have to define it. You have to make it a positive. That's why I used 'Embrace the Target' and we started building off of it. We talked about being the target, pressure, expectations all being positives. Then we used our process as our anchor. At the end of the day if you can stay process-oriented you will not be fearful of anything," Maddon told me.

Maddon handed out "Embrace the Target" t-shirts while bringing fun to almost every day of the six weeks of spring training, maintaining a Maddon-esque flavor in Mesa practices. One morning, the Cubs skipper, attired in tie dye, rolled up onto the field in Mesa driving a large van right out of the '70s. A few weeks later, he had actual bear cubs brought to Sloan Park, as the players posed with the special mascots.

Something that Joe Maddon *didn't* have anything to do with was an infestation of bees on March 27. Jason Heyward was reportedly stung at least 10 times in the top of the third (the bees caused a delay in the game), and then came back to homer in the bottom of the inning. Heroics aside, Heyward struggled through a .164 spring. There would be more offensive struggles to come for the Cubs right fielder.

Things got weird on February 25 during morning stretching, when former Cub and newly signed Baltimore Orioles outfielder (or so we thought) Dexter Fowler appeared out of nowhere and walked onto the field with Theo Epstein at Cubs camp in Mesa. The popular center fielder was back and stunned his teammates (the Orioles deal never having been finalized) when he told them he had agreed to a one-year deal. The move allowed Jason Heyward to shift back to right field (where he was a better fit) and ironically, Jorge Soler, celebrating his 24th birthday, was now on the outside looking in at a starting job. To make room for Fowler, Chris Coghlan was shuttled off to Oakland for RHP Aaron Brooks.

Kyle Schwarber put an exclamation point on some springtime fun by breaking a car windshield with a batting practice home run. The projected starting left fielder, perhaps feeling a little guilty, reached out via Twitter to Safelite, a window repair company, to ask if there was anything they could do (the broken windshield ended up fetching $900 in an auction for charity). By the time spring training ended, the Cubs had a good vibe going and the level of expectation for the 2016 season was off the charts with dozens of national media types spending a lot of their time in Mesa and predicting a championship for the Cubs.

With spring training over it was time to raise the curtain on the 2016 season, and for the first time in Cubs history, they opened the season against an American League team (and they'd finish 2016 against one as well) with a 9–0 shutout in Anaheim against the Angels. It was the biggest opening day shutout in franchise history, with Jake Arrieta picking up where he left off in 2015 with seven scoreless innings.

A 3–0 start while outscoring the opponent 29–7 was definitely ideal. But then came game three of the 2016 season. The injury bug reared its ugly head, claiming its first victim in Kyle Schwarber, who left the game on a cart and was lost for the rest of the regular season with a severe knee injury that included a torn ACL. What initially spelled disaster did allow Joe Maddon to experiment with the depth and flexibility of his lineup, given the previous difficulty of hiding Schwarber's glove.

Despite the injury to one of the Cubs' best offensive players in Schwarber, they didn't lose a step at the plate, especially during a 16–0 rout of the Reds in Cincinnati on April 21. Of course, the offensive output wasn't the story that night. That night, Jake Arrieta hurled his second career no-hitter, making him the first Cubs pitcher to toss no-hitters in consecutive seasons. After a historic 1.77 ERA in 2015, it seemed nearly impossible that Arrieta could get even better, but through four starts in 2016 the numbers were equally eye-popping. Arrieta sported statistics as good as he had posted in his Cy Young season of 2015 with a 4–0 record, a 0.87 ERA, and a .147 Opp BA.

By May 10, the Cubs were 25–6. To find the last time they had a start that strong you had to go back *past* the last time they won the World Series. It was the year before that, in 1907.

The following night, on May 11, the Cubs showed they were human, dropping both ends of a doubleheader to the Padres, perhaps most memorable after San Diego's Christian Bethancourt homered off John Lackey and was perhaps a bit too excited about it.

"I got a long memory" uttered Lackey, one of the more quotable Cubs in 2016.

The Dodgers handed the Cubs a 5–0 defeat to end the month of May but more notably it was the first Cubs (regular season) loss in a Jake Arrieta start since July 25 of 2015. No need for alarm though. The Cubs were 35–15 through 50 games.

Kyle Hendricks posted a career-high 12 strikeouts on June 19, but the headlines were stolen by the just-called-up Willson Contreras, who slugged a pinch-hit home run in his first career major league at-bat. Crazy as it sounds, Contreras has the longest tenure in the Cubs organization of any player on the roster, having been signed as an international free agent in 2009. Fast forward to 2015, when he won the Southern League batting title (.333) and exploded onto the radar of most every scout in baseball. He stayed red hot to start the 2016 season, as he hit .353 in 55 games at Class AAA Iowa prior to his June call up. His spectacular start to the season earned him a promotion to the big leagues and he became the latest Cubs prospect to make waves in the major leagues.

Every day seemed to bring a new hero. On June 27, Kris Bryant stamped his name in the MLB record book by becoming the first player ever to hit three home runs and two doubles in a game. His 5-for-5 performance gave him a Cubs-record 16 total bases, picking up Jake Arrieta, who had a rare off night in an 11–8 win at Cincinnati.

Eventually, though, even the Cubs managed to hit a bump in the road as they posted a 6–15 record over a 21-game stretch heading into the All-Star break, which was closely tied to an injury suffered by Dexter Fowler. Luckily, the break would allow him to get back to 100 percent, even if it meant missing the game he was voted into as a starter.

Also voted in as starters was the entire Cubs infield–Rizzo 1B, Zobrist 2B, Russell SS, Bryant 3B–the second time in MLB history a team's entire infield started an All-Star Game (1963 Cardinals). The Cubs highlight of the game was Kris Bryant marking his return to San Diego (he attended the University of San Diego) by homering off Chicago White Sox star Chris Sale in the first inning.

Apparently the All-Star break was just what the Cubs needed as they reeled off a remarkable 50–23 record after the Midsummer Classic. Theo Epstein and Jed Hoyer weren't just sitting back and enjoying the ride though, as they posted a sign in their Wrigley Field offices that said FIND PITCHING. Their scouts scoured both the American League and the National League in search of arms and the Cubs made a series of trades for relievers.

On July 20, the Cubs acquired LHP Mike Montgomery from the Seattle Mariners for highly touted minor league first baseman Dan Vogelbach and a minor league pitching prospect. The Cubs were one of a number of teams in pursuit of Montgomery, and not only for his ability to pitch out of the bullpen. The Cubs believe that he has a long-term future as starter in their rotation. On July 25, the Cubs made their biggest move of the season when they sent four players, including their number one prospect in minor league shortstop Gleyber Torres, to the New York Yankees for All-Star closer Aroldis Chapman. The Chapman deal was a huge addition to the Cubs bullpen, but it did not come without controversy.

Chapman had been a star with the Cincinnati Reds for several years but he ran afoul of the law in October 2015 when he was involved in a domestic violence incident with his girlfriend at his home in Florida. No charges were filed, but the incident involved Chapman's use of a firearm and Major League Baseball suspended him for the first 30 games of the 2016 season. A trade that would have sent Chapman to the Los Angeles Dodgers fell through because of the incident and he was eventually sent by the Reds to the New York Yankees prior to the start of the 2016 season. He performed well there and once the Yankees fell out of playoff contention he was traded to the Cubs.

The Chapman deal triggered mixed reactions from the Cubs fan base and many members of the media were critical of the addition. Epstein understood the mixed feelings and even said that he was conflicted as he pondered whether or not to make the trade. "We understand there will be lots of different perspectives on this, but we have strong feelings about this," Epstein said. "People will feel differently about that. We understand that and respect it.

"But in the end, we decided it was appropriate to trade for a player who has accepted his discipline, already has been disciplined by MLB, has expressed his sorrow and regret for the incident."

Upon finalizing the deal on July 25, both Aroldis Chapman and Tom Ricketts issued statements addressing the incident and punishment.

Chapman's, in part, read: "As you know, earlier this year I accepted and served a 30-game suspension from Major League Baseball resulting from my actions of October 30, 2015. I regret that I did not exercise better judgment and for that I am truly sorry. Looking back, I feel I have learned from this matter and have grown as a person. My girlfriend and I have worked hard to strengthen our relationship, to raise our daughter together, and would appreciate the opportunity to move forward without revisiting an event we consider part of our past. Out of respect for my family, I will not comment any further on this matter.

"I cannot wait to take the mound at Wrigley Field and look forward to helping my teammates deliver a championship to Chicago."

Ricketts' statement also attempted to make clear the gravity of the issue, along with the fact that he directly addressed that with Chapman. "Obviously, we are aware of the circumstances surrounding Aroldis Chapman's suspension earlier this season. We are also aware that he cooperated fully with the league investigation and takes responsibility for his actions.

"Today, prior to completing the trade, Theo, Jed, and I spoke with Aroldis. I shared with him the high expectations we set for our players and staff both on and off the field. Aroldis indicated he is comfortable with meeting those expectations.

"Finally, my family, this team, and Major League Baseball take the issue of domestic violence very seriously and support efforts to reduce domestic violence through education, awareness, and intervention."

The media looked for comments from other Cubs, at which point Joe Maddon weighed in: "I don't assume bad with anybody for the first time."

"Phenomenal guy," David Ross said, "Great teammate who wants to win and has a great attitude. When [Brian McCann, who gave a positive report on Chapman] says something, I take it to heart.

"You look around the locker room, and all of us have made mistakes in our time in baseball. Hopefully we learn from those mistakes. We're going to welcome him with open arms."

Hector Rondon also spoke on the addition of Chapman, which most likely meant losing his spot as the Cubs closer. "I don't care if I come in in the eighth or seventh," Rondon said. "It only matters to me to come into the game and do my job."

The next day, however, things got even messier when Chapman spoke to the media through translator (and Cubs Quality Assurance Coach) Henry Blanco. When asked about the phone call from Tom Ricketts and Theo Epstein which convinced them to make the trade, Chapman paused and then offered a short response. Blanco, translating, said, "He was sleeping when he got the call so he's trying to remember what they talked about. It has been a long day."

A reporter followed up by asking Chapman if anything Ricketts or Epstein said over the phone made an impact on him. Blanco repeated the question.

"No," he answered.

The answers added fuel to the fire.

After that, Chapman had a one on one interview with ESPN's Pedro Gomez who is bilingual. Speaking in Spanish he said:

> *"I knew that no matter where I was traded to, this would resurface—that the controversy is going to follow me.*
>
> *"But I'm with my girlfriend. Our family is together. We're working toward making things better in our lives. And really, it's going to be with me."*
>
> *"I've grown tremendously from that time. I'm with my girlfriend still, with the family, and I feel that I have absolutely changed as a person. I'm working to be a better person.*
>
> *"And now that I remember—because they just asked me in the previous press conference what the owners asked me—one of the things they did ask me was about being a better person and being a better neighbor to people. And that's something that I think that I am now, much more so."*

An upset Chapman refused to speak to the media later that night following his Cubs debut–a perfect inning with two strike-outs against the White Sox–before deciding to acquiesce at the urging of catcher Miguel Montero. Meanwhile, the Cubs decided to hire a new translator. Joe Maddon defended his reliever when questioned by the Chicago media about the Cubs' controversial addition. "I know there's been some reticence or pushback regarding him to this point. However, understand where he's coming from right now. We don't know him. He doesn't know us. And he really doesn't even know the language."

Quotes from a Cubs pitcher made headlines again about a week later after the Cubs 5–4 walk-off win over the Marlins. This time it was of a more lighthearted nature. John Lackey uncorked what might have been the line of the year. "What are fair expectations?" Lackey said, repeating back part of a question at a postgame press conference after he had pitched. "We're trying to win the World Series. I didn't come here for a haircut. You know what I mean? We're trying to get it on. I came here for jewelry."

Another controversial situation involving a Cubs player occurred on July 29, when infielder Tommy La Stella was optioned to Class AAA Iowa as the Cubs had a numbers crunch with their major league roster. La Stella had minor league options left and that made him an easy target for a demotion, which would have been only for a few weeks as he would have been a lock to be recalled when major league rosters expanded on September 1.

However, the demotion upset La Stella and instead of reporting to the minor leagues, La Stella went back to his home in New Jersey. Cubs officials were rightly upset and had several conversations with their disgruntled player, but La Stella didn't budge for a few weeks. In mid-August he finally reported and was back in the big leagues in September. However, his actions probably cost him a postseason roster spot as La Stella was not a part of the Cubs playoff roster in any of the three rounds they played en route to a World Series title.

"He's not angry," Maddon said before a 5–1 victory over the Los Angeles Angels at Wrigley Field. "He's not upset. He's just at that point now where he doesn't know exactly what he wants to do.

"We all have a different lens for how we view the world. I know when I went through my Kurt Vonnegut stage, I was kind of screwed up when I was 21."

The Cubs front office may not have been as understanding as Joe Maddon, but they didn't react harshly and swiftly, choosing instead to stand behind their infielder. "I think 'disappointed' would be the wrong word," Jed Hoyer said. "Given how much we've talked to him, trying to understand where he's coming from, empathize with him, and give him the space."

La Stella was perhaps very lucky that he played for a manager in Joe Maddon who understood players who were free spirits. Maddon did all he could to support La Stella as he worked through his situation. "Tommy hears his own beat," Maddon said. "I love him for it. He's a very interesting young man, and he's also a very good baseball player. Hopefully, he's going to get back here relatively soon. Like I've said before, he could get up at three o'clock in the morning and hit a line drive on a 1-2 count. That's who he is. So I'd love to have him back."

"We were taken by surprise by his decision, and I think the initial, visceral reaction was to do something punitive, like a suspension or release or something like that," said Epstein, who eventually put La Stella on the temporary inactive list to preserve the minor league roster spot. "But we didn't act on our initial, visceral instinct and instead took time to talk to him and find out what was going on in his head.

"After having those conversations, while I felt like he wasn't handling it the way I would have liked and he may have been making a mistake, I felt like it was the type of mistake that we could work with him, to grow from. And it wasn't a mistake that we wanted to punish him for. We felt it was more misguided and not malevolent, so we wanted to work with him to get him back to this point. I'm glad we did."

La Stella understood that he was going to receive criticism for his decision to not report to the Cubs minor league affiliate but he did not seem affected by what other people thought of his decision. "I understand that there are going to be people out there that kind of draw conclusions and stuff. I'm not necessarily out here to make anybody see anything or explain anything," said La Stella, citing private reasons that he said are baseball related and involve no mental or physical personal problems. "There's not necessarily going to be a cut-and-dried, black-and-white answer," he said. "That answer doesn't really exist."

On September 15, the Cubs became the first team to clinch a division title when the Cardinals lost in San Francisco to reduce the Cubs magic number to zero. St. Louis' loss came late in the evening, long after the Cubs had lost at home to the Milwaukee Brewers. However, the next day on Friday afternoon, a Miguel Montero home run in the ninth inning gave the Cubs a walk-off win over Milwaukee and after the game, it was time to celebrate a division title in the Cubs' new clubhouse. The champagne and beer flowed late into the evening and the Cubs enjoyed the first step on a journey they hoped would involve three more celebrations and a World Series title.

The final two weeks of the regular season saw Joe Maddon rest his regulars as much as possible and he backed off on his pitching staff as well, not allowing his starters to pile up heavy pitch counts as he did his best to preserve their strength and stamina for the extremely draining postseason run that he hoped lay ahead for his team.

The regular season finally came to an end on October 3, and the Cubs ended it in dramatic fashion as they rallied for four runs in the ninth inning to beat the Reds 7–4 at The Great American Ballpark in Cincinnati. Matt Szczur's two-run single in the top of the ninth inning was the game-winning hit and Miguel Montero provided some insurance with a ninth-inning home run to give the Cubs their 103rd victory of the season.

The regular season was finally in the books and now it was time for the playoffs to begin. Nothing less than a championship would be acceptable to the 25 players in the clubhouse and Cubs ace Jon Lester made that clear to the media and the fan base. "This season isn't anything unless we do what we showed up at spring training to do—win a World Series. I don't want to sound like an asshole or anything, but we really haven't done anything yet."

Six days after Jon Lester made that statement, he took the ball and started Game 1 of the NLDS at Wrigley Field against the San Francisco Giants. The season that was a marathon had now turned into a sprint to be the first team to 11 wins and a World Series championship.

14

There Never Was a Curse

The 2016 National League Division Series between the Cubs and the San Francisco Giants began Friday night, October 7, at Wrigley Field in front of a capacity crowd of more than 42,000 fans. The Giants were looking to continue their pattern of World Series championships in even-numbered years (they won in 2010, 2012, and 2014). Wrigleyville was electric from early in the morning as the city of Chicago buzzed with anticipation for what they hoped was the first step of a journey that would finally end the longest championship drought in the history of American professional sports.

Game 1 was a classic pitcher's duel, pitting the starter for the National League in the All-Star Game, Giants star Johnny Cueto, against Cubs star Jon Lester. The game was a scoreless battle featuring outstanding starting pitching into the eighth, until Javier Baez cracked a solo home run in the bottom of the inning to give the Cubs a 1–0 lead. In came Cubs closer Aroldis Chapman to try to close out the victory. He handled the Giants, tossing a scoreless top of the ninth to save the win for Jon Lester and put the Cubs in front in the series 1–0.

Game 2 was a battle of the bullpens, with neither Kyle Hendricks nor former Cub Jeff Samardzija making it past the fourth inning. The Cubs won the game 5–2, with three of those runs driven in by pitchers, including a two-run single by Hendricks and a solo home run by winning pitcher Travis Wood. It was the first postseason home run by a relief pitcher in Major League Baseball since 1924.

Game 3 was supposed to be another marquee pitching matchup, with Jake Arrieta opposing Madison Bumgarner, though it didn't play out that way. Arrieta connected for a three-run home run off the Giants lefty in the second inning, and the Cubs held a 3–2 lead until the bullpen gave up three runs in the eighth. After Travis Wood allowed a leadoff single and Hector Rondon walked a batter, Aroldis Chapman entered the game and struck out Hunter Pence. But he couldn't keep the inherited runners from scoring as Conor Gillaspie tripled and Brandon Crawford singled (both lefties) and the Cubs entered the ninth down 5–3. Kris Bryant hit a two-run homer to tie the game at five, and that's where the game stood until the 13th inning, when Mike Montgomery, in his fifth inning of work, allowed consecutive doubles to give the Giants a 6–5 win.

Giants starter Matt Moore was dominant in Game 4, throwing eight innings of two-hit, two-run (one earned) baseball, while Cubs starter John Lackey was shaky, allowing three runs and lasting just four innings. San Francisco was in complete control and they were on the verge of tying the series at two wins apiece and forcing a winner-take-all Game 5 at Wrigley Field. Having to face Cueto with all of the pressure that a Game 5 would present at Wrigley Field was a scenario that concerned manager Joe Maddon greatly.

"Beating the Giants in Game 4 was crucial for us. Obviously we don't advance if we don't beat them in the series but not having to play Game 5 was big. Truthfully, I did not want to face Cueto back at Wrigley in Game 5. I thought that would have been a really tough get. So once we beat the Giants when we came back late was huge. Just the fact that we came back the way that we did, we came back on the road, we clinched it on the road and we avoided this pitcher, winning the World Series at that point became very believable to me," Maddon told me.

The Cubs faced a 5–2 deficit heading into the ninth inning, but when the players looked out to the mound they saw that Giants starter Matt Moore was done for the night. That decision became controversial for San Francisco manager Bruce Bochy, but with Moore at 120 pitches, Bochy felt he'd had enough. "I don't regret taking Matt out of the game. He had thrown enough pitches and our bullpen should have been able to protect the lead. Matt had gone through Tommy John surgery and I felt 120 pitches was more than enough work for him," Bochy told me.

However, the Cubs offense exploded for four runs and four hits against a quintet of Giants hurlers and took a 6–5 lead into the bottom of the ninth inning, a lead which Aroldis Chapman preserved with three straight strikeouts to end the game and the series. The Cubs were headed to the NLCS to face the Los Angeles Dodgers, who would finish off the Washington Nationals in their NLDS series a few days later.

The battle for the National League pennant began on October 15, when the NLCS opened at Wrigley Field. The pitching matchup favored the Cubs; by virtue of clinching the NLDS on October 11, Joe Maddon was able to set up his pitching rotation, and he tabbed Jon Lester to face Dodgers rookie Kenta Maeda. The Cubs jumped out to an early 3–0 lead on RBI doubles by Kris Bryant and Javy Baez, who also scored a run as he stole home, which was the first steal of home by a Cubs player in a postseason game since 1907.

An Andre Ethier home run closed the gap to 3–1 and the Cubs carried that lead into the eighth inning, when Aroldis Chapman entered the game with the bases loaded. Dodgers star Adrian Gonzalez, another lefty, cracked a two-run single off of Chapman to tie the game at three, stunning the Wrigley Field crowd, who were fully expecting Chapman to blow the Dodgers away with his 103 MPH fastball.

The Cubs loaded the bases, though, in the bottom of the eighth and Wrigley was alive again. With the stands in the old ballpark literally shaking, pinch-hitter Miguel Montero became the most unlikely of heroes as he clobbered a hanging slider on an 0-2 offering from Joe Blanton for the first ever postseason grand slam by a Cubs batter at Wrigley Field. The next batter, Dexter Fowler, then went back to back to make it 8–3 and put the game on ice. The final was 8–4, and the Cubs now had a 1–0 lead in the best-of-seven series.

Maddon had a quick hook in Game 1, pulling starter Jon Lester after just six innings and only 77 pitches with the Cubs leading 3–1. Lester had battled during his outing but he was not as sharp as he had been throughout his 19-win 2016 campaign. Still, the early removal annoyed Lester and led to some criticism about the decision from the Chicago media. Joe Maddon though, was convinced he made the right decision. "If Jon was on top of his game, I may not have done it," Maddon said. "But I didn't think he had his best stuff tonight."

After such a wild ending to the Cubs first NLCS game since 2003, Maddon laughed as he exited the postgame interview room, saying out loud to no one in particular, "Now that was some crazy shit."

The best pitcher in baseball, Dodgers ace Clayton Kershaw, was waiting for the Cubs in Game 2 and he was pitching for the fourth time in a 10-day span. Carrying a 4.59 career postseason

ERA into 2016, Kershaw, unfairly or not, wore the label of a postseason disappointment. But he was trying to spin a different narrative in 2016 and he was coming off perhaps the most critical postseason appearance of his career, a two-out save to close out the NLDS against the Nationals in Washington.

The Cubs started right-hander Kyle Hendricks, who pitched exceptionally well into the sixth inning, allowing just one run and three hits. The only mistake he made all night was an off-speed pitch in the second inning that stayed up on the outer half of the plate, and which Adrian Gonzalez smacked into the left-field bleachers. That would be the game's only run, and with Kershaw magnificent, tossing seven innings of shutout baseball and allowing just two hits, the Wrigley Field crowd was silenced throughout the evening. Dodgers closer Kenley Jansen shut the Cubs out over the final two innings and the series was knotted at one game apiece.

The Cubs offense fared no better in Game 3. With the series shifting to Los Angeles, former Cub Rich Hill was matched up against Jake Arrieta and Hill was outstanding, shutting out the Cubs over his six innings of work. He allowed just two hits and he was in complete control all evening long. Arrieta pitched five innings and allowed four runs on six hits and was not exceptionally sharp with his command. Three Dodgers relievers combined to shut the Cubs out over the final three innings and suddenly there was some concern among the Cubs' massive fan base.

Suffering two straight shutout losses and down two games to one in the series, things didn't look good. With two more games to go out West, the Cubs were staring at a potential clinching game for L.A. in Game 5 if they couldn't locate their missing offense in Game 4.

On Wednesday night, October 19, the fourth matchup of the series saw two struggling Cubs rise to the occasion offensively. In the 2016 postseason, entering Game 4, Anthony Rizzo and

Addison Russell had combined to go 3-for-50 with no HR and no RBI. I had a radio interview scheduled with Rizzo on the afternoon of Game 4. He contacted me and said simply, "I'll do the radio show if you need me to but tomorrow will be a better show. We are going to have a big game tonight and it will be a lot more fun to talk to you and your listeners after we win tonight."

We moved the show to Thursday afternoon and I sat back to watch an offensive explosion from the Cubs superstar first baseman. And what an explosion it was as Rizzo went 3-for-5 with 3 RBI and his first home run of the 2016 postseason. Addison Russell also snapped out of his postseason funk going 3-for-5 and cracked his first home run, a two-run shot in the fourth inning off of Dodgers rookie starter Julio Urias that gave the Cubs a 4–0 lead.

Starting pitcher John Lackey went just four innings as manager Joe Maddon continued his postseason trend of not staying with his starters long into several games, choosing instead to use a handful of relievers that he rode extremely hard en route to the World Series. In Game 4, a collection of five Cubs relievers combined to toss five innings of shutout baseball and sealed the deal on a 10–2 Cubs win.

"We know our offense is too good to keep down for a long time," Ben Zobrist said. "Hopefully, tonight is an indication of what's to come." Zobrist, who shifted from second base which was his position most of the regular season, to the outfield so that Javier Baez could start at second base, had two hits in the Game 4 blowout.

"This is a big win, for sure," Rizzo said. "To even up the series, we have a chance to take another one here [Thursday] and go home with a 3–2 lead. In a way, this is just one game and we know it's going to be a quick turnaround, but this was definitely a big game for us."

"What you've seen so far, it's been a pretty interesting series to this point," Cubs manager Joe Maddon said. "I did not expect it to be such a lopsided victory for us today. Although the Dodgers had theirs yesterday. Like I said, it's two out of three right now. We know it's at least going back home at some point. Tomorrow will be a pretty nice day to come out on top and going back home, having to win one of two. We've been pretty good at Wrigley all year."

Rizzo's breakout game was big for a Cubs offense that had gone 21 innings without scoring a run and while it was the All-Star first baseman who was swinging the big bat that fueled the Cubs offense, he was quick to give credit to one of his teammates for a strategic equipment change that coincided with his outburst. "I hit well with his bat, so he has hits in it," Rizzo said of Matt Szczur, who wasn't on the playoff roster but was traveling with the Cubs. "Same size, just different model and different name and it worked."

Game 5 is considered by many to be the key contest in any best-of-seven series and the Cubs looked at the third game in Los Angeles as no exception. They knew that with a win they would be heading home needing just one win out of the series final two games to advance to their first World Series in 71 years. However, a win for the Dodgers in Game 5 would mean they would be heading back to Chicago needing one win and they would have their ace, Clayton Kershaw waiting for the Cubs.

Continuing their offensive explosion which started in Game 4, the Cubs scored first, grabbing a 1–0 lead in the opening inning on an Anthony Rizzo double which drove in Dexter Fowler, who had singled. The Dodgers tied the game on an Adrian Gonzalez groundout in the bottom of the fourth inning and the game stayed tied until Addison Russell launched a two-run home run to put the Cubs on top to stay. A five-run eighth inning blew the game open and the Cubs cruised to an 8–4 win in a game that wasn't as close as the score indicated. The Cubs led 8–1 heading onto the bottom of the eighth, but reliever Pedro Strop allowed a single run and closer Aroldis Chapman, who hadn't seen work since Game 2, entered the game with a six-run lead and allowed a pair.

The Cubs boarded their team charter to head home, knowing they were one win away from a trip to the World Series. They also knew that the pressure to succeed at Wrigley Field would be unlike anything any of them had ever faced in a Cubs uniform or, for many of the Cubs, at any point in their professional career. "We've heard the history," center fielder Dexter Fowler said, "but at the same time we're trying to make history."

"The city of Chicago has got to be buzzing," manager Joe Maddon said. "We're not going to run away from anything. It's within our reach right now."

While the city was absolutely buzzing about the chance to win the National League pennant for the first time in 71 years and to have a chance to do it at Wrigley Field, another story grabbed some of the headlines. Prior to Game 6, a bit of Cubs news sent shockwaves through the fan base. Sahadev Sharma, a baseball beat writer for Chicago-based TheAthletic.com reported that Cubs slugger Kyle Schwarber, who had been ruled out for the season after his knee injury in April, was in fact in Arizona playing in the Arizona Fall League as a designated hitter with designs on being activated for the World Series. "It was a pleasant surprise," Theo Epstein said before Game 6. "We got news that was better than expected after he saw his orthopedist in Dallas on Monday."

The idea originated with Schwarber, who called Epstein immediately after receiving permission from his doctor, who said his injury was healing faster than expected. "He asked for a chance to do this," Epstein said. "With as hard as Kyle has worked and as much as this means to him—and potentially us—we wanted to give him that opportunity."

"I have full confidence in my knee," Schwarber said. "My knee doesn't bother me. It was my hands that hurt the worst. I've got about eight blisters on them. I guess I should have kept rubbing a bat or something."

"He's made it to a best-case scenario after six months," Epstein said. "We're not ruling anything in; we're not ruling anything out. We're not getting ahead of ourselves. We have a lot of work here before this becomes pertinent."

List of Cubs World Series Appearances

1906 vs White Sox—Lost in 6

1907 vs Tigers—Won in 5 (including a tie)

1908 vs Tigers—Won in 5

1910 vs Athletics—Lost in 5

1918 vs Red Sox—Lost in 6

1929 vs Athletics—Lost in 5

1932 vs Yankees—Lost in 4

1935 vs Tigers—Lost in 6

1938 vs Yankees—Lost in 4

1945 vs Tigers—Lost in 7

2016 vs Indians—Won in 7

As great as the Kyle Schwarber news was, this would potentially not be the biggest news of the day. That of course would be a trip to the World Series if the Cubs could beat the Dodgers to win the National League pennant for the first time since 1945. But, to do that, they would have to solve the best pitcher in the world in Clayton Kershaw.

No problem. The Cubs jumped on Kershaw immediately. Dexter Fowler's ground-rule double to lead off the bottom of the first inning was followed by a Kris Bryant RBI single. Two straight hits to begin the game after being held to two hits total in Game 2 against the Dodgers ace. The score was 2–0 after one inning, and that was all right-hander Kyle Hendricks needed, finishing the day allowing just two hits over 7.1 scoreless innings. Willson Contreras and Anthony Rizzo each homered off Kershaw to pad the lead and Wrigley was electric but nervous. They had been this close in 2003 and that ended in heartbreak. But this time it felt different. This team was different.

Epstein and Hoyer had put together a roster that could handle the intense pressure of not only postseason baseball but the added pressure that came with chasing a championship with the Chicago Cubs. The mixture of veterans who played liked kids and talented youngsters who played like seasoned veterans was the perfect blend of old and young, and the depth that Hoyer had preached about back in February and March was a huge key to this team.

They entered the ninth inning with a 5–0 lead and they had Aroldis Chapman on the mound. There was no way the Dodgers were coming back and a sense of inevitability started to sweep over the venerable old ballpark. Chapman faced Yasiel Puig with one out and a man on and a ground ball rolled towards Addison Russell at second base. Could he turn a double play with the fairly speedy Puig running hard out of the box?

He fielded it smoothly, flipped it to Javy Baez, whose relay throw beat Puig by an eyelash. For an instant, Wrigley was frozen. Had it really happened? Had the Chicago Cubs really clinched a spot in the World Series and won the National League pennant? Then the crowd exploded into deafening noise and feverish celebration. The 42,000 in the ballpark were a mixture of cheers and tears. Many in the crowd were weeping openly, with many holding signs that referenced departed loved ones who hadn't survived to witness this moment.

"There's a lot of pent-up angst and emotion in this city—and all over the nation—Cubs fans who have been loyal through the hard times," Ben Zobrist said. "We know that, but the bottom line is you have to execute at the right time and stay here in 2016. These guys have done it all year long with all the expectations on their backs. We only have four more, so let's go do it now. We're in the exact spot we wanted to be in. We've got a chance to do something that hasn't been done in 108 years. Let's go do it."

The Chicago Cubs were indeed going to the World Series where they would play the American League champions, the Cleveland Indians. There was time to process that later. Now it was time to celebrate—and celebrate the Cubs and their fan base did, late into the night.

A stage that had been constructed a few days earlier in preparation for whoever had clinched the pennant at Wrigley Field was quickly hustled into position behind second base. While the fans cheered wildly the Cubs accepted their National League championship trophy and Jon Lester and Javy Baez were named co-MVPs of the NLCS.

Then the team huddled on the mound for photos and hugs. The tears were still evident with thousands of fans still in their seats more than 45 minutes after the game had ended. No one wanted the moment to end. It had taken 71 years to accomplish this feat and everyone on the field and in the stands wanted to savor such a monumental accomplishment. Then the entire team together walked around the entire field to salute their fans. Reliever Carl Edwards Jr. ran around the outfield waving the W flag and several players sprayed champagne on the fans.

Joe Maddon climbed onto the stage as the trophy presentation was under way and coined a classic line, which was a play on his t-shirts, which were popular among the Cubs fan base: "Try Not To Suck" the shirts read. Speaking to a national TV audience and a fan base hanging on his every word he said, "My first thought is: We did not suck!"

"The thing I preach from [the first] day in spring training is I want us to play the same game regardless of the date on the calendar," Maddon said. "You should not change what you're doing regardless of the time of the year. You want to come out in October and play the same game you've been playing all summer."

Theo Epstein was mobbed by the media, who wanted his thoughts on the moment and what it said about the job his manager had done. "Unbelievable job by Joe ever since he got here. Changed the culture at the major league level. We loved everything that was bubbling up in the organization from the minor leagues, but to finish it off in the big league level, Joe is the best in the business in getting guys to relax, be themselves, focus. We embraced the target this year, his leadership has been everything for a lot of our young guys to settle in and play as well as they did tonight."

"Joe doesn't ever shy away from anything," said Ben Zobrist, who played for Maddon in Tampa Bay. "He's fearless. When it comes to the expectations that have happened for a long time, he told us at the start of the year, we're the best team and we'll have a lot of expectations, but we just need to play our game and we need to keep it simple, and do simple better, one of his other phrases. That's how we approached every game and focused on staying in the moment."

"We're living the dream," Anthony Rizzo said. "This is what you dream of as a kid. I know it's cliché, but we're going to the World Series. This is what you dream of, and we're going to enjoy it as much as we can."

"We're the best team in the National League, we showed that, we won the pennant," Cubs GM Jed Hoyer said. "It hasn't been done here in 71 years. You have to take a brief moment and reflect on that. We did do something special–we're going to the World Series. People are going to watch a World Series in Wrigley Field," he said.

"This is more special," Hoyer said, comparing the Cubs and Red Sox. "The hours from 7:00 PM to 10:00 PM were pretty tough for a bunch of years. To come in here and win and do this in Year Five with all these kids, it really is special. With anything in life, if something is difficult and you have some adversity, it's sweeter. We got swept last year in this round and I don't think anyone liked that taste in their mouth. To play like we did the last three games against the Dodgers was unbelievable."

Perhaps former Cubs pitcher Kerry Wood said it best when he surveyed the wild scene in the Cubs clubhouse and the pandemonium that was evident in and around Wrigley Field.

"I can't put this into words," said Wood, who missed out on his chance to pitch for the Cubs in a World Series in 2003 when his team blew a three games to one series lead and lost the final two games of the NLCS to the eventual champion Florida Marlins. "Now, they've set themselves in history, and they're going to be linked forever. It's epic. It's amazing. What this team has done, and what they've done for the city and for the organization, it's a mind-blowing experience," he told Bob Nightengale of *USA Today*. "These guys come out, unaffected by the history, and we're in a place we haven't been in a long time."

After a night of partying and a day of rest, it was time for the Cubs to turn the page on the celebrations still going on all over Chicago. They still had to win four more games to win the World Series and they would have to do without home-field advantage, despite winning eight more games than any other team in baseball.

The American League representative, the Cleveland Indians, hadn't won a World Series in 68 years and they would host Games 1, 2, 6, and 7, while the Cubs would host Games 3, 4, and 5 at Wrigley Field, because (recently changed) MLB rules awarded home-field advantage to the league that won the All-Star Game. That rule would play a key role because the Cubs would have the use of the designated hitter four times in a seven-game series instead of just three. And they had the perfect guy to fill that role. Kyle Schwarber was coming back, stunning all who had counted him out until the 2017 season opener.

"This past doctor's visit I had right before we went to L.A. for the [NLCS], he looked at my knee," Schwarber said. "He's like, 'Man, it's great. You're strong. I'm not going to hold you back from doing anything.' So then we went from there."

"I tell you what," right-hander Jake Arrieta said, "he's one of the hardest-working kids I've ever been around.... I saw him in and out of the gym three, four, five hours a day with our trainers, doing everything he physically could to get to this point."

The World Series began in Cleveland on Tuesday evening, October 25, and the pitching matchup was a dandy, with the Cubs starting Jon Lester and the Indians going with their ace, Corey Kluber. The Indians had defeated the Boston Red Sox and the Toronto Blue Jays on their way to the World Series, despite being plagued with several key injuries. Star outfielder Michael Brantley was limited to 11 games during the season and starting pitcher Carlos Carrasco was lost for the season with a broken hand suffered in September. Another key member of the starting rotation, Danny Salazar, had been sidelined with a forearm injury, but he was brought back for the World Series to pitch out of the bullpen, though with his effectiveness severely limited.

Despite those injuries, the Tribe still had a ton of talent and a pitching staff led by a former Cy Young Award winner in Kluber, who brought a 0.98 postseason ERA in three postseason starts and a reliever in Andrew Miller, who was not only excellent (no runs allowed in 11.2 IP over six appearances), but willing and able to pitch at any time in a game and for any length his manager needed him for.

Game 1 saw a very cool evening in Cleveland, but the scene at Progressive Field was electric. Thousands of fans, unable to

Players with 6-RBI Game in World Series

Player	Year (Game)	Age
Bobby Richardson	1960 (Game 3)	25 y, 50 d
Hideki Matsui	2009 (Game 6)	35 y, 145 d
Albert Pujols	2011 (Game 3)	31 y, 279 d
Addison Russell	2016 (Game 6)	22 y, 283 d

get tickets for the game, jammed the area around the ballpark; the atmosphere was phenomenal. Thousands of Cubs fans made the journey from Chicago and around the world to witness history in person. However, Game 1 did not go the Cubs way. Cleveland jumped on Jon Lester for two runs in the first on a Jose Ramirez bases-loaded single followed by a Brandon Guyer bases-loaded hit by pitch. Those two runs would be all they would need.

Kluber was sensational, throwing six innings of shutout baseball and allowing just four hits and no walks while striking out nine Cubs hitters. Miller and Indians closer Cody Allen finished up the final three innings and Cleveland grabbed a 1–0 series lead with a 6–0 victory.

It was Jake Arrieta against Trevor Bauer in Game 2 and much attention was given to Bauer's hand, which was injured prior to Game 2 of the ALCS when he had an accident attempting to fix a drone that he had as a toy. Bauer's start was pushed to Game 3 of the ALCS, but he couldn't make it out of the first inning due to excessive bleeding as the wound on his hand opened up.

However, Bauer was healthy and ready to go against the Cubs, who were looking to even the series at a game apiece before the journey home for three straight at Wrigley Field. Jake Arrieta stole the show, taking a no-hitter into the sixth inning before he departed after 5.2 innings of two-hit ball with one run allowed (on a wild pitch).

Offensively, the stars of Game 2 were Ben Zobrist and Kyle Schwarber, who both went 2-for-4, with the latter driving in a pair of runs. The Cubs dominated from the get go and beat the Indians 5–1 to even the series at a game apiece and they were headed back to Wrigley Field.

Game 3 was the scene of the first World Series game at Wrigley Field since 1945. Tens of thousands of fans descended on Wrigleyville starting in the early morning hours for an all-day celebration. Every bar surrounding the stadium was packed, with many demanding exorbitant cover charges to maximize their profits over the season's final three home games.

According to the weather reports the game was supposed to be a slugfest, with wind gusts approaching 40 MPH blowing out at game time. The Indians sent starter Josh Tomlin to the hill, who had an excellent postseason run, but he had still allowed 36 longballs in 174 innings during the regular season. It looked like a high-scoring affair was in store for the Cubs sluggers and with Kyle Hendricks on the mound it looked like the advantage was clearly in Chicago's corner.

Needless to say, the complete opposite of what was expected ended up happening. The Cubs' bats were frigid and mustered only five hits all game long, with only two against Tomlin. Not even actor Bill Murray's stirring rendition of "Take Me Out to the Ballgame"–as Daffy Duck–during the seventh-inning stretch could take the sting out of a 1–0 Indians victory which gave the a Tribe a 2–1 lead in the best-of-seven series.

The Cubs found themselves down three games to one in the series after a 7–2 clunker in Game 4. A run in the bottom of the first inning provided hope that the Cubs could finally solve Kluber but after that first-inning run, Cleveland scored seven straight runs off of John Lackey and four relievers before a late Dexter Fowler solo homer off Andrew Miller closed the gap to five runs. They would get no closer. Suddenly, the Cubs' backs were against the wall and they were one loss from elimination.

No team since the 1985 Royals had come back from a 3–1 deficit in the World Series. No team since the 1979 Pirates did so while winning Games 6 and 7 on the road. The deck was stacked against the Cubs. Their fan base was on the ledge and many believed the team was right there with them. However, inside the Cubs clubhouse there was no such panic.

They had their ace, Jon Lester, starting Game 5, and his outstanding 2016 season and his postseason track record that included two World Series titles while he was pitching for the Boston Red Sox calmed everyone's nerves. Plus, they had a very calm Anthony Rizzo playing the role of Rocky Balboa.

"Just pulled it all out," Rizzo said. "Got to put out the inspirational, underdog. We're saying we're going to battle, we've got to go the distance. There were some speeches in here, some motivational stuff. You've got to keep it loose."

Rizzo had all of the Cubs clubhouse televisions tuned to the movie *Rocky* and he jumped up and was, as veteran catcher David Ross said, "Running around, jumping around, half-naked, doing boxing moves." In fact, when Rizzo reached base he punched the air like a boxer, another nod to his Rocky-inspired theme of going the distance.

Jon Lester took the ball at Wrigley Field for Game 5. The Cubs scratched across three runs against Trevor Bauer in the fourth inning with a Kris Bryant home run, an Addison Russell RBI single, and a David Ross sacrifice fly. The game was 3–2 with one out in the seventh when Aroldis Chapman got the call. The flame-throwing lefty proceeded to shut the door for the final 2.2 innings in a signature performance. The Cubs were still alive. The series was returning to Cleveland with the Indians still in command, leading the best of seven three games to two.

With several thousand Cubs fans making the return trip back to Cleveland, the vibe in and around Progressive Field was tremendous. After freezing cold temperatures greeted the players in Games 1 and 2, the weather in Cleveland was magnificent with the game time temperature at 70 degrees. Game 6 pitted Josh Tomlin against Jake Arrieta and on this night Josh Tomlin's luck finally ran out. Some MLB analysts believed that Tomlin would struggle because of the appearance of Joe West as the home plate umpire. West was extremely strict with his strike zone and Tomlin was considered a nibbler who liked to live on the edge of the strike zone. That was exactly what happened as Tomlin was roughed up early, with the Cubs jumping on him in the top of the first inning.

The Cubs plated three in the first on a Kris Bryant solo home run and a two-run double by Addison Russell on a blooper to right-center field that the Cleveland outfield badly misplayed. And Russell was just getting warmed up. In the third inning, after a walk and two singles (which forced Josh Tomlin from the game), the 22-year-old shortstop stepped up to the plate against reliever Dan Otero and crushed a 2-0 offering over the fence for a grand slam which gave the Cubs a 7–0 lead.

Russell became the second youngest player in major league history (after Mickey Mantle) to hit a grand slam in the World Series. Jake Arrieta gave way to Mike Montgomery with two outs in the bottom of the sixth and the score 7–2. An inning later, Joe Maddon made the controversial decision to bring in Aroldis Chapman with a five-run lead. Chapman escaped the seventh and pitched a scoreless eighth before a Rizzo two-run home run made the score a comfortable 9–2. Yet, back came Chapman for the bottom of the ninth. Was Maddon running a risk by continuing to use Chapman? Would he be as effective if needed in Game 7? Chapman issued a leadoff walk and was replaced by Pedro Strop, and another run scored to make it 9–3, but questions remained regarding Maddon's usage of his star reliever.

After the game, Maddon defended his move: "It was just the middle of their batting order. There was just no other way to look at that and feel good, man," he said. "That could have been the ballgame right there.... I thought the game could have been lost right there if we did not take care of it properly."

Teams to Come Back From 3–1 World Series Deficits in 7-Game Series

2016 Cubs (vs Indians)
1985 Royals (vs Cardinals)
1979 Pirates (vs Orioles)
1968 Tigers (vs Cardinals)
1958 Yankees (vs Braves)
1925 Pirates (vs Senators)

Chapman backed his manager, telling the media through an interpreter, "I don't worry about a few extra pitches.... I have all the strength and mentality to pitch in this scenario. I'm ready for Game 7, 100 percent. It's the last game of the season. You cannot save anything. Time to leave it all on the field. I feel blessed that I'm just healthy to pitch in this situation. This is why the Cubs brought me over." What many observers don't know is that Maddon had met with Chapman before the game to map out his strategy.

In any event, the series was even at three games apiece, setting the stage for an epic Game 7. And the game would not disappoint. Television ratings were sky-high, tickets prices were in the thousands, and the highways between Chicago and Cleveland were jammed with cars filled with fans who wanted a chance to witness history, whether that was inside the stadium or in the plaza and the bars surrounding it. In fact, several rest stops in Indiana and Ohio reported running out of food in the middle of the day due to the large numbers of Cubs fans that were stopping on their way to Cleveland.

"I was sick to my stomach all day, just nervous," Ben Zobrist told MLB TV. "One team was going to go home with all the marbles and the other was going to go home shattered and broken and we knew that we could be either one."

Anthony Rizzo told MLB TV, "Every time I shut my eyes, just start thinking, *Wow, this is Game 7.* All of the possibilities of winning–but what if you lose? All of the self-doubt. There were a lot of emotions going into that game."

With the season on the line, Corey Kluber came back for his third start of the World Series, opposite Kyle Hendricks. This was also Kluber's third start in just eight days, and many wondered if he could again dominate the Cubs' powerful lineup. Dexter Fowler made history with the first leadoff home run in a Game 7 in World Series history, giving the Cubs an early 1–0 lead.

The Indians retaliated in the bottom of the third with an RBI single off the bat of Carlos Santana. But the Cubs added a pair in the top of the fourth on an Addison Russell sacrifice fly and a Willson Contreras RBI double, and to lead off the fifth, Javier Baez hit a solo HR to drive Kluber from the game. Even Andrew Miller couldn't put out the fire in the fifth before Rizzo knocked in a run. It was 5–1 Cubs heading into the Indians' half of the fifth. Kyle Hendricks got a quick two outs before walking Carlos Santana after a pitch that looked to be right down the middle was called a ball. Joe Maddon surprisingly popped out of the dugout and signaled for Jon Lester. This despite agreeing with Theo Epstein in a pregame meeting that Lester would only come into the game to start an inning, not with men on base.

David Ross couldn't corral a dribbler by Jason Kipnis, and an errant throw by Ross put Kipnis on second and Santana on third. Santana and Kipnis both then scored on a wild pitch which hit the dirt and bounced up to hit Ross on the mask and squirted away before he could corral it. Lester then settled down to get the third out but now it was 5–3 Cubs. David Ross, in his final career game, got one of those runs back when he homered off of the previously invincible Andrew Miller to make it 6–3 Cubs. Lester held the Tribe at bay for three innings before another early pull by Maddon in the bottom of the eighth. Lester, like Hendricks in the fifth, got the first two outs of the inning before allowing a baserunner (a Jose Ramirez single). Enter Aroldis Chapman.

The questions that had been debated all day long about Chapman's effectiveness after his lengthy outing in Game 6 were quickly answered. His fastball, usually in the 100–103 range, was in the 97–99 range and he started his night by throwing 18 consecutive fastballs, showing little confidence in his slider, which he had used during his time as a Cubs pitcher to keep hitters off balance. Brandon Guyer connected with Chapman's seventh fastball for a double, scoring Ramirez, which brought light-hitting Rajai Davis to the plate.

Davis battled Chapman for six pitches—ball, foul, foul, ball, foul, foul—before pitch number seven brought about the unthinkable. Choking up on his bat heavily, Davis drilled a line drive over the left-field wall to tie the game, sending Progressive Field into a frenzy. Chapman had only allowed two home runs all year—and they oddly enough had come back-to-back in a June game with the Yankees. Now was another home run—at the worst possible time. Chapman collected himself after a Coco Crisp single and struck out Yan Gomes. The game was suddenly tied at six, heading to the ninth and Cubs fans everywhere were in a state of shock.

"It looks like we're going to win the World Series and all of sudden, boom, it's tied in the eighth," David Ross said to MLB TV. "Oh God. And all I thought about was, *How are the fans?* And I thought, *They've got to be miserable right now.*"

"I'd be lying if I said I didn't think about the curse at that moment," Zobrist said.

Indians star Jason Kipnis told me, "As soon as he hit it we were thinking, *Holy crap, the curse is real. This is ours.* Why wouldn't we be thinking that? To not be optimistic at that point—Why wouldn't we think the momentum had come over to our side?"

The Cubs tried to rally in the top of the ninth and seemed poised to push a run across as David Ross coaxed a leadoff walk. Jason Heyward reached on a fielder's choice, and then stole second and took third on a bad throw with Javy Baez at the plate. With a full count, Baez attempted a bunt and fouled it off for a strikeout. The decision to ask Baez to bunt was a puzzling call by Joe Maddon and Baez was clearly upset. Was the pressure of the moment seizing the Cubs?

Dexter Fowler grounded one up the middle that looked like it might get through and drive in the go-ahead run but Indians shortstop Francisco Lindor made a sensational play to snare the ball and throw out Fowler to end the inning.

Kipnis nearly ended the game in the ninth with a walk-off home run but the ball ended up going foul down the right-field line. When the ball left the bat it appeared the Indians had just won the World Series and stunned the Cubs in the cruelest possible fashion. And many don't know that Kipnis grew up 200 yards from infamous Cubs fan Steve Bartman and he remembers walking by his house after Bartman's role in the Cubs collapse in the 2003 NLCS against the Florida Marlins.

"Kipnis would have gone down as the biggest villain in Chicago sports history and maybe the biggest villain in American sports history," CSN Chicago sportscaster and lifelong Cubs fan Luke Stuckmeyer said.

"It would have been a headline writer's dream for a local kid to win the World Series that way and my heart sank when it left the bat," Jed Hoyer said.

"I'd have loved every second of it," Kipnis told me. "That's not a bad thing. That doesn't make me a bad person. Maybe it would have made me a bad person to Cubs fans, but I'm an athlete going out there competing and doing my job. It would have been an amazing moment in sports history. I've watched the replay and I can see from the TV angle how people might have thought it was a home run but I knew as soon as I hit it that it was going to go foul. And by the way, I keep hearing that Chapman was gassed, but I don't feel too sorry for him. Your gassed closer was still throwing 99 miles an hour and he has one of the best pitches in the game."

The game was headed to extra innings.

Then came the rain. And a 17-minute delay.

With the Cubs reeling and the tarp on the field, right fielder Jason Heyward called a team meeting.

"Guys, weight room! Won't take long!" Heyward implored. "We're the best team in baseball, and we're the best team in baseball for a reason," Heyward said once the team had gathered. "Now we're going to show it. We play like the score is nothing-nothing. We've got to stay positive and fight for your brothers. Stick together and we're going to win this game."

There were players with tears in their eyes as Heyward spoke. "It was really emotional. Heyward spoke from the heart and he told us we won 103 games in the regular season because we were the best team in baseball and we had to come together and win this game," catcher Willson Contreras told me.

Closer Aroldis Chapman, who had surrendered the game-tying home run, was weeping. His teammates told him they had his back and that they would pick him up and win the game when play resumed. Rizzo left the meeting knowing he was about to be a world champion. "All game long I was burning nervous energy. I was a wreck. I thought about all the people in Chicago and how much this meant to them. But after we had that meeting, I knew we were going to win. It was only a matter of how and when. That rain delay was the most important thing to happen to the Chicago Cubs in the past 100 years. I don't think there's any way we win the game without it," said Anthony Rizzo.

When play resumed after the 17-minute delay, Kyle Schwarber got things started in the top of the 10th with a single off reliever Bryan Shaw. Albert Almora was then summoned as a pinch runner and he showed impressive baseball savvy, tagging up and advancing to second base on Kris Bryant's long flyout to the warning tack in center field. Rizzo was intentionally walked to set the stage for Ben Zobrist, who poked a double down the left-field line on a 1-2 pitch. Russell was then intentionally walked to bring up Miguel Montero, who promptly singled home Rizzo. Trevor Bauer was summoned from the bullpen, but it was too late.

The Cubs took an 8–6 lead into the bottom of the 10th, three outs away from a World Series title.

It wouldn't be easy. It never was. Carl Edwards Jr. got two quick outs, but a Brandon Guyer walk turned into a run when he advanced on defensive indifference and scored on a Rajai Davis single. In came Mike Montgomery to face Michael Martinez. Montgomery had warmed up four times in the game and was quietly hoping not to pitch in extra innings, fearing he had nothing left in his arm. Nonetheless, Joe Maddon summoned him to close out the game and give the Cubs their first World Series title in 108 years.

Montgomery battled and spun a curveball with the count on Martinez 0-1. Martinez hit a roller toward Kris Bryant at third. Fox play-by-play man Joe Buck called it a tough play on the broadcast but Bryant, with a huge grin on his face, fielded the ball cleanly and, despite slipping on the wet grass, he fired the ball to Rizzo at first. Martinez was out and the game was finally over.

The Chicago Cubs were world champions at last.

15

Celebration Time in Chicago

"I said before the Series that a sweep wouldn't do it," Cubs chairman Tom Ricketts told me after the Game 7 victory. "It would have to be something epic. And that was epic, wasn't it?"

"Nothing's been easy, nothing's been given to us," Jon Lester said. "Every series has been a battle and been a grind for us. We played three really good opponents to get here, and here we stand. It's an unbelievable feeling to be a part of this. You wouldn't expect it any other way."

Cubs GM Jed Hoyer was emotionally drained after the game and as he reflected on the dramatic victory, he said that he knew that the 17-minute rain delay was crucial to helping his team steady themselves after the Indians had tied the game at six.

"I think the rain delay was the best thing that ever happened to us, to be honest," Hoyer said. "Theo and I saw all the hitters were huddled in the weight room during the delay and kind of getting pumped up. I felt great and thought, 'We're going to win this inning and we're world champions.' Maybe after 108 years, you get some divine intervention?

"Theo and I were laughing about that–it had to be super hard," Hoyer said of winning the Series. "We're down three games to one, we have a big lead in the game, 6–3. You don't feel good, but things were lined up pretty well for us. It was a roller coaster. We'll be talking about that game for decades. It was incredible."

After seeing the impact that a World Series title had on the fans in Boston when the Curse of the Bambino was finally erased, Hoyer knew immediately what the Game 7 victory would mean to the Cubs' title-starved fan base.

"I know so many people who are thinking of their grandfathers and fathers now in Chicago and that's what it's all about. It's bigger than these 25 guys, it's bigger than this organization. It's about this city and the fans who have stuck by this team forever. I'm sure there will be a lot of people visiting their departed loved ones in cemeteries over the next several days," he said.

While the fan base dealt with the ups and downs of the thrilling playoff run, their emotions had been tested at both ends of the spectrum. From the highs of the wins and the lows of the defeats, the Cubs fan base had felt the stress of the past month. But the players said they paid little attention to the past 108 years and the pressure that was evident throughout the city of Chicago.

"I don't think they know about the history, they know to go out there and play baseball," David Ross said. "They know they're really, really good. You have a lot of successful, young talented players who have been successful their whole careers, and they expect to succeed. There's not a whole lot of guys talking about what's happened in the past. They're looking to the future, and the future is bright for that group."

From veterans like Ross, Jon Lester, and John Lackey, who had all tasted World Series success, to the youngsters who were the backbone of the Cubs bright future, they all focused on the day-to-day process that got them to the brink of a title.

"There was no weight on our shoulders," shortstop Addison Russell said. "It's either we do it or we don't. We go out there and compete and try our best. If we don't, we'll feel really bad, but we gave it all we had.... This is in the history books, we made our mark.

"It's such a young core," he added, "and we're just getting started."

With the title now secure and the pressure-packed run through the playoffs finally over, Jed Hoyer had a message for this massive fan base who had seen so much heartbreak and losing for so many years.

"Enjoy it. Just enjoy it," Hoyer said. "There's no curses—there never was a curse. It's about having the best team and playing well over seven games in a World Series, and we did that. Enjoy it. The Cubs are no different than any other team. When we're the best team, we can win, and we were the best team."

The World Series parade was Friday, November 4, and it was everything everyone believed it would be whenever the Cubs won the World Series, but it was also so much more. The parade route began outside Wrigley Field, eventually working its way from Wrigleyville to Grant Park.

Jon Lester was a hit and a must-follow on Twitter as he live-tweeted the event. Some highlights:

These buses are too high up! We almost got taken out by the power lines! Lost my hat! Haha

Lotta love for everyone's favorite grandpa out here!

Woody is rocking a sleeveless cammo vest. What a maniac!

They keep yelling at us to sit down! Rossy almost got decapitated!

GRANT PARK!! Just a sea of the best people in the world!!! #FlyTheW

When the Cubs finally arrived at Grant Park, Cubs radio play-by-play man Pat Hughes emceed the event, introducing all the staff and players. The Grant Park crowd went wild as each name was called.

When Cubs chairman Tom Ricketts got up to speak he received a thunderous ovation. It was a long way from the days just a few years earlier when people were questioning his ability to run a baseball team. Or when they questioned whether or not he and his family were too cheap to spend the money it would take to put a championship team on the field.

"You know, I've said it for seven years, I have the most unique job in the world. Because almost every single day, a complete stranger comes up to me and they always say the same thing. They say, 'Mr. Ricketts, I'm 71 years old, please win the World Series before I die.' Now I normally say something like ,'Okay, eat right, take care of yourself, exercise, how much time do I have?' Well, for the thousands of people who have said that to me, and are still with us, there you go."

With the crowd roaring their approval throughout his speech, Ricketts beamed as he spoke about his world championship team. Then he ended with this:

"So, I'm gonna finish with a trivia question, and just yell out the answer if you know it. How long has it been since the Cubs have won the World Series?

"The answer is *ZERO* years since the Cubs won the World Series! Thank you."[1]

With signs throughout the crowd that said "Theo for President" or "Theo for Mayor," the loudest cheers were saved perhaps for the architect of the Cubs miraculous turnaround. Team President Theo Epstein acknowledged the patience of the Cubs' fan base.

"One hundred and eight years. Ridiculous. A hundred and eight years of support, patience, love for this team, waiting for what happened two nights ago in Cleveland. I've been here for five years in particular, and we've asked a lot of you. We've put you through a lot over the last five years. A hundred and one losses. Traded players you've come to know and love for guys you never heard of. Trading 40 percent of the rotation three years in a row, asking you guys to follow the draft, follow the minor leagues. Let's be honest, for a while there we forgot the 'not' in 'try not to suck.' But you stayed with us...."

Then it was time to introduce the manager. In 108 years, 49 full-time managers and a handful of others on an interim basis had tried to win a World Series managing the Chicago Cubs. Only Joe Maddon was able to turn the trick. His speech started with a nod to his age and his love of old-time rock 'n' roll. "Welcome to Cubstock 2016. Look at this thing!"

The first curse word of the afternoon belonged to Jon Lester, who kept it short and sweet. "How about this shit? Sorry, kids... Really, the only thing I wanna say is one more time for David Ross. I love you, buddy. Woody, keep your shirt on. Thank you."

Miguel Montero, who had first coined the term "We Are Good" at the start of the 2015 season, stepped up to the microphone briefly. "We are good, boys!" as the crowd roared its

1. For Tom Ricketts' letter to all Cubs fans following the season, World series, and parade, please see Appendix V.

approval with many waving signs that said #WeAreGood or wearing t-shirts with the popular hashtag.

Then Anthony Rizzo, one of only two players left from the 2012 team that had lost 101 games, stepped up and exclaimed, "It happened, baby. It happened."

He then gave a heartfelt speech, being overcome with emotion when he honored his friend and mentor David Ross, who he called up to the podium. "Chicagooooo," Ross bellowed. "Look what the boys got me [holding up the World Series trophy]!" And he finished with a selfie on stage with the team and the hundreds of thousands at the rally in the background.

Then Anthony Rizzo came back to the microphone and surprised the crowd by presenting Tom Ricketts with the ball from the final out of the World Series. "Someone told me this ball is worth $3 million. Well, there is no one else more deserving of this ball than our owner, Mr. Tom Ricketts," Rizzo said as the crowd roared its approval.

To conclude the festivities, David Ross came back to the podium and introduced country music star Brett Eldredge, who led the crowd in a rousing rendition of the Cubs victory song, "Go Cubs Go."

The turnout to celebrate the 2016 World Series champions was huge. Bigger than most anyone believed was possible when a Cubs World Series title was just a dream. The city of Chicago estimated that 5 million fans were in attendance along the parade route and at the rally in Grant Park. It is believed to be the seventh largest gathering of people in human history.

1. Kumbh Mela pilgrimage, India, 2013 (30 million)
2. Arba'een festival, Iraq, 2014 (17 million)
3. Funeral of C.N. Annadurai, India, 1969 (15 million)
4. Funeral of Ayatollah Khomeini, Iran, 1989 (10 million)

5. Pope Francis in the Philippines, 2015 (6 million)
6. World Youth Day, 1995 (5 million)
7. Cubs World Series parade (5 million)
8. Funeral of Gamal Abdel Nasser, 1970 (5 million)
9. Rod Stewart concert, Brazil, 1994 (3.5 million)
10. Hajj pilgrimage, Mecca, Saudi Arabia, 2012 (3 million)

Whether or not you believe that figure, it was indeed an unbelievable turnout. There were incredible numbers of people from the start of the parade early in the morning outside Wrigley Field, along the parade route, and ending up at Grant Park. "Way more people are here than I ever could've imagined," said Kyle Hendricks "This is wild–we want to do it again and again."

With a World Series title belonging to the Cubs after a 108-year wait, Theo Epstein finally realized that he belonged. That making the move from the Red Sox to the Cubs was the right thing for him and his family. Yes, he had been a die-hard Boston Red Sox fan, and yes, he had won and won big there. But the run in Boston had ended badly, with strained relationships with his bosses and a collapse by his 2011 Red Sox team and that affected him deeply.

Chicago had presented Epstein a chance to cleanse himself of the final tough days of his Red Sox regime and now, with millions of fans ecstatic over the Cubs championship, Epstein realized how the moment the ball settled into Anthony Rizzo's glove for the final out of Game 7 had changed his life and his perspective forever.

"I just feel completely at peace with my decision to come here now, like it was meant to be and absolutely the right thing for me to do. There was more to it than simply switching employers. I had to leave my hometown team. I had to uproot my family. I had to commute between Boston and Chicago for the first nine

Roundup of Cubs 2016 Awards

NL Gold Glove: Anthony Rizzo (1B), Jason Heyward (RF)

Wilson Defensive Player of the Year: Anthony Rizzo (1B)

NL Platinum Glove: Anthony Rizzo (1B)

NL Silver Slugger: Anthony Rizzo (1B), Jake Arrieta (P)

NL MVP: Kris Bryant

NL Hank Aaron Award: Kris Bryant

NLCS MVP: Javier Baez & Jon Lester

World Series MVP: Ben Zobrist

months. I put my professional reputation on the line to an extent. And, on the flip side, I was being entrusted with the future of this franchise and wanted desperately to reward Tom and the fans for putting faith in me.

"Baseball, like life, can be really arbitrary. You can do a good job with a good process and not get the results. You can be the best team and not win. You can make the playoffs year after year but never win a ring. I had already developed a real kinship with and appreciation for Cubs fans. It took a few years, but I was hooked. That last out made everything fall perfectly into line. I knew why I had come here, knew all the sacrifices were worth it, knew why I had felt so connected to Cubs fans, knew how much it meant to them, and knew how much it meant to me. It was a feeling of tremendous joy, unmatched relief, and of, I guess, belonging," he told me.

The Chicago Cubs had accomplished something many fans believed they would never see in their lifetime. It brought unbridled happiness and for many, tears of joy. Their dream of seeing their beloved Cubs on top of the baseball world was finally a reality.

Why did it take so long to become a World Series winner? Before Tom Ricketts and his family bought the franchise, no one had the willingness or the foresight to put a plan in place to build a team from the ground up and to stay loyal to that plan until it succeeded. Now you know how it happened, but for loyal Cubs fans across the world they also know how much this title meant to the fan base. They know because they lived their lives waiting and dreaming of this moment. It is a reality, and as Jed Hoyer said, it's time to enjoy it, Cubs fans. You finally are World Series champions.

AFTERWORD

The Inside Story of What Went Wrong After 2016

"I can't even put it into words... it's unbelievable. We're in the books. We're in history forever. This team is brothers forever no matter what."

—Anthony Rizzo, on the field in Cleveland
just minutes after catching a throw from Kris Bryant
to clinch the Cubs 2016 World Series championship.

So, after winning 103 games and finally capturing a World Series title after a 108-year drought, we're all left wondering why the Cubs didn't achieve more postseason success after 2016 ended in such glorious fashion.

There are so many layers to unpack as we ponder that question. First, with the extremely young roster that the Cubs had after beating the Cleveland Indians in one of the greatest Game 7s in baseball history, their success was something that many assumed would continue for the foreseeable future.

But after winning the World Series the Cubs stumbled in a number of key areas. Management made critical mistakes that short-circuited the team's chances to build a long-term championship contender. While the players that were the core pieces of the 2016 team severely underperformed, especially offensively, after dominating in both 2015 and 2016.

Just three years after winning it all on that magical night in Cleveland, Ohio, the Cubs parted ways with Joe Maddon, the manager who led the way to the title and looked to be the answer in the dugout for as long as he wanted to be there.

Maddon's looser management style irritated the Cubs star-studded front office, and when his original five-year contract was up after the 2019 season, the two sides agreed it would be best to part ways. The Cubs needed a shot of discipline and Maddon needed a new challenge, one where his skill set would be more appreciated than it was his last couple of seasons in Chicago.

The front office also made its share of critical mistakes, some of which were such major errors that they would hamstring the club for several years going forward. From a lack of production from the Cubs' farm system beyond the handful of homegrown players that were key parts of the World Series team to a devastating inability to develop any solid major league pitching, the Cubs were forced to try to stay on top through free agent spending and major trades.

Add in the decision to cut ties with center fielder and leadoff man Dexter Fowler, who parlayed his outstanding 2016 season into an $82.5-million deal with the St. Louis Cardinals, and the Cubs feared lineup suddenly struggled to score runs on a consistent basis.

So where did it all go wrong? Why did the Cubs achieve only moderate levels of success after 2016? Why were they unable to reach baseball's mountaintop again?

"If you look at the five-year rebuild, it was just about perfect. It was probably one of the best in history, if not the best," Theo Epstein said. "And why? It wasn't because it was a grand strategy or a new paradigm of how to run a baseball operation. It was because we performed at an extraordinarily high level. We hit on an incredible number of deals and got impact players back in deals where we shouldn't have.... And we haven't performed at that level since then."

To answer the multitude of questions surrounding the franchise's failure to develop the dynasty that so many were predicting, let's start with the off-season following the 2016 title. The Cubs knew that defending their title would be difficult enough, as no one had repeated as World Series champions since the New York Yankees in 1998, '99, and 2000. Add in the 108-year drought between championships and the attention that the Cubs garnered was unprecedented.

After winning their title in such dramatic fashion, it seemed that everyone wanted a piece of the Cubs. From a *Saturday Night Live* appearance to commercial endorsements for almost everyone on the roster, the Chicago Cubs were cashing in on the next-level celebrity that their championship provided. And who could blame them?

However, there was a downside to all of the attention. It clouded the judgement of some of the team's biggest stars, as nearly every one of them rejected an opportunity to sign long-term, big-money contract extensions. Instead, players like Kris Bryant, Javy Baez, Willson Contreras, Kyle Schwarber, and former Cub Addison Russell all said "no thank you" and elected to go year to year on one-year deals.

Had the front office done a better job hitting on trades and signings post 2016, and if the same players had performed better offensively, perhaps the players who turned down extensions would have gotten paid because their value would have skyrocketed with multiple World Series titles on their résumés.

Only star pitcher Kyle Hendricks saw the value of getting guaranteed money to play in a city he truly loves, and he signed a $55-million deal that will keep him in Chicago through at least the 2023 season.

While the Cubs front office preferred to keep all negotiations in house, privately their frustration at seeing many of their young stars say no to big-money offers was evident. In fact, former Cubs president of baseball operations Theo Epstein said this on my radio show when I asked him a direct question about not getting his young stars signed to long-term deals.

"We made long-term, big-dollar extension offers to all of our core guys and other than Hendricks everyone said 'no thank you.' That is their right. We can't force someone to sign a contract extension."

So while the "other" team in Chicago, the White Sox, were able to sign long-term extensions with many of their young up-and-coming stars, such as Tim Anderson, Eloy Jimenez, Luis Robert, Yoan Moncada, and Aaron Bummer, the Cubs were not.

One rival executive said to me after it became apparent that the Cubs young stars would not sign long-term contract extensions, "the Cubs youngsters were feeling the power of being on one of the youngest championship rosters in baseball history. 'We are the Cubs. We will win again, and the money will just keep going up. Why should we settle for less money now? We don't need the security.'"

That cast doubt on the long-term future of the roster and that, combined with serious offensive struggles, hamstrung the franchise going forward.

"If you look at my track record in Boston and then here, in the first six years or so we did some pretty epic things, and then the last couple years weren't as impressive. Maybe what that tells me is I think I'm great at and really enjoy building and transformation and triumphing. Maybe I'm not as good and not as motivated at maintenance, so to speak," Epstein said.

So, let's look at the moves and decisions that were made after the 2016 season and how they worked out for the Cubs moving forward.

2017

The starting pitching staff that combined to win 81 games in 2016 won just 48 in 2017 and appeared fatigued throughout the season. The Cubs found themselves 5½ games behind the division-leading

Brewers at the All-Star break, forcing Epstein to consider trading what he called short-term assets to make changes to his roster.

However, after trading his two best prospects (Eloy Jimenez and Dylan Cease) to the White Sox to acquire veteran left-handed starter Jose Quintana, the Cubs erased the deficit and took control of the NL Central. They would go on to win 92 games and, after defeating the Washington Nationals in five games in the Division Series, the Cubs found themselves back in the NLCS for the third consecutive season.

However, after going 0–14 with runners in scoring position in the series, the Cubs were steamrollered by the Los Angeles Dodgers, four games to one, and the dream of repeating as World Series champions was dead.

A look back at the 2017 team shows a club that had a gaping hole in the leadoff spot after the departure of Fowler to free agency. While the decision to not pay Fowler $82.5 million was the right one, the mistake was not replacing his productivity at the top of the lineup. In fact, the lack of a leadoff hitter was something the Cubs would never quite answer for the rest of Epstein's tenure on the north side of Chicago.

Instead, manager Joe Maddon installed Kyle Schwarber in the leadoff role, and he struggled mightily. He had spent the off-season continuing to rehab from the knee injury that had sidelined him for almost all of the 2016 season, before his surprising return in the World Series.

But while he was rehabbing, it prevented him from truly preparing for the leadoff spot, and in late June he was sent back to the minor leagues to work on his hitting. In fact, while his power returned, Schwarber would never again be the hitter the Cubs thought they had drafted when he was chosen fourth overall in the 2014 draft.

Between the overall struggles of the pitching staff—including off-season acquisition Brett Anderson, who made only six starts and developed a rift with the front office—and the decline of aging starter John Lackey, the Cubs once dominant rotation was a long way from where it was in 2016.

Plus, the Cubs made a deal with the Kansas City Royals in which they traded outfield prospect Jorge Soler, who had played briefly in the big leagues and had shown flashes of stardom. Soler had four years of club control left and projected as a potential All-Star.

In return, the Cubs received standout closer Wade Davis, who had just one year left on his contract before free agency. Davis had a solid season for the Cubs and then departed for a multiyear deal with the Colorado Rockies. Soler, after struggling early in his time with the Royals, broke out in 2019, when he smashed 48 home runs and drove in 117 runs.

Was it a trade that the Cubs regretted making when Davis left Chicago after just one season? No, because Soler was blocked by several players in the Cubs outfield and more importantly, he projected as a DH and not as an everyday outfielder.

Davis gave the Cubs exactly what they were looking for as he was a hard-throwing closer who filled the role that Aroldis Chapman held in 2016 after coming over from the New York Yankees. And, for a team trying to win back-to-back World Series, Davis was exactly what the Cubs needed.

After considering a trade with Detroit for future–Hall of Famer Justin Verlander, Epstein and GM Jed Hoyer decided his injury concerns and hefty contract were too risky and they pulled the trigger on the Quintana deal.

That decision would turn out to be one of the worst post–World Series moves for the Cubs' star-studded front office. Verlander, after waiting on the Cubs' decision almost up until the July 31st trade deadline, finally got the message that the Cubs weren't interested and approved a trade to the Houston Astros.

He would go on to be part of a World Series champion in 2017, when he went 5–0 after the trade, and he would also win the 2019 Cy Young Award, when he compiled a 21–6 record. Since arriving in Houston, Verlander has put up a 43–15 record with a second-place finish in the Cy Young voting in 2018 as well as his first-place finish in 2019.

Not only did the Cubs make the wrong decision on the Verlander trade opportunity, but they also used the very best prospects in their farm system to acquire a very average starter in Quintana, who never achieved the results that the Cubs envisioned for him when they traded away two tremendous prospects in Jimenez and Cease. Those two would go on to play roles in the White Sox franchise resurgence and playoff appearance in 2020.

Believing in their core of young talent and confident in their ability to rebound, the Cubs front office chose to make only cosmetic changes to the offensive part of the roster. They did shake up their coaching staff though, firing both pitching coach Chris Bosio and hitting coach John Mallee and replacing them with veterans Jim Hickey and Chili Davis.

Davis was a longtime major leaguer, and his philosophy was old school. It would not be well-received by the Cubs players. Hickey had been manager Joe Maddon's longtime pitching coach and confidante in Tampa Bay, and he jumped at the chance to reunite with his friend on the Cubs staff. However, he had some personal issues that circumvented his ability to help the Cubs pitching staff. He left the organization less than a year after he was hired.

2018

After writing off the 2017 playoff elimination to the hangover of winning the World Series, the Cubs believed they would return to their winning ways and playoff success when the 2018 season began.

Epstein and Hoyer spent the off-season acquiring more pitching again, by spending huge sums of money to augment a rotation that still had not one homegrown pitcher in it. After signing Tyler Chatwood early in free agency for $38 million, the Cubs added closer Brandon Morrow for another $21 million, veteran reliever Steve Cishek signed for another $13 million, and the Cubs finished their off-season spending spree when they inked Yu Darvish to a six-year, $126-million deal.

The Darvish deal looked on paper to be a huge win for the Cubs. He was coveted by many contenders and chose the Cubs because he believed they were ready to win another World Series.

By signing Darvish, the Cubs also said goodbye to World Series hero Jake Arrieta, who eventually signed with the Philadelphia Phillies. Arrieta struggled to stay healthy with the Phillies and the club declined to pick up his option after the conclusion of the 2020 season. He underwent arm surgery in 2019 and battled a hamstring injury that ended his season prematurely in 2020. He is currently a free agent and is throwing for interested teams, including the Cubs, who are (as of January 2021) in dire need of starting pitching.

But, while Arrieta struggled, so did Darvish. He never felt right in spring training and eventually he was forced to undergo elbow surgery in May of 2018, ending his season and leading many to call the signing a bust. He did return and had a solid second half of the 2019 season and he finished second in Cy Young voting in 2020.

However, the Cubs did nothing to improve their struggling offense or address the leadoff spot, which was still a major problem. Ian Happ was next up at the top of the Cubs lineup and after he homered on the first pitch of the 2018 season, many around the Cubs believed they had solved the lineup's biggest weakness.

But that optimism was short-lived. Happ struggled mightily and lost his starting job a month later. In fact, he would end up back in the minor leagues to begin the 2019 season, before finally cementing a spot on the roster in 2020.

And after trading away so much of their once-vaunted farm system, they did not have much left to include in any in-season trade talks. But, with Chatwood struggling to find the strike zone and Darvish out after arm surgery, Epstein and Hoyer had no choice but to swing a trade with the Texas Rangers for veteran pitcher Cole Hamels. Hamels had a great relationship with Rangers GM Jon Daniels, and he made it clear that the Cubs were the only place he wanted to be traded. Daniels acquiesced and made the deal easy for Chicago to complete. Hamels pitched well in a Cubs uniform and helped the team stay in the race by going 4–3 with a sparkling 2.36 ERA as the Cubs tied for the NL Central title.

The 2018 season saw the Cubs win 95 games, but they finished the 162-game regular season tied atop the NL Central with the Milwaukee Brewers and were forced to play a one-game playoff at Wrigley Field.

The Brewers won that game 3–1, which forced the Cubs to play the Colorado Rockies in the Wild Card Game the very next night, also at Wrigley Field. Again, the Cubs came up short, scoring just one run in a 2–1, 13-inning loss, and the once-promising season was over just one game into the postseason.

Epstein addressed the media after the season, and he did not mince words when he said that the Cubs offense was broken. He also said changes could be in the offing to jumpstart his struggling club. He was right when he said the offense was broken but again the front office did virtually nothing to improve the roster. Instead, they chose to have faith in their core of talent and the only changes they made were to the coaching staff.

Davis was out as hitting coach and had this to say after he was fired. "I guess I need to make some adjustments in the way I deliver my message to the millennial players now. I need to make those adjustments for the next job I get, if there is one. I hope the next guy connects better with the players, because I felt that there were multiple players there I didn't connect with. It wasn't that I didn't try. It just wasn't there," he told Gordon Wittenmyer of the *Chicago Sun-Times*.

With Davis and pitching coach Jim Hickey both out, it meant the Cubs were changing their most important coaches for the second consecutive off-season. Hardly the type of stability that a championship-contending team strives for as they try to win another World Series.

2019

With the Cubs top players seeing their window of contention closing after the 2021 season, spring training opened with an air of change which was evident even if the roster did not show much in the way of movement. The core of Anthony Rizzo, Kris Bryant, Willson Contreras, and Kyle Schwarber were all still on the roster and manager Joe Maddon was still at the helm.

However, after seeing both 2017 and 2018 end short of the World Series, the Cubs front office demanded change from their championship-winning manager. Epstein and Hoyer asked Joe Maddon to cut down on his twice-daily media briefings and to be more hands on with the day-to-day teaching they wanted from the coaching staff.

"It was plenty," Maddon told ESPN. "Philosophically, Theo needed to do what he needed to do separately. At some point I began to interfere with his train of thought a little bit. And it's not that I'm hardheaded. I'm inclusive. But when I started there–'15, '16, '17–it was pretty much my methods. And then all of a sudden, after '18 going into '19, they wanted to change everything."

So with this backdrop of change and uncertainty, the curtain rose on the 2019 season, with many around the game doubting the Cubs ability to reach the top of the mountain as they were constructed.

Especially considering that no drastic moves were made to improve the offense which had struggled for the better part of the past two seasons. The farm system had nothing in it to impact the roster and the pitching staff was starting to show signs of age. The bullpen wasn't nearly as dominant as it had been, and the closer's role was in flux after the signing of Brandon Morrow proved to be a major flop.

The Cubs struggled throughout the season to score runs consistently and while they were still a talented roster, they were nowhere near the dynasty that so many had predicted.

As the season unfolded, it became obvious that the once-anticipated run to multiple championships was a pipedream. Maddon would be gone as soon as the season ended, no matter what the outcome was.

The end was coming quickly, like an oncoming train shining its light as it approached the station and there was not much anyone could do about it. Not even a deadline deal for a star hitter could reverse the struggles of the rest of the roster.

The front office tried mightily though, getting approval from ownership to add the salary of Detroit Tigers star Nicholas Castellanos, who provided a jolt of adrenaline into the lineup and perhaps more importantly, the clubhouse.

In fact, his infectious attitude was noticed by many around the team, including his new manager. "He's reminding us what hunger looks like. This guy, he's really happy to be here and play in this ballpark and he wants to get to the postseason badly. I love what he's doing. Every day, conversationally, his work–everything about him indicates, 'Let's go, I want to play in October!' And I love it," Maddon told NBC Sports Chicago.

But, despite a sensational run with the Cubs, Castellanos' heroics were not enough, as the team limped to the finish line with an 84–78 record and missed the playoffs for the first time in five seasons.

And in a move that surprised no one around the organization, or around the sport, the Cubs announced in late September that the organization and their World Series–winning manager were parting ways. "There was just, you can say, philosophical differences," Maddon told ESPN as he referenced his relationship with Epstein.

"But he and I are still good friends. And I like the man a lot. It was just time for him to get someone else and time for me to work somewhere else. That's all. A five-year shelf life in Chicago is almost equivalent to... 10 somewhere else. At the end of the day, man, there's nothing to lament there. That was the most successful five years that the Cubs have ever had."

When Epstein was asked about Maddon's comments to ESPN, he had an interesting response. "Maddon's version would conflict with some of the things that he and his agent were saying and doing towards the end of the season," Epstein told reporters.

"It doesn't mean it's not true. And if that's how he feels, especially with the benefit of hindsight, I'm not going to dispute it. But it doesn't really reflect the conversations we were having up until the very, very end—the last day or two—when we talked about a parting of the ways being best for everybody," Epstein said.

He went on. "Joe and I aren't exactly the same. I think his approach was more that things would work themselves out—these are great players, let them play, these things will work out. But from my perspective, there was a little bit more cause for concern."

So, with Maddon out and the last two years of club control of many of the stars staring the front office in the face, it was widely assumed that Epstein and GM Jed Hoyer would finally start to overhaul the roster and trade some of their stars.

But bubbling under the surface was a financial stranglehold that was preventing the Cubs from adding more talent. In fact, star free agent Bryce Harper had the Cubs at the top of his list of destinations after playing out his contract in Washington. Most Cubs fans, after hearing that Harper had named his dog Wrigley, figured he was going to be the next big star to make Chicago his home.

However, over the past few seasons, ownership had been putting the lion's share of their available resources into renovating Wrigley Field and rebuilding the footprint that the ballpark had in the surrounding community. That meant taking on new investors and taking on huge debt to finance all of the construction and property acquisitions, such as the rooftops that overlook the playing field.

A new hotel and many new restaurants were built across the street and a new office building with more eating and drinking options were also part of the renovations.

Those commitments turned Wrigley Field into a tremendous destination to watch a ballgame, but unfortunately the product on the field could not keep up.

And then COVID-19 hit.

When the pandemic struck, the 2020 MLB season was about to begin. The Cubs went from expecting to draw in excess of 3 million fans to an empty ballpark. Revenue streams that the Cubs counted on to service their debt dried up instantly. And while it affected everyone in the sports world, perhaps no team was more adversely affected than the Chicago Cubs.

Most teams have stadiums that were paid for by their local municipalities, thus shielding them from the major expenditures that the Ricketts family had to shoulder to improve Wrigley Field's antiquated facilities.

Suddenly, the 162-game MLB season was thrust into doubt. Instead, a three-plus-month shutdown hit the sports world, forcing teams to cut expenses dramatically. The Cubs kept their employees working but asked their highest-compensated staff members to take large pay cuts. In fact, Theo Epstein reportedly took a 35 percent cut from his $10-million salary to try to help the franchise and to try to keep as many employees in their jobs as possible.

The Cubs also picked an extremely poor time to launch their own TV network. After finishing a 15-year deal with NBC Sports Chicago, as well as smaller deals with both WGN-TV and ABC-7 Chicago, the Cubs, at the urging of business operations president Crane Kenney, spurned opportunities to stay on the same channel with the crosstown White Sox, the Chicago Bulls (NBA), and the Chicago Blackhawks (NHL).

Thus, the Marquee Network was born. The Cubs partnered with the Sinclair Broadcasting Group to create a Cubs-only channel. But what do you show if there are no Cubs games?

In addition, the Cubs had trouble getting clearance on the most popular cable system in the area, Xfinity, which has almost 60 percent of the Chicagoland area's cable TV subscribers. Xfinity is owned by, you guessed it, Comcast/NBC, which also obviously owns the Cubs' former home, NBC Sports Chicago.

Eventually the two sides came to an agreement, but not before several months had passed with no deal, costing the Cubs millions of dollars in carriage fees. Carriage fees are the per-subscriber dollars that each channel gets when they are available on a cable or satellite TV provider.

Another problem that hit the Cubs and their owners was the political climate that was dividing much of the U.S. population. President Donald Trump became a hot-button topic that divided the country in a way that had not been seen before.

With the city of Chicago and the surrounding suburbs decidedly leaning Democratic, any support for Trump was not well-received by large portions of the Cubs fan base. However, the Ricketts family (with the exception of sister Laura, who is very active in the Democratic party), were *very* supportive of Trump.

In fact, the Cubs board of directors was originally made up of the four Ricketts siblings (Tom, Pete, Todd, and Laura) and both Pete and Todd played active roles in trying to get Trump re-elected in 2020. Pete is currently the Republican governor of Nebraska, and has been a vocal supporter of Trump, while Todd was the chief of fundraising for the Trump re-election campaign. At one point, Todd even used Wrigley Field for a Trump fundraiser. That move angered many Cubs fans, who openly complained about the team mixing politics with their favorite baseball team. Pete Ricketts would go on to step down from his board of directors' role while he is serving his term as governor. Tom Ricketts has wisely stayed out of mixing his politics with his ownership of a baseball team.

All of this drama combined with the financial fallout from the pandemic made for a very precarious situation for the Cubs. Tom Ricketts feels he did all he could to keep his employees on the payroll for as long as he could despite the massive drop in revenue.

However, a quote from the Cubs chairman received national attention and raised eyebrows around the sport, with Ricketts saying this in an interview with Jesse Rogers of ESPN: "The scale of losses is biblical. The timing of the work stoppage, the inability to play was right before the season started. We're looking at 30 teams with zero revenue. To cover the losses, all teams have gone out and borrowed. There's no other way to do it in the short run. In the long run, we may be able to sell equity to cover some of our losses but that's in the long run. Who would invest at the moment?"

In fact, while some teams were already trimming the size of their front-office staff, Ricketts was holding out, trying to keep paying his employees. He was receiving internal advice to lay off a large number of employees as early as June, but he resisted until the season was over in early October, at which point the Cubs dismissed approximately 100 staffers, many of whom had been with the organization for 10–20 years, and in some cases even longer.

Then, in a story that I broke, came the news that Epstein was not interested in a contract extension and that he would be leaving the organization with a year left on his contract.

The extremely unselfish move by Epstein provided the Cubs a savings of $10 million for 2021 and paved the way for his close friend, Cubs GM Jed Hoyer, to move up into Epstein's role as president of baseball operations.

So what will Epstein do to occupy his time? As the calendar flipped to 2021 he accepted two different opportunities that could both lead to his next full-time occupation in sports. Commissioner Rob Manfred hired Epstein as a consultant to the commissioner's office, with an emphasis on helping make the sport more exciting and appealing to younger fans. Also, it's expected that Epstein will play a role in helping MLB and the MLBPA negotiate the next CBA, which will expire after the '21 season. He has long been speculated as a potential future commissioner of the sport.

Epstein also accepted a position with Arctos Sports Partners, a private equity platform that works to increase liquidity and financial flexibility for current ownership groups. They also acquire passive minority stakes in sports franchises, and I've long believed that Epstein will someday be a large part of an ownership group of an MLB team, so this partnership with Arctos could be the runway he needs to start moving his career in that direction.

Since the transfer of power to Hoyer, the Cubs have said goodbye to tens of millions in payroll commitments, including fan favorites in Lester, Schwarber, and, in the most stunning move of all, the trade of 2020 Cy Young runner-up Yu Darvish to the resurgent Padres.

The Darvish deal saved the Cubs approximately $52 million, but the return in player capital outraged the Cubs loyal fan base. Chicago received a 17-year-old prospect, two 18-year-old prospects, a 20-year-old prospect, and journeyman starting pitcher Zach Davies. None of the prospects ranked in San Diego's top 10 minor leaguers, but as one rival executive told me when I asked him about the trade, "when you get San Diego to take almost all of the money that Darvish is owed you aren't going to get their best prospects back."

In short, the Cubs saved a ton of money and bought four lottery tickets from the Padres system. Will any of them hit? Check back in three to four years to find out.

In recent weeks, the Cubs have declined to offer a contract to power-hitting left fielder Kyle Schwarber. He signed a one-year contract with the Washington Nationals in late December for $10 million.

Another fan favorite, and one of the most important Cubs in the history of the franchise, star pitcher Jon Lester, became a free agent after the 2020 season, and he made it clear to team management that he would take less money to return to Chicago and finish his career as a member of the Cubs. He never received a competitive offer, despite personally calling Tom Ricketts to attempt to get a deal done.

In fact, the only offer he received from the Cubs came after he received an offer from the Washington Nationals. Lester had been told that the Cubs had to move more money off of the payroll before they could make any offers, but once the Washington offer came in, the Cubs raced to make their pitch. It was far inferior to the $5 million he settled on to play for the Nationals. He agreed to a one-year deal with a club option for a second year, ending his dream of retiring as a Chicago Cub.

So, who goes next? Gone off of the 2020 roster are some very recognizable names, many with big salaries. Sources have confirmed to me that the Cubs are hoping to trim their payroll by $80 million before the start of the 2021 season.

C Victor Caratini	$592,000
P Yu Darvish	$22 million
P Jon Lester	$20 million ($10 million buyout)
P Jose Quintana	$10.5 million
P Tyler Chatwood	$13 million
LF Kyle Schwarber	$7.01 million
2B Jason Kipnis	$1 million

It seems like such a long time ago that the Cubs were on top of the baseball world on that magical night in Cleveland. They were jumping around on the field with such joy after third baseman Kris Bryant fielded a slow roller and threw it across the diamond to first baseman Anthony Rizzo.

Who could have predicted that just four years later the roster would be in flux, the World Series–winning manager would be entering his second season as the manager of the Los Angeles Angels, and the club would be in the midst of a roster teardown to save money?

And, in perhaps the most surprising move of all, their future Hall of Fame team president would leave $10 million on the table and walk away from what he had built with a year left on his contract.

Could all of the club's on-field struggles been avoided to capitalize on the momentum of the 2016 title? Had they been able to develop just one or two pitchers in their system, Epstein and the front office would not have been forced to spend so much money on their pitching staff. The inability to develop *any* homegrown pitching is the single biggest reason the Cubs never returned to the World Series.

By the time they got to 2019, trying to keep their window of championship contention open, their pitching staff alone was being paid $138 million—more than the *combined entire* payrolls of the Rays and Orioles. And that was the one Cubs team that *didn't* make the playoffs during the Cubs six-year run.

New team president Jed Hoyer is a savvy baseball man and is exceptionally well-liked by everyone who deals with him. But with his hands tied from a financial perspective, his only hope at getting the Cubs back to the World Series is if he has a "Plan" Part Two. For his sake, and the Cubs sake, he's going to need it.

—David Kaplan
January 27, 2021

Appendices

Appendix I

Cubs Drafts of Amateur Prospects, 1994–2011

Andy MacPhail (Ed Lynch) 1994–2002

1994

1st round: Jay Peterson, RHP (High School)

Other notables: Kyle Farnsworth (RHP, 47th round)

Notes: Pitchers selected with each of first 10 picks (Round 1-10)

Combined WAR in Cubs uniform: 0

1995

1st round: Kerry Wood, RHP (High School)

Other notables: Adam Everett (SS, 4th round, did not sign); Justin Speier (C, 55th round; eventually pitched)

Notes: Pitcher selected in Rounds 1-3

Combined WAR in Cubs uniform: 26.3

1996

1st round: Todd Noel, RHP (High School)

Other notables: Kyle Lohse (RHP, 29th round)

Combined WAR in Cubs uniform: -1.4

Notes: Pitchers selected with 3 of first 4 picks

1997

1st round: Jon Garland, RHP (High School)

Other notables: Scott Downs (LHP, 3rd round);
Michael Wuertz (RHP, 11th round)

Notes: Pitchers selected with first 3 picks

Combined WAR in Cubs uniform: 3.7

1998

1st round: Corey Patterson, OF (High School)

Other notables: Will Ohman (LHP, 8th round);
Eric Hinske (3B, 17th round)

Notes: Position players seleted with first 4 picks

Combined WAR in Cubs uniform: 5.5

1999

1st round: Ben Christensen, RHP (College)

Combined WAR in Cubs uniform: -0.9

2000

1st round: Luis Montanez, SS (High School)

Other notables: Dontrelle Willis (LHP, 8th round)

Notes: Shortstops picked with first 2 picks

Combined WAR in Cubs uniform: -2.0

2001

1st round: Mark Prior, RHP (College)

Other notables: Ryan Theriot (SS, 3rd round);
Ricky Nolasco (RHP, 4th round);

Geovany Soto (C, 11th round);
Khalil Greene (SS, 14th round, did not sign);
Tony Sipp (LHP, 28th round, did not sign)
Notes: Pitchers selected with 5 of first 7 picks
Combined WAR in Cubs uniform: 31.3

2002

1st round: Bobby Brownlie, RHP (College);
Luke Hagerty, LHP (College);
Chadd Blasko, RHP (College);
Matt Clanton, RHP (Jr. College)
Other notables: Rich Hill (LHP, 4th round);
Randy Wells (C, 38th round, pitched)
Notes: Pitchers selected with 6 of first 7 picks
Combined WAR in Cubs uniform: 11.6

Jim Hendry 2003–2011

2003

1st round: Matt Harvey, OF (High School)
Other notables: Sean Marshall (LHP, 6th round);
Sam Fuld (OF, 24th round did not sign);
Tim Lincecum (RHP, 48th round, did not sign)
Notes: Position players selected with first 3 picks
Combined WAR in Cubs uniform: 7.8

2004

No First Rounder
Other notables: Sam Fuld (OF, 10th round);
Jerry Blevins (LHP, 18th round);
Micah Owings (RHP, 19th round, did not sign)
Combined WAR in Cubs uniform: 0.4

2005

1st round: Mark Pawelek, LHP (High School)

Notes: Pitchers selected with first 4 picks

Combined WAR in Cubs uniform: 0.0

2006

1st round: Tyler Colvin, OF (College)

Other notables: Jeff Samardzija (RHP, 5th round)

Notes: Position players selected with 4 of first 6 picks

Combined WAR in Cubs uniform: 5.0

2007

1st round: Josh Vitters, 3B (High School);

Josh Donaldson, C (College)

Other notables: Darwin Barney (SS, 4th round);

Brandon Guyer (OF, 5th round);

Andrew Cashner (RHP, 29th round, did not sign)

Notes: Position players selected with 9 of first 10 picks

High Schooler taken 3rd overall; then 10 straight college players

Combined WAR in Cubs uniform: 6.2

2008

1st round: Andrew Cashner, RHP (College)

Other notables: Josh Harrison (2B, 6th round)

Sonny Gray (RHP, 27th round, did not sign)

Notes: Pitchers taken with 4 of first 6 picks

College or JuCo players taken with 20 of first 21 picks

Combined WAR in Cubs uniform: 1.0

2009

1st round: Brett Jackson, CF (College)

Other notables: DJ Lemahieu (IF, 2nd round)

Justin Bour (1B, 25th round)

Combined WAR in Cubs uniform: 0.8

2010

1st round: Hayden Simpson, RHP (College)
Other notables: Matt Szczur (OF, 5th round);
Jerad Eickhoff (RHP, 46th round, did not sign)
Combined WAR in Cubs uniform: -0.8

2011

1st round: Javier Baez, SS (High School)
Other notables: Dan Vogelbach (1B, 2nd round)
Notes: Position players taken with 9 of first 11 picks (including 1-3)
Combined WAR in Cubs uniform: 1.2

Baseball America lists draft spending

No	Team	2012	2013	2014	2015	Four-Year
1	Astros	$12,074,200	$11,441,000	$6,154,500	$17,865,000	$47,534,700
2	Rockies	6,978,700	10,368,200	8,853,800	13,648,900	39,849,600
3	Cubs	9,164,700	11,724,900	9,783,000	7,578,700	38,251,300
4	Twins	12,602,400	8,776,400	8,067,600	6,511,400	35,957,800
5	Royals	7,573,000	9,581,900	9,888,700	7,162,300	34,205,900
6	Cardinals	9,909,490	8,526,400	7,613,800	7,539,400	33,589,090
7	Marlins	5,755,700	7,951,000	13,112,900	6,613,100	33,432,700
8	D-backs	4,594,800	8,049,100	8,357,900	11,128,900	32,130,700
9	Rangers	7,394,400	7,696,500	6,089,200	9,533,300	30,713,400
10	Reds	7,450,400	6,757,800	7,929,900	7,740,050	29,878,150
11	Red Sox	7,908,000	7,210,900	7,814,800	6,454,500	29,388,200
12	Padres	10,993,000	7,895,000	6,637,600	3,709,100	29,234,700
13	Pirates	3,830,700	9,887,400	8,186,400	7,305,000	29,209,500
14	Mariners	9,325,200	7,376,700	8,237,500	4,163,100	29,102,500
15	Indinas	5,330,000	6,713,600	9,317,800	7,594,380	28,955,780
16	White Sox	6,452,100	5,810,800	10,460,600	5,283,600	28,007,100

No	Team	2012	2013	2014	2015	Four-Year
17	Blue Jays	10,486,000	3,747,280	9,308,700	4,154,800	27,696,780
18	Brewers	7,200,100	4,637,300	8,102,300	7,254,100	27,193,800
19	Yankees	4,898,400	9,197,400	4,050,200	8,252,800	26,398,800
20	Braves	4,758,000	5,410,500	5,069,800	11,151,400	26,389,700
21	Giants	4,630,500	6,063,800	7,275,900	7,890,300	25,860,500
22	Athletics	8,301,600	6,506,100	5,386,000	5,600,000	25,793,700
23	Rays	4,427,300	7,147,000	7,141,319	6,589,900	25,305,519
24	Phillies	4,787,800	6,186,900	7,187,800	6,876,700	25,039,200
25	Dodgers	6,277,300	6,366,100	5,901,100	6,323,600	24,868,100
26	Mets	7,007,400	7,854,400	6,488,800	3,427,700	24,778,300
27	Orioles	7,433,200	7,235,000	3,410,600	5,959,700	24,038,500
28	Tigers	3,172,300	6,839,100	5,405,300	6,904,200	22,320,900
29	Nationals	4,880,500	3,176,200	5,188,600	4,229,800	17,475,100
30	Angels	2,289,800	3,168,200	6,387,500	4,978,800	16,824,300
	Total	207,886,990	219,302,880	222,809,919	219,424,530	869,424,319
	Average	6,929,566	7,310,096	7,426,997	7,314,151	28,980,811

Appendix II

Partners and Sponsors

Cubs Legacy Partners

Nuveen Investments	Sloan Valve
Toyota	Under Armour
American Airlines	Starwood Hotels (SPG)
Anheuser Busch	ATI Physical Therapy
Wintrust Financial	Advocate Health Care

Cubs Advertisers and Sponsors (2015 Season)

Wine	E.J. Gallo
Baked Goods	Gonnella Baking/Matin's Famous Pastry Shoppe
Beef and Hot Dogs	Vienna Beef
Candy	Hi Chew
Chewing Gum	Wrigley
Chips	Frito-Lay
Condiments	Heinz, Cholula, Weber Sauces and Seasonings
Cookies, etc.	Prairie City Bakery
Dairy Products/Ice Cream	Joe and Ross Ice Cream (Multiple brands)
Donuts	Dunkin Brands
Fast Food	Portillo's
Fruit	Testa Produce
Pizza	Giordano's

Soft Pretzel	J&J Snack Foods
Miscellaneous Food	Fisher Nuts, Nuts on Clark, Illinois Pork Producers
Beer	Anheuser-Busch
Carbonated Soft Drinks	Pepsi
Coffee	Peet's Coffee & Tea, Dunkin Brands
Sports Drink	Gatorade
Liquor	Jack Daniels, Diageo, Rum Chata, Jim Beam, Inc., CH Distillery
Miscellaneous Beverages	Bigelow Tea, Bob Chinn's Premium Beverages
Water	Pepsi
Computer Retailer	PCM
Television	Comcast SportsNet, WGN, ABC
Radio	CBS Radio
Credit Cards	MasterCard
Banking	Wintrust
Investments	Nuveen/Charles Schwab
Supermarket	Jewel-Osco
Accounting Firm	Grant Thornton LLP
Airline	American Airlines
Apparel	Under Armour, Majestic, Nike
Headwear	New Era
Automotive	Audi/Toyota
Energy Provider	AEP
Concourse Advertiser	Access 360
Express Mail Delivery	FedEx
Government	Las Vegas Convention and Visitors Authority
Healthcare/Hospital	Advocate Health Care/ATI Physical Therapy
Health Insurance	Blue Cross/Blue Shield of Illinois
Hotel	Starwood
Insurance	State Farm, Assurance
Lawn Care	Scott's
Limousine	Top Fleet, Inc.
Lottery	Illinois Lottery
Machinery Equipment	Caterpillar
Misc. Products	Weber-Stephen Products, Reynolds Consumer Products

Misc. Service	Magellan Corporation, Aon, Jani-King, TransUnion, Draft Kings
Paint	Benjamin Moore
Publishing	Professional Sports Publications
Rail Service	Amtrak
Sanitary Supply	Sloan Valve Company, Blue Lizard, Nivea Men
Sports Cards	Topps
Cable TV	Xfinity
Ticket Company	StubHub
Tires	Hankook
Travel	Lyft
University/College Services	Northwestern University
Waste Management Co.	Allied Waste

Appendix III

List of Critical Clauses in Rooftop Contract

Key Points in the Chicago Cubs Rooftop Contract

3. Payment obligations.

3.1 Royalty

a) Each Rooftop shall pay the Cubs, on an annual basis, an amount equal to 17 percent of its Gross Revenues and 11 percent of its Billboard Revenues, if any (together, the "Royalty").

b) The Parties agree Rooftops are currently prohibited from displaying Billboards under City of Chicago law. Nothing in this Agreement will preclude the Cubs from opposing any change to the current law, including the placement of Billboards or any other advertising visible from inside Wrigley Field on any of the buildings in the Wrigley Field Adjacent Area.

6. Wrigley Field bleacher expansion.

6.1 If the Cubs expand the Wrigley Field bleacher seating and such expansion so impairs the view from any Rooftop into Wrigley Field such that the Rooftop's business is no longer viable unless it increases the height of its available seating, then such Rooftop may in its discretion elect to undertake construction to raise the height of its seating to allow views into Wrigley Field and the Cubs shall reimburse the Rooftop for 17 percent of the actual cost of such construction.

6.2 If the Cubs expand the Wrigley Field bleacher seating and such expansion so impairs the view from any Rooftop into Wrigley Field such that the Rooftop's business is no longer viable even if it were to to increase its available seating to the maximum height permitted by law, and if such bleacher expansion is completed within eight years from the Effective Date, then if such Rooftop elects to cease operations before the beginning of the next baseball season following completion of such expansion, the Cubs shall reimburse that Rooftop for 50 percent of the royalties paid by the Rooftop to the Cubs during the time between the Effective Date and the date of expansion of the Wrigley Field bleachers. The Cubs shall pay such reimbursement to the Rooftop within 30 days of receiving notice from the Rooftop it is no longer viable and has ceased operations. Any Rooftop receiving payment from the Cubs pursuant to this provision shall cease operations for the remainder of the Term and shall not seek or accept any compensation or benefit related to activity on a Rooftop on a day of a Game.

6.3 In the event of a dispute between the Cubs and any Rooftop regarding whether such Rooftop remains viable pursuant to Section 6.1 or 6.2 or whether (or to what extent) construction of new seating is required pursuant to Section 6.1, either Party may request such dispute be resolved pursuant to binding arbitration between the Parties pursuant to Section 9 below.

6.4 If the Cubs expand the Wrigley Field bleacher seating and such expansion impairs the view from any Rooftop into Wrigley Field such that Rooftop's Gross Revenue in the year of expansion is more than 10 percent below the average Gross Revenue for that Rooftop in the two years prior to expansion (normalizing for number of Games played, in rain-outs and doubleheaders, playoff games, work stoppage, replacement players, and the like), then the affected Rooftop can seek a reduction in the Royalty rate for all subsequent years of the Term. Upon such request, the parties shall meet and negotiate in good faith a new Royalty. If the Parties cannot agree, then the Rooftop may submit the issue of its appropriate Royalty rate to binding arbitration pursuant to Section 9.

a.) In the event any Royalty is reduced pursuant to this section 6.3, the Cubs may seek to raise or restore the Royalty at a later date (e.g., in the event the Rooftop subsequently builds higher or the Rooftop's drop in the business proves temporary). Such revision may be negotiated between the parties or submitted to arbitration. Notwithstanding the foregoing, in no event may the Royalty exceed the 17 percent.

6.5 Nothing in this Agreement limits the Cubs' rights to seek approval of the right to expand Wrigley Field or the Rooftops' right to oppose any request for expansion of Wrigley Field.

6.6 The Cubs shall not erect windscreens or other barriers to obstruct the views of the Rooftops, provided however that temporary items such as banners, flags and decorations for special occasions, shall not be considered as having been erected to obstruct views of the Rooftops. Any expansion of Wrigley Field approved by governmental authorities shall not be a violation of this Agreement, including this section.

7. Marketing

7.1 WGN-TV will show and comment upon the Rooftops' facilities during broadcasts of Cubs games and the Cubs will request other Cubs television broadcasting partners to do the same. If, however, there is a Billboard or other advertising on a Rooftop, WGN will not be required to show that Rooftop or comment on it and Cubs may request others not to show or comment.

7.2 Each Rooftop shall have a license during the Term to use the Cubs' Marks identified in Exhibit B solely for the purpose of marketing and promoting the sale of admissions to its Rooftop. The Cubs will not object to the Rooftops' use, solely for the same purpose, of the term "Wrigley Field". Each use of the Cubs Marks must include a trademark notice of registration or protection as shown on Exhibit B. The Cubs revise Exhibit B from time to time in their discretion. Rooftops may not use Cubs' Marks on merchandise, apparel, Billboard or to promote the sale of any other product or service.

7.3 From time to time during each season, the Cubs shall authorize WGN-TV or other Cubs broadcasting partner (s) to identify a phone number where fans can call to reserve Rooftop seating. Such phone number will provided to Cubs by the Rooftops jointly. The Rooftops shall determine how calls to that phone number will be apportioned among the various Rooftop businesses.

7.4 The Rooftops shall have the right to inform the public that they are endorsed by the Cubs.

7.5 The Cubs director of marketing shall meet with Rooftops before the start of each Major League Baseball season to discuss opportunities for joint marketing.

7.6 The Cubs shall include a discussion about the Rooftops on their tour of Wrigley Field and shall include stories positive about the Rooftops in The Vine Line.

7.7 Each of the Rooftops may display broadcasts of Cubs games to patrons at its facility, including displaying such broadcasts on multiple television sets, without any infringement of any copyright owned by the Cubs or its assignees.

8. Non-disparagement.

8.1 Each Rooftop agrees that it will not publicly disparage, abuse, or insult the business of the Cubs or the moral character of the Cubs or any of its employees.

8.2 The Cubs will not publicly disparage, abuse, or insult the business of any Rooftop or the moral character of any Rooftop or any Rooftop employee.

9. Arbitration.

9.1 The arbitrators shall be chosen as follows: each of the Cubs and the Rooftop shall nominate three individuals to serve as arbitrator. None of these persons may be an employee of the Cubs or any Rooftop nor have any financial interest in the Cubs or any Rooftop. The affected Rooftop will then choose one of the three individuals nominated by the Rooftop. The two individuals selected as arbitrators will then meet and choose a third arbitrator to complete the panel, which third arbitrator must be an independent, third party with no relationship to or interest in (including without limitation any related or unrelated financial or business relationship) the Cubs or any Rooftop. If the arbitrators cannot agree on a third arbitrator, then each Party's arbitrator shall nominate one independent, third party who shall have no relationship or interest in (including without limitation any related or unrelated financial or business relationship) the Cubs or any Rooftop and who is not a current or former elected official or employee of the City of Chicago or any organization or entity who has received money form the Cubs or any Rooftop.

The third arbitrator shall be chosen by lot from among those two individuals.

9.2 In the event more than-one Rooftop is involved in a similar dispute related to this Agreement, the Parties may agree, but are not required to, arbitrate such dispute collectively. In such event, the affected Rooftops will agree on arbitrators pursuant to section 9.2 and collectively submit one set of choices to the Cubs.

9.3 Each Arbitration decision shall be binding on the Parties to that Arbitration and, unless the Cubs and all Rooftops agree in advance of the decision, shall be binding vis-à-vis each other only.

9.4 The losing party in the Arbitration shall bear the costs and fees of the Arbitration as well as the costs and fees of the prevailing party.

Appendix IV

Theo Epstein's Letter to Red Sox fans

(published in the *Boston Globe* on October 25, 2011)

I grew up in Brookline just down the road from Fenway Park, living and dying with every pitch, every win or loss, and every Red Sox season that fell painfully short. My whole outlook on life changed at age 12 as my twin brother and I writhed on the living room floor, devastated by Game Six of the '86 Series.

Had you told me then that the Red Sox would go on to raise not one but two World Series flags, I wouldn't have believed you. And had you told the 12-year-old me that I would someday walk away from my dream job as general manager of the Red Sox completely of my own volition, I would have thought you were crazy.

I think that kid would appreciate an explanation—and so might some of you.

For the last decade, I gave everything I had to the Red Sox and received even more in return. I grew enormously as a person, had some successes, and made a lot of mistakes, too. I still love the organization, enjoy close relationships with owners John Henry and Tom Werner—as well as a complicated but ultimately productive and rewarding relationship with Larry Lucchino—and count many of my co-workers among my dearest friends. The reason I am leaving has nothing to do with power, pressure, money, or relationships. It has nothing to do with September, either.

Football legend Bill Walsh used to say that coaches and executives should seek change after 10 years with the same team. The theory is that both the individual and the organization benefit from a change after so much time together. The executive gets rebirth and the energy that comes with a new challenge; the organization gets a fresh perspective, and the chance for true change that comes with new leadership. This idea resonated with me. Although I tried my best to fight it, I couldn't escape the conclusion that both the Red Sox and I would benefit from a change sometime soon.

With this thought in mind, my assistant general manager, Ben Cherington, and I discussed how best to finish preparing him to take over as general manager, likely after the 2012 season, and how to ensure that the Red Sox could maintain continuity within our talented baseball operations group. Those steps were important for me before I could begin to feel comfortable making a transition. This summer, when ownership and I first discussed Ben as my successor, the Red Sox were stable, thriving, and talented enough in the big leagues and in the farm system to compete as one of the best clubs in baseball this year and for many years to come.

Then, September happened.

All of a sudden, we found ourselves needing to pick a new manager, a decision with long-term implications and one best made by someone who could lead the Red Sox baseball operation for the foreseeable future. Then the Cubs asked permission to interview me. The Cubs—with their passionate fans, dedicated ownership, tradition, and World Series drought—represented the ultimate new challenge and the one team I could imagine working for after such a fulfilling Red Sox experience.

So, knowing my time as the general manager was drawing to an end, I had a decision to make: stay one more year and do my best to conduct the manager's search under less than ideal circumstances, or recommend the succession plan, allow Ben to run the search process, and join the Cubs. I wrestled with leaving during a time when criticism, deserved and otherwise, surrounded the organization. But Walsh's words kept popping into my head, and I recalled how important it was for me as a relatively new general manager to bond with Terry Francona during the interview process back in 2003.

It was very difficult deciding to leave the place where I grew up, where I met my wife, where my son was born, where my family and closest friends live, and where I help run a charitable foundation. And it was equally hard to part with the organization and the people, including John, Tom, and Larry, who entrusted me with this role at such a young age and supported me along the way. But it was the right thing to do.

What a privilege it has been to be a part of the Red Sox these last 10 years. The first title in 2004, born from the heartbreak of Aaron Boone, was unforgettable: The Steal, Papi, the Bloody Sock, the Greatest Comeback Ever, the end of The Curse. The second, 2007, was equally rewarding as it solidified the franchise's rise and marked the emergence of a core drafted, developed, and trained in the "Red Sox Way" so many had worked so hard to establish.

Beyond the results on the field, I believe the Red Sox came to stand for certain things over the last decade. Pride in the uniform. Appreciation of our history. Controlling the strike zone. Grinding at-bats. Having each other's backs. Rising to the moment. Never backing down. Connection to the fans. Hard work. Playing with passion and urgency. These concepts were taught in the minor leagues and reinforced at the big-league level by our homegrown players and by Tito, a selfless leader who always put the Red Sox first. These principles united the organization and came to define us.

This is why September—when we let fans down by falling short of these ideals—was so crushing. But the Red Sox will recover. What was built up with pride and passion over so long cannot be torn down in one bad month. The same is true, I know, of the fans' loyalty.

Yes, September was a collective failure. As the general manager, I am the person ultimately responsible. Things did indeed happen in the clubhouse that do not have a place at the Red Sox or anywhere in sports. But the reports about team-wide apathy and indulgence are exaggerated. It may not seem this way now, but the team did care about winning, about the fans, and about each other; unfortunately, we failed when we let less important things get in the way. I tried desperately to reverse our slide, as did Tito, the coaches, and the players. But we just could not play well, and then we did not handle the adversity well.

Everyone involved is taking responsibility. The players I've talked to are embarrassed by our performance in September and are rededicating themselves this winter—not only to their training in the gym and on the field but also to their growth as leaders. September was a wake-up call to those of us in management as well; there are plans to raise standards in several areas, and Ben will work hard with the new manager to ensure those standards are met.

If not for the complete confidence I have in Ben to address these issues, I could not in good conscience leave the organization at this time. But there is no one in baseball more qualified to be the next general manager of the Red Sox.

Ben is infinitely more prepared than I was when I took over nine years ago. He's been an area scout, an international scout, an advance scout, a farm director, and he's supervised drafts. Ben is honest and insightful, fearless and friendly—and he is ready to lead this organization forward.

Lost in the cacophony of the last few weeks is the fact that the Boston Red Sox remain one of the preeminent organizations in baseball, with an extremely bright future. Ben will head the same scouting and baseball operations staff that engineered much of the club's success the last nine years. There is tremendous talent on the major league club and significant depth in the farm system after a decade of strong drafts.

Despite recent criticism, Red Sox ownership remains a model for others to follow. John, Tom, and Larry demonstrate their commitment to winning in the most fundamental way possible: If something needs to be done to help the team on the field, it gets done. September happened despite them, not because of them. It may not seem this way now, but I am convinced that we will look back at September of 2011 not as some harbinger of the demise of the Red Sox, but as an anomaly in the midst of a decades-long run of success for the franchise. Some good may even come from it. I know the climate is especially hostile right now, and our mistakes are well documented, but I encourage fans not to lose faith in the players or in the organization. Red Sox Nation is a fantastic place, and it's even better when we take a deep breath and give each other the benefit of the doubt.

In Fort Myers next spring, a rededicated, revitalized, reborn Red Sox team will take the field for its first workout of 2012. September will seem like a long time ago. So will 2004 and 2007. I won't be there, but the 12-year-old in me will be rooting for the Red Sox (except, of course, when they play the Cubs in June). From afar, I think I'll finally be able to enjoy the experience more, to pull for the players with appreciation for their hard work and better perspective when things don't go the way we—or they—want. I hope you will join me.

Thank you for all the incredible support this last decade. I will never forget it. May we meet again in an October not too many years from now.

Appendix V

Tom Ricketts' Letter to Fans

Dear Cubs Fans,

It happened! From this season's many magical moments to Game 7's epic ending, your 2016 World Champion Chicago Cubs made history.

Throughout the entire season, our team never quit and you never lost faith. From the first pitch to the last out, we felt your energy and enthusiasm. It's only fitting the greatest journey in all of sports was fueled by the most loyal fans in the history of the game. While no fan base should have to wait more than a century, your love for the Cubs never wavered.

I'd like to offer a heartfelt thank you for your support of my family, our team and the entire Cubs organization over the past few years. Your patience and trust enabled us to build a championship organization the right way.

They say a team is a group of individuals working together to achieve a common goal. All year long, our talented team played for each other and for you. They persevered in the moments that mattered most in their quest to win the World Series. Last year, they had us believing in magic. This year, through their character, chemistry and no-quit attitude, they proved dreams really do come true.

None of this is possible without the tireless efforts of our baseball operations staff working throughout the farm system and at the major league level. Thank you to Theo, Jed, Jason, and their incredible teams. And to Joe, our entire coaching staff, and the best players in the game, thank you for bringing the World Series trophy home to Chicago.

It was a true joy to watch Cubs fans, whether young in age or young at heart, embrace old traditions and create new ones while cheering our team to victory. You flew your W Flags with pride, crafted thoughtful chalk memorials on our beloved bleacher walls and participated in the largest parade and rally in U.S. history. We'll never forget the cheers of our few million friends as the team's double-decker buses rolled down Michigan Avenue and the sea of blue that greeted us at Grant Park.

While our number one goal was to deliver a championship to our deserving fans, we've also made great progress on preserving Wrigley Field and set records for our fundraising and community contributions. In addition to baseball operations, our business operations, from Crane and senior leadership to our front office associates and nearly 2,000 dedicated individuals who make Wrigley Field such a special place, deserve thanks for helping us deliver on all three of our organizational goals.

Only a week removed from achieving our ultimate goal, it's hard to think about the future. With that said, I truly believe this is just the beginning. With one of the youngest starting lineups in World Series history, our team is built for sustained success. As we cherish the moment and enjoy our championship together, work is already underway to defend our title in 2017.

Let's Go Cubs,
Tom Ricketts

Acknowledgments

This book would not have been possible without the tireless efforts of my lead researcher, Christopher Kamka.

Chris has worked in research and production in the Comcast SportsNet newsroom since 2009 and he has also worked as Associate Producer on Cubs and White Sox television broadcasts for several seasons. Chris is an extremely popular follow around the baseball world and he can be found on Twitter @ckamka.

Thank you to Tom Ricketts and the Ricketts family. You were exceptionally open and honest and I thank you for your willingness to cooperate as I wrote this book. Thank you to PR maven and good friend Dennis Culloton.

Also, a huge thank you to Cubs President of Baseball Operations Theo Epstein, Vice President and General Manager Jed Hoyer, VP of Scouting and Player Development Jason McLeod, and manager Joe Maddon and his staff.

Thank you to Cubs President of Business Operations Crane Kenney and Cubs Vice President Colin Faulkner. In addition, thank you to Wally Hayward of W Partners.

In addition, thank you to Cubs Media Relations Director Peter Chase and his assistant, Jason Carr. Your cooperation was vital to this project's success.

Also, a huge thank you to everyone connected with the Chicago Cubs for their cooperation throughout the season and over the past 22 years that I have hosted their pre- and postgame shows. It is an unbelievable honor to work around such a tremendous organization.

Thank you to all of my friends and co-workers at CSN and ESPN 1000 who had to put up with my constantly asking them to read rough drafts or asking for their opinion on this book. Your support will never be forgotten.

And a special thank you to my family, including my wife, Mindy, who had to deal with late nights, constant revisions, and a distracted dad who was always thinking about *The Plan* and the Cubs.

Finally, I say this as a fan first and a media member second: Thank you to the members of the 2016 World Series champion Chicago Cubs. You accomplished something that many believed would never happen. You will be remembered forever for what you overcame and for what you achieved.

—David Kaplan
December 2016